GREAT BIRDS
OF BRITAIN & EUROPE

DUNCAN BAIRD PUBLISHERS
·LONDON

GREAT BIRDS
OF BRITAIN & EUROPE

200 STAR SPECIES

JONATHAN ELPHICK
DAVID TIPLING

GREAT BIRDS
OF BRITAIN & EUROPE

JONATHAN ELPHICK
DAVID TIPLING

AUTHOR'S DEDICATION
To Linda Smith (1958–2006),
who loved birds almost as much as she loved making people laugh

CHIEF PHOTOGRAPHER'S DEDICATION
To Jayne,
with thanks for her understanding

First published in the United Kingdom and Ireland in 2008 by
Duncan Baird Publishers Ltd
Sixth Floor, Castle House
75–76 Wells Street
London W1T 3QH

Conceived, created and designed by Duncan Baird Publishers

Managing Designer: Manisha Patel
Design Assistant: Saskia Janssen
Picture Research: David Tipling
Commissioned maps: Sailesh Patel

British Library Cataloguing-in-Publication Data:
A CIP record for this book is available from the British Library

ISBN: 978-1-84483-686-4

10 9 8 7 6 5 4 3 2 1

Typeset in Gill Sans
Colour reproduction by Scanhouse, Malaysia
Printed in Malaysia for Imago

CONTENTS

KEY TO DISTRIBUTION MAPS

- summer
- resident
- winter

INTRODUCTION by Jonathan Elphick

My aim in writing this book was to provide concise but informative and evocative word portraits of some of the most remarkable birds to be found in Europe. My definition is deliberately broad: there are various ways in which the 200 species I have chosen can be considered remarkable. Some of these birds, such as the Red-necked Phalarope or Bluethroat, are particularly beautiful. Others are intimately associated with certain habitats or regions – for example, the Greater Flamingo, Alpine Swift, Siberian Tit, Rook and Citril Finch. These include birds that are restricted to a particular place, such as the Harlequin Duck and Corsican Nuthatch. All too many birds are special because they are increasingly scarce and threatened – sometimes, as in the case of the White-headed Duck or Spanish Imperial Eagle, grievously so. By contrast, some species, especially the Wren, are remarkable for being very widespread, and the Fulmar and Cattle Egret have made dramatic expansions in their range. Birds such as the Dotterel and Puffin can be remarkably approachable, while the Bittern and Dupont's Lark are challengingly elusive.

Many birds are special because of their interesting or unusual behaviour. Good examples are the Lammergeier's extraordinary dietary specialism as a bone-digester and the brood parasitism of the Cuckoo and Great Spotted Cuckoo. Some birds I have selected, such as the Dipper and Bearded Reedling, are the sole representatives of their family in Europe – or even in the world, as with the Hoopoe and Wallcreeper.

What exactly is meant by the "great" in the book's title? Dictionary definitions of the word include "significant, distinguished, remarkable, prominent, pre-eminent, important, outstanding, most worthy of consideration". I would maintain that all the birds in the following pages deserve such accolades.

As for another key word, "Europe", there are numerous alternative definitions from which to choose. Some include such far-flung outposts as the Canary Islands, Madeira,

the Azores and the Cape Verde islands, as well as the great island of Greenland. Although the avifaunas of these places have undeniable affinities with the birdlife of Europe, I decided not to cover them, and the same applies to Turkey – although many European birds, including a good proportion of those found in this book, can also be seen in that country, and in North Africa. Although the distribution map for each species shows these regions, none of the species that are found there but not in Europe (except perhaps as rare wanderers) are included. The Europe of this book extends from Ireland and Iberia in the west to the watershed of the Ural Mountains in the east; and from Iceland, Svalbard and the Russian island of Novaya Zemlaya in the north to extreme southern Spain, the islands of Crete, Cyprus, the western and northern shores of the Black Sea and the Caucasus Mountains in the south.

Once the basic parameters had been established, the far more difficult task had to be faced of choosing precisely which species to include. The work of the author, photographer, editor and designer of a book such as this one involves careful planning and, later on, as with bespoke tailoring, accurate cutting and fitting. Throughout the process, the real difficulty lay more in what each one of the team could bear to excise than in what to include. As my first draft of species was circulated beyond the inner circle, a variety of people with an interest in birds and books made their pitches for favourite birds. Eventually, after much discourse and some disagreements, we all settled on what we thought was the final list – although there were a few more deletions and additions after picture research and writing were well underway, to ensure we had the best coverage and the finest images.

I could make a different list each week, each day, but there would always be a core of species that no one of sound judgment with reasonably functioning eyes and ears could sensibly omit: Chough, Kingfisher, Nightingale, Lammergeier,

Golden Eagle, Golden Oriole, Peregrine Falcon, Nightjar, Woodcock, Curlew, Barn Owl, Puffin... to name just a random dozen off the top of my head – and from the bottom of my heart. As for the rest, one can argue the toss for ever. But one man's – this man's – Chough is another man's Chukar or Cetti's Warbler, so in the end the selection, though heavily influenced by committee, was essentially my personal choice. Because some families (for example, gannets, storks, nightjars, accentors, dippers and shrikes) are represented in Europe by only a single species or a few species, they are disproportionately represented here – as are other families (such as falcons, owls, woodpeckers and finches) that have a large number of particularly charismatic birds. Nevertheless, virtually every family with European representatives is included.

Ornithologists think that more than one-and-a-half million species of birds have existed since these remarkable creatures evolved from dinosaurs some 150 million years ago. Just 200, then, is a minuscule percentage. Even set against the global total of 9,800 or so species that exists today, it is a mere two percent, or one in every fifty. But within the subcontinent of Europe, where there are about 700 species, the proportion looks more impressive. And as far as possible I have tried to include a balanced selection.

Thus, the range includes some of the region's smallest birds, such as the Firecrest and Wren, and some of its largest (Great Bustard, Black Vulture, Bewick's Swan, Dalmatian Pelican, Common Crane). It takes in the spectacularly plumaged and flamboyant (Bee-eater, Kingfisher, White-winged Black Tern) and the relatively plain (Thekla's and Dupont's Larks) or super-cryptic (Woodcock, Nightjar, Scops Owl). It spans the most graceful or elegant (including Avocet, Arctic Tern and Wax-wing) and the most bizarre (Bald Ibis).

As a temperate to Arctic region, Europe – like northern Asia and North America – cannot rival the tropics for sheer biodiversity. Nevertheless, it contains a great variety of habitats and a correspondingly exciting range of birds. With a long and complex coastline, off which lie many offshore islands, Europe is a splendid place in which to enjoy a wide range of seabirds. The north-west is rich in cliffs and remote islands, supporting huge, noisy, densely packed breeding colonies of Gannets, Manx Shearwaters, Fulmars, storm-petrels, auks and Kittiwakes. The North Sea and Irish Sea coasts, in particular, have big estuaries with mud and sand banks that result from large tidal ranges. These are the haunts of a great variety of waders and wildfowl, both common breeders or visitors from Arctic Europe and rarities from Asia and North America.

The ornithological specialities of different geographical regions of Europe and its varied habitats are well reflected in the choice of birds in the book. There are birds restricted to the far north, such as Ivory Gull, Snowy Owl, Arctic Redpoll and Siberian Jay; species restricted to extensive forests, such as Capercaillie, Great Grey Owl and Black Woodpecker; others characteristic of open grasslands, steppe and desert, such as Sociable Plover, Dupont's Lark and Trumpeter Finch; and Mediterranean specialities, including Spanish Imperial Eagle, Eleonora's Falcon, Azure-winged Magpie and Citril Finch. The increasingly visited and bird-rich Caucasus merits two little-known and much sought-after species that in the European context are endemic to the region: the Caucasian Snowcock and Great Rosefinch.

The lives of some of the birds I have selected, such as the Snowcock, Lammergeier and Leach's Petrel, are intimately bound to wild places where few people venture, on land or sea; while at the other extreme are birds like the Lapwing, White Stork, Cattle Egret, Skylark and Rook that make their homes in farmland, and those, such as Swift and Wren, that thrive as our cohabitants in villages and towns or even in the most noisome and congested cities.

And since birds are famously mobile and adaptable, there are those individuals that ignore what the species is supposed to do and confound the expectations of habitat-based guides and their neat compartments – such as the Peregrines that nest on cathedral spires or high-rise office buildings as a substitute for cliff ledges, or the Wallcreepers that have (albeit very rarely) chosen a similar alternative by wintering in such atypical spots as the Free University in Amsterdam (visited by an individual in 1989 and again in 1990) or the Panthéon in Paris in 2004.

Sometimes birds turn up on cue at a reliable site, while on other occasions the encounter is a result of pure luck – as with the above-mentioned Wallcreeper sightings, or even more amazingly, the extremely fortunate ornithologist who came upon a group of 48 individuals of that stunning high-mountain speciality on a single sunlit rock face in the mountains of the Haute Savoie, in the French Alps.

Birds such as the Wallcreeper or Eleonora's Falcon are undeniably special. But hopefully, as with children or friends, one can say, "You're *all* special." This rings true for me, at any rate.

Alas, far too many birds need more attention to their welfare if they are to survive and if we are to delight in watching them and learning more about their lives. Habitat destruction has had a massive impact on the fortunes of many European birds, with species such as Grey Partridge, Corn-crake, Lapwing and Skylark having vanished from areas where they were once among the most familiar of birds, as a result of agricultural intensification. The plethora of other threats includes wetland drainage, pollution, collision with power lines or windfarm turbines, overhunting, drowning in fishing nets and deliberate or accidental poisoning of raptors.

The much-publicized but too-little-heeded spectre of global warming will have a massive impact on the bird life of Europe. The changing climate will drive many species out of environments to which they have evolved an intricate mesh of adaptations over millions of years. For a large percentage of affected species these traumatic events will prove disastrous, as they are already suffering from other manmade blights such as those outlined above. There is a very real chance that unless we can forestall this outcome very soon, many of the birds celebrated within these pages will follow the Great Auk into extinction.

I have reflected this concern for the future in the accounts of many of the birds in this book, within the overall aim of portraying the essence of each bird and making it clear why it has been chosen. Drawing on the privilege of a scientific education, a passion for ornithology, over 50 years of watching and learning about birds, and the help of specialists who have reported their research in many books and journals, I have tried to include some interesting aspects of each species' biology. But no matter how aware we are of the facts, our reactions to wildlife cannot be purely objective: they also reveal much about our own nature. While trying to avoid indulging in the excesses of gross anthropomorphism, I have attempted to convey something of my own emotional and aesthetic responses to these exceptional creatures – and those of others who have studied and loved them from early history to the present day. I hope I have succeeded in enthusing and entertaining the already-converted and in encouraging those who have yet to do so to discover the rewards of getting closer in every way to the birds around us.

INTRODUCTION by David Tipling

Bird photography dates back almost to the very origins of photography itself. It is difficult to trace who took the first bird picture, and what it showed, but we do know that the first published bird photograph, certainly in Britain, was of a Song Thrush's nest and eggs taken in 1892 by the Kearton brothers. Until then, birdwatchers and the general public had made do with illustrations. Now suddenly a new way of showing the natural world was at the fingertips of those early pioneers.

The early part of the 21st century has witnessed a new technological dawn. Not only has the digital age brought with it an explosion in interest across the whole of Europe and beyond, but most importantly the bird photographer of the 21st century has the tools at his or her disposal to take images that just a decade ago were impossible. Bird photographers today are no longer held back by limitations with equipment: the limit now is their inventiveness and the strength of their desire to make exciting new pictures that will push the art forward – just as the Keartons and many others did over a century ago.

We live in an age in which it appears there is an over-supply of great bird images, and perhaps there is for some species, but for many more we have only just scratched the surface. In researching pictures for this book it became apparent to me that there are still many challenges left for the intrepid bird photographer in Europe. I set out to fill some gaps myself.

Embarking on an adventure in the Great Caucasus in Georgia in pursuit of Caucasian Snowcocks, I failed in that quest but came home with pictures of some of our continent's most charismatic birds. Those mouth-watering species included the Great Rosefinch. On that same trip I was treated to a memorable day in the company of a pair of Wallcreepers and on another occasion marvelled at over 100,000 migrants passing through a mountain valley in a single day. Just half a mile from my home that same summer I spent every available evening with a pair of Nightjars, finally capturing an image of a displaying male after many failed attempts.

Good pictures do not usually come without a great deal of planning and often much persistence. This book is testament to the dedication and skills of the current crop of the best European bird photographers at large across the continent. It is not just a showcase but a celebration of both the beauty and character of some of Europe's most sought-after species. It would have been easy to pack the book full of amazing action sequences and stunning flight shots, but that would have defeated the intention, which is to impart in words and pictures the character of each bird. I hope we have gone some way toward achieving this aim.

FROM WILDFOWL TO GAMEBIRDS

BEWICK'S SWAN

Cygnus columbianus bewickii

Over 90 percent of the western population winters at fewer than 15 sites in Europe. Some 60 percent of the peak count is in the Netherlands; about 35 percent in England (more than half in the Ouse Washes). The main threats are collisions with power lines and illegal hunting across its range.

All swans are special, particularly in flight, by virtue of their size, grace and power. Among the white northern swans, Bewick's has a more gentle appearance and an extra wildness that makes it harder to approach. Notably goose-like, it is more compact and shorter-necked than the Whooper, with which it was lumped in the catch-all name "wild swans" until 1830. Differences were recorded then by the English ornithologist William Yarrell, who gave it its name, honouring the great wood engraver and naturalist Thomas Bewick. Relatively dainty compared to Whooper and Mute, it is still huge, with a wingspan of up to 1.95 m.

Today regarded as a race of the Tundra Swan, this beautiful bird is one of the most intensively studied of all wildfowl. A vast amount of research has been amassed by ornithologists from many countries, especially those working for Britain's Wildfowl and Wetlands Trust (formerly the Wildfowl Trust). Foremost was the founder of the Trust, Sir Peter Scott. He and his wife Lady Philippa used to crawl across their floor to greet guests at their house so that they would not disturb the first of the wary swans to grace the lake just outside their living room at the Slimbridge wildfowl centre in 1964. He meticulously painted semi-stylized views of both sides and front of individual Bewick's Swans that migrated each year some 2,500 miles from their breeding grounds on the Siberian tundra. His alert artist's eye had observed that each bore a unique pattern of black and yellow on the bill, by which they could be identified. Giving each bird a name further personalized them. The recording of bill patterns over the last 40 years has extended to some 7,600 individual swans.

BEAN GOOSE
Anser fabalis

The Taiga Bean Goose breeds from N. Scandinavia to N.W. Russia, and winters in S. Sweden and Denmark, also N. Germany and Poland, with a few in the Netherlands and just two areas of Britain. The Tundra Bean Goose nests in N. Russia and W. Siberia, and winters more widely in Europe.

One of nature's most stirring sights is a great skein of geese passing high overhead on migration each spring and autumn, the wild music of their calls making the experience even more en-thralling. Dramatic too is the sight of a flock coming in to land.

To most birdwatchers, this is the least familiar of the grey geese that winter regularly in western Europe. It was only in 1833 that it was separated from the Pink-footed Goose. While confusion is understandable, this is a striking bird with a strong character of its own. Two distinct subspecies (sometimes regarded as full species) occur in Europe. The race *fabalis* (Taiga or Western Bean Goose) breeds in small numbers across the western part of the vast belt of coniferous woodland known as the taiga. The slightly smaller race *rossicus* (Tundra or Russian Bean Goose) breeds mainly farther east on the Arctic tundra.

Not nearly as bulky as Greylags, Bean Geese have a far more elegant air, thanks to their long proportions, in particular the long neck and almost triangular head. In all but bright sunlight, they look dark brown like the finest chocolate, the colour of the dark peaty soil where they breed. Their shyness and readiness to take flight at the least alarm make them a challenge to see well – and, more important, without disturbing them unduly. They usually hold the neck very upright, more like a swan. Indeed, while Bewick's Swan is the most goose-like of the European swans, the Bean Goose is the most swan-like of the European geese.

LESSER WHITE-FRONTED GOOSE
Anser erythropus

Globally scarce, with three fragmented sub-populations: an E. Asian one wintering in China, a C. Asian one wintering around the Black Sea and a tiny N. European one that winters in Ukraine, Azerbaijan, Greece, Bulgaria, Hungary and the Netherlands with staging sites in Estonia, Lithuania and Poland.

The most beautiful of the world's grey geese, the Lesser White-front, is also the rarest. It can be hard to pick out among a flock of "carrier" species – in western Europe usually the White-fronted Goose. Smaller and neater, it has a rounded head and a shorter bill of a brighter reddish pink. The smart uniform body plumage contrasts with the dark brown neck and head, the latter set off by a yellow eye-ring that often looks slightly raised and swollen. The white blaze on the forehead extends farther up and ends in more of a point than a rounded margin.

Lesser White-fronts breed across the relatively narrow zone of low-Arctic and sub-Arctic willow and birch scrub between the high-Arctic tundra and the great taiga belt to the south. It is on their wintering grounds far to the south, and on migration and at stopovers in between, that they face their major threat – the hunter's gun. Numbers have plummeted globally from 100,000 to fewer than 30,000 in under 50 years, and of these fewer than 500 pairs now breed within Europe, almost all in Russia. The rest are spread thinly across Finnmark in the far north of Norway, where there was an estimated 30–50 pairs in the 1990s, representing a huge decline from the 10,000 or so believed to breed there in the early 1900s. There may still be a few in Finland, but the wild Swedish population is now extinct. A reintroduction scheme in Swedish Lapland has restored a small population, using Barnacle Geese as foster parents, migrating with them to protected wintering areas in the Netherlands.

BARNACLE GOOSE
Branta leucopsis

Plump-bodied, with a shortish, ample neck, a gently rounded head and a short bill, these are among the loveliest of all geese. Their essentially pied plumage gives them a crisp pattern, bolder than that of any other goose native to Europe. At closer range in good light the face can be seen as not pure white but a lovely warm pale buttermilk, and the black barring of the back and wings is interlaced with steel grey that may take on an exquisite lavender hue. The pattern of black and white plumage on the head and neck of Barnacles shows individual variation. At one extreme, some have all black necks with just the face (apart from the lores) white and the black extending forwards along the crown as far as eye level; while at the other, the white extends down the foreneck as a wedge and the crown is black only at the rear.

Though usually forming only loose colonies at their Arctic breeding sites on virtually inaccessible cliffs and rocky seabird islands, these are intensely gregarious birds in winter, with flocks

Greenland breeders winter in Ireland and W. Scotland; the Svalbard population on the Solway Firth; and those nesting on Novaya Zemlya and Sweden on the coasts of Germany and the Netherlands. The world population has soared from 30,000 breeding pairs in the 1950s to almost double that today.

often numbering in the thousands. They are concentrated at just a small number of sites, with two-thirds of the entire Greenland breeding population on the Scottish island of Islay. Their stubby bills and fast pecking rate make them very efficient grazers as they feed in big, tightly packed flocks on saltmarsh plants and nutrient-rich swards of grass and clover on cattle pasture.

As they fly from their roosts in large, irregular lines or ragged U's, they utter a shrill yapping, like excited little dogs. Close up, the creaking noise of the wings is apparent. On the ground, flocks keep up a conversational murmur while feeding.

RED-BREASTED GOOSE
Branta ruficollis

Breeds in small colonies only on the Taimyr, Gydan and Yamal peninsulas in Siberia; majority of population winters on western coasts of the Black Sea, in Romania and Bulgaria, with very small numbers regularly wintering in the Netherlands, Greece and Turkey, and vagrants elsewhere in Europe.

A linocut on legs would be an apt if fanciful description; but this lovely bird is far more than just the most colourful and boldly patterned of all geese. Neat and small for a goose, with a tiny, stubby bill, it is special because of its relative rarity on a global scale. Its breeding range is restricted to just three peninsulas in the west Siberian tundra, with about 70 percent on the Taimyr Peninsula. Its wintering range, too, is limited, with 80–90 percent of the entire world population (which may number fewer than 38,000 birds) dependent on just five areas in Bulgaria and Romania. Here they are vulnerable to agricultural intensification.

Despite its jigsaw of bright colours, those seeking it out are often surprised by its ability on the ground to melt into the background of a mass of larger congeners – usually White-fronted, Brent or Barnacle geese. For the bird, such a bold crazy-paving-like pattern, well named "disruptive" by biologists, is an adaptation evolved to break up its outline against a background of other shapes. This reflects the relatively high risk of predation, especially from the Arctic fox (as well as outlaw human hunters). It has a habit of using Peregrines, or sometimes Rough-legged Buzzards, Snowy Owls or Herring Gulls, as bodyguards by breeding very near the nests of these species.

For those who do not venture out of western Europe, seeing this exotic little goose in the wild is a lifetime, or at best occasional, treat, usually depending on a rare bird alert. Even better, it might just be a lucky find suddenly standing out in that flock of larger geese as they take flight across an estuary saltmarsh or a field of winter wheat.

RUDDY SHELDUCK
Tadorna ferruginea

Worldwide, the second commonest shelduck (after Common). Wild birds are in Europe restricted largely to the S.E., where it is widespread but local. Perhaps over 90 percent of the total of 19,000–32,000 breeding pairs occur in Russia and Turkey. Has suffered large declines recently, at least in Turkey.

The problem often facing a birder in western Europe who encounters this handsome bird is whether it is a truly wild individual or not. Many do escape from waterfowl collections, where they are valued for the subtle beauty of their plumage, the richly glowing cinnamon body contrasting with the orange-buff head – though not for their belligerent nature.

To be sure of seeing wild birds, you must travel to south-eastern Europe. Here, on the fringes of its (overwhelmingly Asian) range, it has a scattered but widespread distribution.

The Spanish name *Tarro canelo*, or "Cinammon Pot", refers to this duck's stout body, as well as its colour. Some North African breeders used to migrate in autumn to Spain (a rare example of a bird migrating north to winter in Europe), but this exodus has declined to just the odd individual in most years. With the decline of native European birds, the small feral population well established in the Netherlands, Germany and a few other European countries has assumed greater conservation importance.

All shelduck are very vocal, but none more so than this species. When disturbed, it will produce an incessant volley of loud calls once likened to a cross between the strident cries of a large gull and a person gargling, and transliterated in a classic work on wildfowl by the French ornithologist Jean Delacour as *ka-ha-ha* (for the female) and *ho-ho-ho* (for the male). In Hindu myth the male and female are lovers torn asunder, doomed to pour out their hearts to one another with cries of grief.

PINTAIL
Anas acuta

Strong contenders for most beautiful of all ducks, and so well loved by bird artists, the drakes are among that select band of birds that look beautiful whatever they are doing – from sailing serenely on fresh water in summer like sharp-prowed, long-sterned schooners or riding the waves in a grey winter estuary, to impressing a female by holding their "pin" tails at jaunty angles. The colour combinations and patterns they sport are exquisite, and could not be improved on by a top fashion designer or interior decorator – the chocolate head and neck, neatly slashed at the rear by the white peninsula extending up from the breast; the long cream and black lanceolate feathers cascading over the delicately barred grey and white flanks. As with some other ducks, such as the drake Gadwall, these fine barrings are referred to by one of those Latin-derived words beloved of biologists – "vermiculations", meaning a worm-like pattern. The drake's buttermilk and black stern pattern is a

One of the most widespread of all ducks, breeds across northern Eurasia, N. Africa and N. America, wintering south as far as central Africa, S. Asia, various Pacific islands and Central America. In Europe, hunting and habitat loss, with dependence on a few vulnerable wintering sites, have caused recent declines.

variation on that displayed by the much smaller but almost as elegant drake Teal. The females, too, are a cut above the average female dabbling duck, with their battleship grey bill outlined in black and their paler, greyer plumage. Although they lack the rakishness of the males, their tails are relatively long and pointed.

In flight, too, these are elegant birds. Flocks dash about fast and often high in neat V's, when the small head, long slender neck and long, tapering rear body combine with the long, slender wings to add to their élan.

GARGANEY

Anas querquedula

Breeds over a huge range right across Eurasia, from Britain and France to far eastern Russia. Most western European countries have relatively small and varying numbers, with 90 percent of pairs in Russia and Ukraine. European birds winter across a broad belt in Africa south of the Sahara.

European birders associate duck-watching chiefly with winter, when huge concentrations fly across the continent to their wintering grounds. While it has a similar size and structure to the equally beautiful Eurasian Teal, a common breeder and winter visitor in Europe, the scarcer Garganey is the exception to this general rule. It is the only European wildfowl species in which virtually the entire population migrates to winter in the northern tropics of Africa. Its exclusive status as a visitor is reflected in the old English name of Summer Teal. While watching other wildfowl in western Europe tends to be associated with cold and blustery weather, the Garganey evokes drowsy days with the buzz of insects and a shimmer of heat haze over the reedy or swampy shallow freshwaters it loves to haunt.

Adding to the effect, the male's advertising call sounds rather insect-like – hence another of its old English common names, Cricket Teal – or, since it is lower and fuller than a cricket, more like a singing frog. Drake Garganey music has also been compared to the sound of breaking ice, or even to that made by a stick run along the teeth of a large comb, like the often-mentioned way of imitating the staccato two-phrase song of the male Corncrake, but with the hand moving more hesitantly to produce a more variable single note. But to my ears at least, it is closest to the noise made by trailing a stick along metal railings, or of a fishing reel being wound in.

Shyness, scattered distribution and difficulties of female identification mean that the true picture of the species' status in much of its range is hard to assess. Hunting is a threat.

MARBLED DUCK
Marmaronetta angustirostris

Uniquely among European dabbling ducks, the male and female of this subtly attractive bird look alike. With its grey-brown plumage and pointed tail, at a distance it could look like a small female Pintail, but a good view reveals that it really resembles no other European duck. The marbling that accounts for its common and generic names is formed by pale feather edges; the other features on what is essentially an all-brown and buff bird are the large dark smudge around each eye and, in the male, the shaggy crest hanging from the nape. Another distinction resides in the absence rather than the presence of a feature: that its plain brown wings lack the metallic-coloured speculum on other dabbling ducks. Although it has been assigned often to the main dabbling duck genus *Anas*, it generally merits a genus of its own nowadays.

Once this small duck was more common, and in places one of the most abundant species of wildfowl. Until Saddam Hussein's destruction of its habitat by draining, the bulk of the world population lived in the vast marshes of southern Iraq. It was probably never common

Today one of the rarest European wildfowl, threatened elsewhere in its fragmented range in N. Africa, Canary and Cape Verde Is., and central and S. Asia. The two European breeding populations, in S. Spain and the Caucasus, are small relics of their former numbers – just a few hundred breeding pairs.

in most of Europe, owing to its dependence on shallow wetlands and its preference for seasonal or sporadic waters such as brackish coastal lagoons and shallow marshes – the kinds of places favoured for drainage by land developers. Compounding the problem is its fondness for remaining on a single water body rather than commuting to a safe roosting site, like most other wildfowl. Also, it is depressingly easy to shoot. Although it has been recorded increasingly in northern Europe in recent years, most birds are regarded as escapes from wildfowl collections.

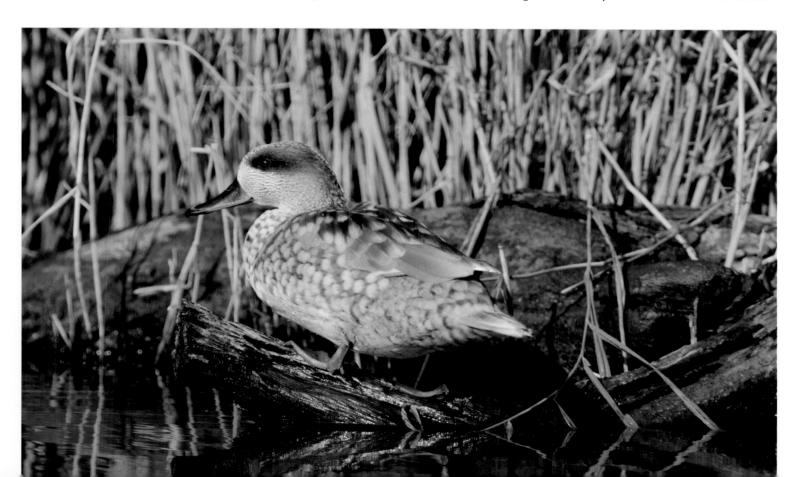

FERRUGINOUS DUCK

Aythya nyroca

Breeds discontinuously from western Europe to western China, but despite being regarded as recently as the 1920s as one of the most plentiful of all wildfowl over much of this huge range, it has undergone massive declines, especially in Europe; for example, it is now greatly reduced in Spain.

"Ferruginous" means "rust-coloured", but the dictionary definition does scant justice to the splendour of the male's head and body plumage, which runs the gamut from deep mahogany under an overcast sky to a rich lambent chestnut in sunlight.

The specific name *nyroca* originates from a Russian word *nyrok* for a type of waterbird, while the usual vernacular name in Spain is *Porrón Pardo*, literally translating as "brown wine-jar" and presumably referring to the elongated neck (*porrón* is the word for a particular type of jar with a long spout). An old English name for this unusual diving duck was the Common White-eye, and indeed the male's eyes have creamy white irides that can blaze across the water at surprisingly long range. The neat white stern adds to the bird's dapper appearance and is found in both sexes. The "Common" part of the old name may produce a hollow laugh from birders who have sought this increasingly hard-to-find species. It has undergone catastrophic declines in much of its range, due chiefly to habitat alteration and hunting. Today, BirdLife International places Ferruginous Duck in the Near-threatened category on a global scale. Although there may be as many as 24,000 pairs left in Europe, this is the most optimistic recent estimate, and the true number may be nearer 13,000. It is not only scarcity that makes the Ferruginous Duck such a hard-won prize: compared to most other *Aythya* species, it is far less sociable, and doubtless often overlooked as it swims unobtrusively among dense rafts of its commoner relatives.

STELLER'S EIDER
Polysticta stelleri

The fact that this species is normally just a winter visitor to the far northern rim of Europe makes it one of the most exciting birds for an adventurous birder to find on a visit to the handful of regular European wintering sites such as Varangerfjord in northern Norway or one of the Baltic Sea sites off Lithuania or Estonia. Here these smallest and least typically eider-like of the world's four species of eider may form large, densely packed rafts that perform impressive feats of group diving, as synchronized as a Busby Berkeley spectacular, powering down to the seabed in search of mussels and other molluscs as well as crustaceans and marine worms.

The drake has lovely iridescent, deep purplish-blue scapular and tertial feathers – a cascade of broad curving stripes against the snow-white colour of the rest of the inner wings, contrasting with the delicate warm peach of the breast plumage that subtly darkens to chestnut and almost black on the belly. Even the more sober female is brighter than the females

Breeds along the coasts of the Arctic Ocean and Bering Sea from the Yamal Peninsula to the Kolyma Delta in Siberia and Barrow and North Slope of Alaska. In winter the western Siberian population migrates westward to the Kola Peninsula, extreme northern Finland and Scandinavia and parts of the Baltic Sea.

of other eiders, flaunting a slightly more subdued version of the male's long tertials and a Mallard-like blue-and-white speculum.

As well as being the smallest eider, Steller's Eider also has the most restricted breeding range, along remote coasts of far eastern Siberia and northern Alaska. There is concern about its future: populations have plummeted in the last thirty years or so, as a result of hunting, pollution, drowning in fishing nets, depletion of food stocks and an increase in predation by Ravens and large gulls, which thrive on waste food as humans spend more time in the eiders' formerly pristine homelands.

KING EIDER

Somateria spectabilis

Apart from the Long-tailed Duck, the King Eider breeds farther north than any other waterfowl, across much of the coast of Russia. European sites are in western Russia and Svalbard, Norway. It also occurs from Alaska across Canada to Greenland. It winters on coasts to the south of its breeding range.

This striking bird arguably has the widest range of any species of eider. Its common name is well chosen: with his brilliant crown-like headgear, a frontal shield of bare orange skin bulging upwards from the equally bright coral-red bill, the drake is certainly a regal sight – especially when an individual turns up as a vagrant to temperate waters among groups of lovely but less spectacular Common Eiders. Of the common names in various languages, only the usual French name, *Eider à tête grise* (Grey-headed Eider), fails to do it justice; an alternative – *Eider remarquable* – is far more apposite.

King Eiders often fade from view rapidly when a group dives in unison. Favouring deeper water than Common Eiders, Kings usually descend more than 20 m (55 m has been noted) to forage for molluscs, sea urchins and other prey on the sea-bed.

Tameness in a totally wild creature always makes it special, and the female King Eider is one of that select group of incubators that sits tightly on her eggs – some especially confiding females can even be touched or picked up off the nest. The duck feeds seldom during the three-week incubation period. One female never left her nest for seven days before being flushed by an Arctic fox. Another endearing feature of the female is that, in contrast to the Common Eider, she appears to have an expression, and a cheerful smile at that, thanks to the angle of her gape line. King Eiders sometimes breed alongside the nests of Long-tailed Skuas and (during years of lemming abundance, when presumably they do not need to bother with other prey) Snowy Owls, which rarely bother the ducks but keep predators away.

HARLEQUIN DUCK
Histrionicus histrionicus

In Europe, some 3,000 or so pairs at most breed only in Iceland, where it remains all year and is vulnerable to the possibility of aluminium smelting, not least because of an associated dam and hydroelectric scheme. Elsewhere it is more abundant, in eastern Russia, Alaska, Canada and Greenland.

The word "dapper" could almost have been invented to describe this characterful, colourful pigeon-sized duck. Unlike typical sea ducks, the dainty but incredibly tough Harlequin lives along fast-flowing, food-rich streams and rivers, where it feeds by diving to the bottom and then walking against the current, searching for aquatic insects and their larvae among the rocks, like an outsized Dipper. Also like a Dipper, a Harlequin can dive into the water from flight and is loath to fly over land. The birds seem to positively relish the fastest, most turbulent waters, but they do occasionally suffer broken bones, as evidenced by fractures that have mended. No other European or indeed Northern Hemisphere duck has this ultra-adventurous lifestyle.

With the coming of winter, as many freshwater feeding sites freeze, Harlequin Ducks move down to the sea. Still they favour the roughest waters, diving now for molluscs and crustaceans along rocky shores and headlands, seemingly heedless of the waves crashing about them.

The unique, bright pattern of grey-blue, black, chestnut-red and white making up the drake's plumage is, of course, what gave the species its name, from the tradition of the stage Harlequin, Columbine's young lover in the Commedia dell'Arte (the specific name, *histrionicus*, is the Latin word whose original meaning was "theatrical"). Despite its boldness, this pattern is surprisingly cryptic against a background of broken water and wave-splashed rocks, breaking up the bird's outline.

VELVET SCOTER

Melanitta fusca

Unless you travel north to its mainly freshwater breeding haunts in northern Europe, this is a winter bird. Often encountered tucked among offshore flocks of the more abundant Common Scoter, this cousin is handsomer, bigger and heavier. Although there may be as many as a million in north-west Europe in winter, the bird mainly occurs singly or in small groups. The flashes of white are always a pleasant surprise, clinching identification as a swimming bird flaps its wings – fortunately a frequent habit – during a telescope sweep of a big raft of Common Scoter riding the waves offshore. Even on the closed wing this major field mark, celebrated in the alternative name of White-winged Scoter, is often visible as a thin white line. If its owner obliges even further, and shows its legs as it rises half out of the water, or when it dives, these can be seen to be red, brighter in the male. Together with his mainly golden-yellow, red-tipped bill, they add a touch of colour to a bird that is essentially velvety black. Even quite close to, the drake's small crescent-shaped white

Breeds in N. and central Norway and in Sweden, Finland, Estonia and N. Russia (with a smaller population in the Caucasus). Major concentrations of wintering birds are in the eastern North Sea (20 percent off Denmark) and the Baltic, including the Gulf of Pommern and the Gulf of Riga.

marking under the white-irised eye can be hard to make out, but when seen it gives the bird an almost comical "expression". The common name relates, apparently, not to fast movement but to a historical printing error for "sooter", referring to the sooty black plumage of the drake. Be that as it may, these are, like other sea-ducks, fast fliers. But their flight looks heavier, more laboured than that of their common relative, and take-off is more of an effort. Along with some other sea ducks, Velvets partly open their wings when diving to provide extra thrust, as they plunge down far below the surface to feed off the sea-bed.

LONG-TAILED DUCK

Clangula hyemalis

Probably the most northerly breeding duck, nesting mainly north of the Arctic Circle in Iceland, Norway, Sweden, Finland, across Russia, and from Alaska to Greenland. It has bred in Britain. Many winter in the far north, others rarely move farther than Britain, Japan, Vancouver or Virginia.

It would surprise many birders to discover that the most abundant duck species worldwide appears to be the Long-tailed Duck. Major threats include fishing nets (they are deep divers, venturing to as much as 60 m down), oiling and hunting. These handsome sea ducks may still have a population of about 7.5 million right around the top of the world – though given their inaccessible habitats, such estimates are educated guesses.

Although very abundant, these compact-bodied little ducks remain special every time you have the good fortune to see a flock bobbing about like corks in a rough winter sea or a big loose skein flying out to roost, a fine last sight at dusk. All their seasonal and age-related plumages are attractive but it is the drakes' greatly elongated central tail feathers, lost only during the flightless late summer eclipse, that make them so arresting visually. These 13 cm-long appendages wave about like black whips with a life of their own.

Long-tails are also memorable for their far-carrying voices. Among the most garrulous of all wildfowl, the drakes can be heard for much of the year, often answered by the harsh, gruff calls of the females. Their wild yodelling is supremely evocative and appropriate to their wild habitat, be it the offshore waters of their wintering range or the lonely tundra pools, lakes and marshes where they breed in the brief Arctic summer. Comparisons have included the baying of distant hounds or, more fancifully still, bagpipes played by some aquatic Highland pipe major.

BARROW'S GOLDENEYE

Bucephala islandica

In the Old World, this bird breeds only in Iceland, where it is normally resident. The two N. American populations are a larger one in S. Alaska and W. Canada, south as far as N. California; and a smaller one in coastal Labrador, eastern Canada, which winters on coasts to the south, as far as New York.

Species pairs often include one bird that – to some observers at least – has the slight edge on its sibling. Even more dapper than the Common Goldeneye, the male Barrow's Goldeneye is distinguished by a neat row of six or seven white "windows" along the black scapulars. All ducks have something of a toy boat look about them, but this plumage feature adds to it by resembling a row of portholes. Further, more subtle distinctions from the more familiar relative are the crescent shape of the white cheek patch and the black of the head reflecting the light with a more regal gloss – purple and violet rather than green.

In Europe, it is restricted to Iceland, where just 500–600 pairs breed – fewer than 0.5 percent of numbers in the species' main range in western North America. Up to 90 percent of the Iceland birds breed in one of the country's prime bird sites, Lake Myvatn and its outflow, the River Laxa. Myvatn means "Midges", and it is the abundance of these insects that accounts for the ducks' concentration, forming their major summer diet. Unlike the tree-nesting Goldeneye, in the treeless landscape it haunts in Iceland Barrow's Goldeneye has to nest in deep crevices – found in abundance in the strange landscape of the lava fields around this beautiful lake. They will also use nest boxes provided for them, some on the sides of houses.

In contrast to most northerly breeding wildfowl, Barrow's Goldeneye do not move far after breeding. Icelandic breeders rarely stray from their island, making their occasional appearances in western Europe exciting for birders – if they can be shown to be truly wild.

SMEW

Mergellus albellus

Breeds in the taiga zone of northern Eurasia, from northern Scandinavia through Finland and across Russia. European breeders winter in N.W. and central Europe, with the largest numbers in the countries bordering the Baltic Sea and in the Netherlands, especially in the IJsselmeer.

If ever a wildfowl species epitomized a habitat, it is the especially stunning drake of this very distinctive, beautiful little sawbilled duck in its winter haunts, on a part-frozen lake or reservoir. His plumage varies with the light, from the blue-tinged colour often seen in ice to a pale buttermilk hue; the subtle tracery of spidery black lines and black patches rend the pristine white, like cracks in the ice. The smaller females and juveniles – and males in their flightless eclipse plumage – have a more subtle beauty, with the distinctive cap that earns them the generic

birdwatchers' name of "redhead" having the deep, rich russet colour of a weasel (an old name was Weasel Duck).

The sharp, cold beauty of the male reflects his toughness in remaining in winter as long as possible despite harsh weather on fresh waters that may be more solid than liquid: he fishes by diving into openings in the ice. Females are more likely to move out when the temperature plummets than males, with the result that concentrations of either sex build up in different parts of their winter range. Wintering flocks both large and small are often shy and restless. Big flocks are impressive to see as they synchronize their diving, while rival males in winter and early spring courtship parties frequently perform breast-pumping and crest-raising, with attacking lunges.

Their northern European breeding range offers the delight of seeing these cavity-nesting ducks emerge from a tree hole, often one previously tenanted by a Black Woodpecker.

WHITE-HEADED DUCK

Oxyura leucocephala

This remarkable-looking bird is special as the only duck native to Europe that belongs to the small and strange stifftail group. Thought to have diverged from other wildfowl early in the family's evolution, these birds earn their name from their habit of cocking their tails stiffly erect at right angles, like a miniature terrier. Grebe-like in their devotion to water, they are the most aquatic of all ducks and their *modus vivendi* is above all as diving birds. Like grebes, too, they have their legs placed so far back on the body that they can only shuffle awkwardly on land.

Any mention of this bird – and its very survival in the continent – is intimately bound up with its close relative, the Ruddy Duck, a relatively recent introduction from North America. Defenders of the newcomer are outraged at the idea of a blanket cull to prevent interbreeding with its rare cousin. Whatever the rights and wrongs, the bald statistics are that there are thought to be over half a million Ruddies flourishing

Reintroductions aimed at increasing breeding populations are underway in Corsica, Italy and Mallorca. Control measures against Ruddy Ducks are being taken in the UK, France, Spain and Portugal. Wintering birds can be seen in the lagoons at Cadiz, the Burgas area of Bulgaria and Porto Lagos, Greece.

in North America, while the world population of White-headed Ducks in Europe and Asia has undergone a 50 percent decline over the past 10 years to only 8,000–13,000 pairs.

Compared with the drake Ruddy Duck, the male of this species is a bigger, bulkier bird, with a less rich red plumage and, as the name suggests, an almost all-white head. Its equally startling bright blue bill differs in being distinctly swollen at the base, making the bird look even odder and more clown-like than its relative.

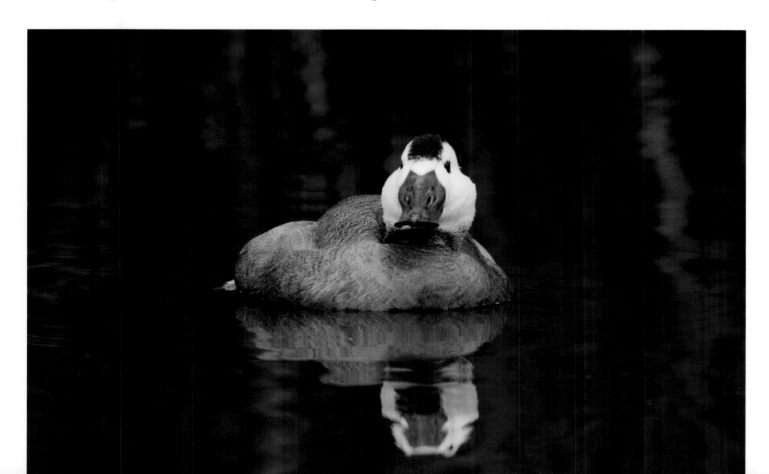

PTARMIGAN
Lagopus mutus

A scattered distribution in the mountains of south-central Europe, with a northern outpost in the Scottish Highlands. In the tundra, much more widespread, from Iceland across N. Scandinavia and Russia and around Arctic N. America. Largest European populations: Iceland, Norway and Russia.

As soft and white as the snow that surrounds it for much of the year, the Ptarmigan is Europe's high-altitude grouse par excellence. It is well provided with adaptations that fit it for life on the bleak wastes of high mountain plateaux where few other creatures make a permanent home.

Ptarmigan have a sequence of three adult seasonal plumages each year, instead of the more usual two. This ensures that in all seasons they are perfectly camouflaged, blending in seamlessly with the changing background as snow melts, rocks are revealed and the sparse mosaic of vegetation spreads. As well as being wrapped in soft, down-lined plumage that traps warmth, Ptarmigan gain further insulation from their habit of digging out a shelter in which a pair or family group can sit out the bitter cold of the night, huddled together beneath the thick blanket of snow. Their feathered feet serve as snowshoes, so that they can run at speed across snow fields as well as bare ground.

Although this splendid bird's specific name is *mutus*, it is often far from silent, having a range of guttural snoring, belching and cackling calls. Most distinctive is the flight display "song" of the male, its usual rhythm during take-off recalling "Here comes the bride" from Wagner's *Lohengrin*.

Global warming will shrink what is already a relatively restricted alpine habitat and the far larger Arctic tundra populations will also be at risk. These fleet-footed gamebirds will have nowhere to run to and nowhere to hide from Golden Eagles and other predators, as the snow vanishes and their previously invisible white plumage stands out like a beacon.

BLACK GROUSE
Tetrao tetrix

Widespread across northern and central Europe, more patchily distributed farther south, its range extends across northern Asia, mainly on uplands but lower down further north. In most of Europe, especially Britain, numbers and range are greatly diminished; very large populations in Russia.

On a cold spring dawn in the moors, assembled at their traditional display ground, or lek, male Black Grouse are ready to perform to the gathering female greyhens. Advancing and retreating like boxers, pairs of males circle round, facing one another. Their wings droop almost to the ground, the lyre-shaped tail expands to reveal the white powder-puff of undertail feathers and the red wattle above each eye is distended. As the displays become more intense, the birds start leaping into the air and sparring with one another, grabbing at their opponents with their bills.

Lekking sites are traditional, and some have been in regular use for up to 50 or more years. Nowadays, leks typically contain up to ten or so males, and only occasionally more than 40. This is a measure of the species' decline in Europe, where up to 150 males or even more could once be seen at the largest leks.

The performance is accompanied by remarkable, atmospheric sounds. The main theme is rookooing: a soft but insistent bubbling like the cooing of a roomful of demented doves. Rising and falling in pitch, this continuo is overlain with loud wing-flaps and harsh, hissing sneezes as the blackcocks leap into the air. This vocal *tour de force* can be heard from a distance of up to almost two miles in the still dawn air. All the while the subtly plumaged brown-barred greyhens observe the performance from a discrete distance, like high-school girls shyly eyeing the boys at an old-fashioned dance. The males that mate with most females tend to have the biggest combs.

CAPERCAILLIE
Tetrao urogallus

The largest numbers and most continuous distributions are in the boreal forests of northern Europe through Russia east to halfway across Siberia. Populations in W. and central Europe are fragmented. Most populations (including the reintroduced Scottish one) are small and endangered.

As with the Mute Swan (thought capable of breaking bones) the cock Capercaillie has at times been demonized as a serious threat to people. True, this largest and heaviest of all the world's 19 species of grouse can be menacing to humans, dogs and even vehicles that intrude into its deep, dark forest domain. Looking even bigger with its throat feathers bristled out into a bulging beard, broad wings beating and great tail fanned out like a turkey cock, a displaying male is certainly one of the most impressive of all European birds as it stands its ground. The odd charging male has even on occasion been known to put a man flat on his back. But in fact the bird is infinitely more threatened by humankind than the other way round.

The Capercaillie has a long history as a gamebird. In Scotland it was rendered extinct by the late 18th century. Since the 1970s, hunting has been restricted or banned in all western and central European countries. However, the main threat today, of habitat loss and degradation, remains.

These are dwellers in old-growth boreal forests of tall conifers interspersed with open patches rich in ericaceous shrubs and wildflowers. After enduring a tough winter diet consisting almost exclusively of conifer needles, which these heavy birds obtain by climbing about in the treetops with surprising agility, in summer they relish a mixed salad of leaves, buds, flowers and fruits of various herbs and shrubs. Their chicks rely on invertebrates, especially caterpillars on bilberry leaves.

CAUCASIAN SNOWCOCK

Tetraogallus caucasicus

Snowcocks form a subgroup of partridges with various features more typical of grouse – such as dense, cold-resistant plumage. The five species are specialized high-mountain denizens found mainly in central or southern Asia with two species just reaching Europe. The Caucasian Snowcock has the smallest range of these mysterious, exciting gamebirds. Its appeal is bound up with its extreme habitat: high above the tree and even scrub lines, it roams a broken world of snow and rock where few humans venture. It seldom occurs below 2,500 m in summer, and can be encountered as high as 4,000 m or more. Even in severe winters it rarely descends as far as the foothills. In its lofty domain it favours remote grassy slopes with jumbles of rocks and patches of snow relieved by alpine meadows and riven by impenetrable ravines and dramatic cliffs.

Although marginally the smallest of the snowcocks, this is a sizeable bird, the bulkier male twice the size of a Grey Partridge and about the same size as a female Capercaillie.

Endemic to the Greater Caucasus (and thus to europe), from N. Georgia and adjacent areas of Russia to N. Azerbaijan. Although the species is hunted, its remote habitat limits pressure from this potential threat. There may be as many as 67,000 breeding pairs, about 75 percent of them in Georgia.

Apart from being distinctly smaller than males, females are very similar, although their plumage is slightly duller, and unless seen well may be hard to distinguish.

These are very cautious and elusive birds, hard to find in the great expanse of mountain. When flushed, a family party will run, cackling, to the nearest ridge and then take off and descend over the top. They can only glide downhill, their heavy bodies and short wings making ascent impossible.

The Caucasian Snowcock resembles the other species found in Europe, the Caspian, but their ranges do not overlap.

GREY PARTRIDGE
Perdix perdix

Although Europe accounts for less than half its global range, the huge decline of this gamebird (for example, over 85 percent over the past 30 years in Britain) in much of its European range is cause for concern. Some of the least depleted populations occur in parts of northern France and Poland.

The Spanish equivalent of the familiar saying "And they lived happily ever after" is "*Fueron felices, y comieron perdices*" – "They were happy and dined on partridges." In Iberia, as in Britain and some other parts of Europe, this is one of the most prized of all gamebirds, both as a challenging bird to shoot and as one of the tastiest of all roasts. Although hunting is bound to have an impact on this acutely declining species, more significant is habitat loss. Across most of western and central Europe, and increasingly in the east, too, as modern farming methods replace age-old tradition, the birds are failing. Hedgerow havens and wide field margins for nesting are grubbed out, and both insect and plant food supplies are devastated by insecticides and herbicides, as well as by the loss of stubble to autumn cereal sowing.

It is not just their increasing scarcity that makes it a challenge to find these birds in a field. Beautiful, subtly patterned mottled upperparts and the broken-horseshoe marking on the underparts camouflage them superbly against a background of clods of earth or stubble. Often your first encounter with a covey is when its tight-packed members burst up into the air with a heart-stopping whirr of wings just as you are about to step on them – such disturbance is not to be encouraged during the breeding season, of course. A recent study in Germany found that in open arable farmland, population density was reduced even along roads bordered by hedgerows, suggesting that traffic noise was a critical factor. Ironically, it is sound that one misses first when the birds are gone – the wonderfully atmospheric "creaking gate" contact calls of the partridges themselves.

QUAIL

Coturnix coturnix

There are some birds that one can almost guarantee to see by going to the right place at the right time, and there are others whose presence is often utterly unpredictable. The Quail certainly falls into the latter category for most birdwatchers in Europe, making an encounter all the more rewarding. Add to that the furtiveness of a gamebird that, by contrast with the bold strutting Pheasant or the plump whirring partridges, is a diminutive recluse, and you have an exciting mixture. Usually the only evidence of the bird is the far-carrying, three-note whiplash whistle that is the male's advertising call. The traditional transliteration "wet-my-lips", while accurate and charming, cannot do justice to the power of this sound. It can be maddeningly ventriloquial. And as with the Wren or Cetti's Warbler, it seems astonishing that such a volume of penetrating sound can be produced by a bird of this size, no longer than a Skylark – a feat that often misleads you into thinking it is much

This is a widespread summer visitor to much of Europe. Numbers fluctuate, especially in some areas such as Britain, where it is scarce. It has declined over much of its European range owing to agricultural intensification, hunting, and drought in its winter quarters in central Africa.

nearer than it really is. When it stops, perhaps to make a rare flight to proclaim its presence from another field of barley or clover, you are even more aware than before of the quietness of a hot, drowsy rural summer's day. Then there it is again, more distant this time, using sound like a net to snare a mate. If that disembodied voice ever leads you to the right spot, you may be lucky and come suddenly upon its owner, when it is likely to spring up with a low, direct, fast and twisting flight on surprisingly long wings before disappearing once again into cover.

FROM DIVERS TO FLAMINGOS

BLACK-THROATED DIVER
Gavia arctica

Breeding extends from UK through Scandinavia and across the far north to eastern Siberia. It also extends into the west of Alaska, where it is known as the Arctic Loon; replaced by the similar Pacific Loon across the rest of northern N. America. It winters in coastal waters south of its breeding range.

This is one of the most striking of all European birds in both appearance and voice. A bird in pristine breeding plumage is a creature of great beauty. The crown and cheeks of its almost snake-like head and rear neck are clothed in velvety, dove-grey feathers, in which glow a pair of ruby-red eyes. The op-art theme of black and white vertical stripes up the front of the neck is continued in a much smaller "necklace" beneath the bill. Its wonderfully wild wailing calls echo through and epitomize the majestic landscapes in which it breeds.

Divers are, above all, lovers of water. Unlike ducks, they have very flattened tarsi (the bones forming the lower parts of the legs). The legs can be rotated so that on the forward stroke, they present the narrower face foremost, offering least resistance to the water, then, on the backstroke, the broader surface, adding to the overall propulsive power.

The Black-throated Diver, unlike the smaller sea-fishing Red-throated, fishes in fresh waters in the breeding season. Accordingly, it needs a large area of water by its nest to provide enough fish, crustaceans and molluscs to sustain the pair and their two chicks. Nor will just any old lake do: the birds must gain possession of a large stretch of water that will not rise after heavy rainfall or the eggs or chicks will be flooded. So many lakes that otherwise look perfect are bereft of these gorgeous birds. Artificial nesting rafts at some sites have helped against flooding. Wind farms and human disturbance are also threats.

BLACK-NECKED GREBE

Podiceps nigricollis

One of the most wide-ranging grebe species, occurring in Europe, East and southern Africa, Asia and central and western North America. A widespread but scattered breeder in Europe, with the bulk of the population in the east, especially in Poland, Russia and the Ukraine.

Grebes share a whole suite of strange traits. One that is unique to the family is that they generally build a special platform of waterweed on which to copulate: unlike male ducks and other wildfowl, the male grebe cannot mate by balancing on top of his partner as she almost submerges in the water. Another habit is that of eating their own feathers (and feeding them to their chicks) to prevent puncture of the digestive tube, fore and aft of the stomach, by cushioning it from sharp fish bones.

Grebes are also known for their striking breeding plumage, and the Black-necked is no exception, with its spray of gold and yellow plumes standing out against velvet black. At a distance, these ear-coverts can look like big floppy ears: the old English name of Eared Grebe was used for the species in Britain until 1912 and is still the official North American name. The shape of the head, too, is remarkable – high and peaked, with the almost vertical forehead sweeping up from the jauntily uptilted bill. This can be seen throughout the year, as can the brilliant ruby eyes.

Even experienced birders can struggle to distinguish a distant winter-plumaged Black-necked from a Slavonian. But the two are not as closely related as this might suggest: the Black-necked is believed to form a superspecies with four grebe species (one of them extinct) from South America, where the grebe family probably originated. It is by far the most abundant of the world's grebes, but its population in Europe of 53,000–96,000 breeding pairs probably accounts for less than 5 percent of the world total (with about 90 percent in North America), this relative scarcity adding to its specialness here.

FULMAR
Fulmarus glacialis

Originally bred in Europe only in Iceland. From there, it spread to the Faeroes and St Kilda. Now, it breeds all around Britain as well as on various other north-western coasts. Largest populations: Iceland, Svalbard, the Faeroes, Britain. Small numbers nest as far south as northern France.

Despite their abundance in northern Europe, Fulmars are always exciting to watch at their coastal nesting sites, which they visit for much of the year. Breeding pairs spend much time head-waving, jabbing their thick tube-nosed bills at one another, nibbling one another's napes, and gaping to reveal the blue-grey or purplish interiors of their mouths, all the while cackling and crooning loudly. Ornithologists who ring fulmar chicks on their nest ledges, sometimes high above the waves, must beware of the hiccoughs that herald the ejection of a stream of foul-smelling stomach oil – the species' chief defence against rivals or predators. Clothes matted with this orange or (in chicks) lumpy grey liquid wax are usually thrown away, as otherwise they retain the evil odour for many years despite repeated washings.

Fulmars are equally dramatic out to sea, coping with apparent nonchalance during a squall or storm. Their flight then is a stirring aerobatic performance, in which the bird makes skilful use of the immense power of the battering air currents. Using the technique of "dynamic soaring" shared with its huge relatives the albatrosses, it is propelled downwind in long swooping glides into a wave trough, then turns to breast the wind and shoot up high before slanting down again.

Few other European birds have undergone such dramatic range expansion. A major cause is its propensity for taking advantage of offal, originally the remains of the giant victims of large-scale whaling in the late 18th and early 19th centuries, and then, after that savage industry's decline, the massive amounts of fish offal cast overboard by trawlers.

CORY'S SHEARWATER
Calonectris diomedea

Breeds in burrows and in crevices and caves on rocky coasts and islands in the Mediterranean and Atlantic, with over 75 percent of its range within Europe. Largest colonies by far are in the Azores, with other big ones in the Canary Islands, Madeira, Italy, Malta, and on islands off the coast of Spain and in Greece.

Of all the European shearwaters, Cory's is the biggest, with a powerful two-toned bill and bulky body longer than a Great Shearwater's or Fulmar's. Often seen following ships, it has a different flight style from the stiffer action of its smaller relatives. In calm conditions, it can seem relaxed and leisurely, almost gull-like and at times even lumbering, with a few fluid beats of its long wings alternating with glides low over the water. In high winds it shoots high into the air in great bounding arcs, then banks down again to repeat the process. Characteristic at all times are the bowed wings, flexed at the tips.

Its size and power make it look rather like an albatross, albeit a relatively miniature version. The specific name *diomedea* reflects this superficial resemblance, *Diomedea* being the name given to the main genus of those far larger birds. The generic name *Calonectris*, which it shares with just two other shearwater species, means "good or beautiful swimmer". The common name celebrates Charles Barney Cory, an American, who was not only an ornithologist, bird collector and museum curator but also a millionaire and a golfing, billiards and pistol-shooting champion. Cory was the first to describe the Atlantic race *borealis* in 1881, from a specimen obtained off Cape Cod. The species was first described by the Italian-Austrian Johannes Scopoli over a century earlier, with reference to the nominate Mediterranean race. This latter race is sometimes regarded as a full species, Scopoli's Shearwater — as is the smaller and darker form, the Cape Verde Shearwater, which breeds on the Cape Verde Islands, far out in the Atlantic, 300 miles west of the coast of Senegal.

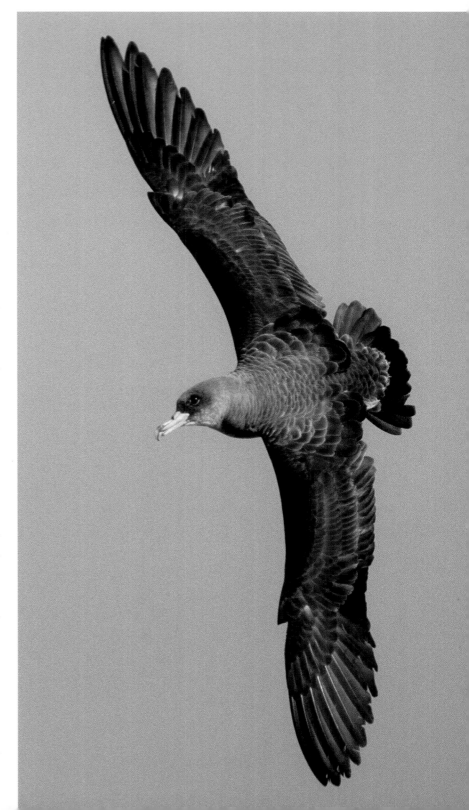

MANX SHEARWATER
Puffinus puffinus

Over 90 percent of the world population breeds in Britain and Ireland, most on offshore, rat-free islands such as Rum off W. Scotland, Skomer off S.W. Wales and the Copeland Is. off N. Ireland; the species also breeds in Iceland, the Faeroes, islands off Brittany, and in the Canaries and Madeira.

This is one of a few European birds with almost all of its population breeding in Britain. A visit to a colony is an unforgettable – and potentially unnerving – experience, as the birds that rested in great "rafts" offshore visit their nest burrows at night, and utter their spine-tingling calls, a cacophony of screaming, howling, crooning, crowing, cooing and chuckling notes.

Like others of their tribe, these seabirds are masters of dynamic soaring. In a stiff wind, their rocketing, roller-coaster progress is one of the high spots of any sea-watch as long lines of birds pass by, flashing alternately black and white as they bank and turn. The birds make skilful use of the air currents travelling at different speeds above the ocean surface, their narrow, rigid wings almost shearing the water as they descend into the troughs between the waves.

Among the greatest of all ocean navigators, Manx Shearwaters make huge, rapid annual migrations to winter mainly off the Atlantic coast of South America: this is the only European bird species to migrate regularly to this region. Even at their breeding colonies, they travel far and fast when collecting food to satisfy their plump young. Birds from Welsh colonies are thought to fly as far as the Bay of Biscay to take advantage of large shoals of sardines – a round trip of about 1,200 miles.

Manx Shearwaters are extraordinarily long-lived. One breeding on the Copeland Islands, ringed when five years old at least in July 1953, was retrapped in July 2003, making it at least 55. It had probably travelled well over 600,000 miles – equivalent to circumnavigating the globe 24 times – on migration alone.

LEACH'S STORM-PETREL

Oceanodroma leucorhoa

Reassuringly, the European breeders account for just 0.5 percent of the 10 million-pair world population, which nest mainly on islands off Newfoundland and the Pacific coasts of North America. From 1997, small numbers of these wide-ranging birds have been found breeding in the S. Hemisphere.

This is Europe's most enigmatic seabird. Until recently there was total uncertainty over its true numbers, with only the widest range of estimates of minimum and maximum numbers to go on – for example, from 10,000 to 100,000 pairs in the British Isles in 1991. This was due to the difficulty of censusing a bird that is merely the size of a Starling and nests down a burrow on remote islands which it visits only during the breeding season at night.

But recently the technique of playing back tape recordings of the eerie, other-worldly calls of the bird, memorably described by Andrew Stevenson, bird recorder for the Outer Hebrides and Western Isles, as sounding like "a goblin on acid", has resulted in a far more accurate assessment. This is a sound that only relatively few, privileged birders will hear. However, every so often severe weather blows large numbers of these oceanic wanderers onshore or even inland.

Leach's Petrel breeds in fair numbers in the British Isles, almost all on remote islands off northern Scotland (48,000–65,000 pairs), with almost 95 percent of the total on the St Kilda group. In Ireland, there are just 300 pairs or so at one site, the Stags of Broadhaven off County Mayo. The largest European colonies are in Iceland, totalling between 80,000 and 150,000 pairs. The European population is concentrated at relatively few sites, and though these are all remote, they are potentially vulnerable to the introduction of mink, rats or other predators, as well as Great Skuas on St Kilda.

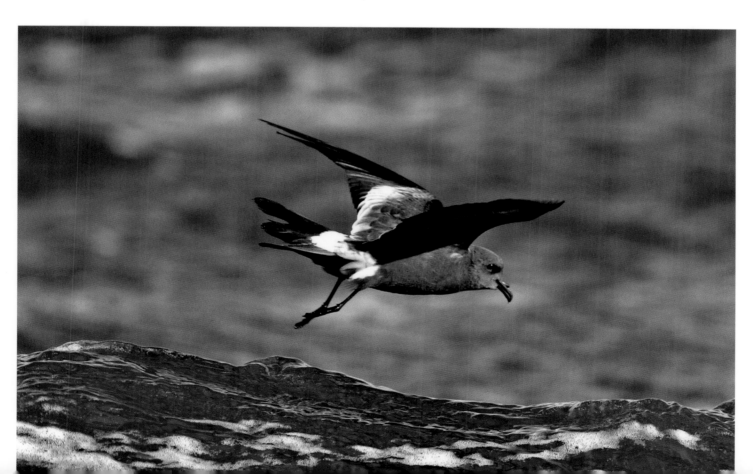

DALMATIAN PELICAN
Pelecanus crispus

The small European population (fewer than 1,800 breeding pairs) breeds colonially in freshwater wetlands, river deltas and coastal lagoons; numbers have increased at the largest colony, in N.W. Greece, but elsewhere declines continue and the species remains threatened by loss of habitat.

The world's seven species of pelicans include some of the largest and heaviest of all flying birds, and the two European species, Great White and Dalmatian, are the largest of all. The latter, on average, just takes championship position, at least in terms of length; it weighs almost as much, making it one of the heaviest waterbirds in the world. Next to the Australian and Great White, it has the longest bill of any bird.

Pelicans are ungainly-looking birds on the water or when roosting or nesting. In the air, though, they are supremely majestic, whether soaring on thermals in lazy spirals or in steady powered flight low over the water. Birds from some Dalmatian Pelican colonies may commute 6–30 miles each day to find food, and many make annual migrations.

Unlike the White Pelican, which fishes only in the shallows, Dalmatian Pelicans often feed in deep waters. With the bill submerged, the pouch is used to net fish, crabs and shrimps. Like other pelicans, these are among the relatively few birds that feed co-operatively. Forming a horseshoe-shaped phalanx, they swim slowly, wings flapping every 15–20 seconds, to drive the fish into the shallows. Here the great bills can rapidly scoop up their prey in quantity. Sometimes a bird will plunge its body below the surface to reach fish deeper down. Another use for the capacious pouch is as a huge living bowl, into which parents returning from a fishing expedition regurgitate a lukewarm fish soup for the young to stick their heads into and sup from.

GANNET
Morus bassanus

The most dramatic and powerful of all European seabirds, this is the biggest member of the gannet and booby family worldwide, and the only one to breed on this continent. Like its relatives, it has a cigar-shaped body, its tapering shape accentuated forward by the powerful, pointed dagger of a bill and aft by its long pointed tail.

The display of mass plunge-diving by feeding flocks is one of the world's greatest wildlife spectacles. They hurtle down like a giant's quiver of gleaming white arrowheads shot at a steep slant into the sea. The birds' paths cross one another in a dizzying blizzard of bodies that throw up great plumes of spray as they hit the water with tremendous thwacks. Being a species that lives in colonies containing up to tens of thousands, nesting only about 60 cm apart, Gannets have evolved a complex suite of precise, ritualized behavioural actions and responses that help them maintain social order. Even so, fights over nest sites are common, and often vicious.

A large colony is awe-inspiring. As you approach in a small boat, from a distance the carpet of gleaming white bodies along the top of an island cliff resembles a giant iced cake. When you get nearer, you are faced with a phenomenal assault on your senses of smell and hearing. The intense sharp tang of guano hits the nostrils as the cacophony of strident guttural *arrrah arrrah arrrah* calls swells into a deafening chorus. Counting such densely packed colonies is no easy task, but aerial surveys have proved their value in increased accuracy at censusing large ones or those on particularly remote or dangerous sites. Indeed, more is known about the world population of this species about than any other common seabird. Satellite tracking provides evidence of the astonishing distances birds will travel from the colonies to dive for fish for their young – as far as 335 miles from the big colony on the Bass Rock off the south-east coast of Scotland. It is to this long-studied colony that the Gannet's specific name refers.

Over 70 percent of the world population breeds in the British Isles at 18 colonies, all on islands apart from those on mainland cliffs at two colonies in Yorkshire and the Moray Firth. The rest are in Iceland, Norway, the Faeroes, Germany, France and the Channel Islands; and in eastern Canada.

PYGMY CORMORANT

Phalacrocorax pygmaeus

Present in a few wetland areas across S.E. Europe and in Russia, Ukraine and the Caucasus. Largest populations in Romania and Azerbaijan. Other sites: Lake Kerkini and Mikri Prespa (Greece), Lake Skutari/Shkodra (Montenegro/Albania) and Sultan marshes (Turkey). Far more secure than 40 years ago.

This is a good example of the appeal of a bird that is a diminutive version of far more familiar close relatives. One of a small group of "microcormorants", it is only half the size of the Cormorant, being about as big as a Coot. Furthermore, the rounded profile of its head, the thick neck and the short, deep bill give it a very different profile, making the Pygmy look less reptilian, even a bit like a duckling or gosling. The sepulchral tones of the typical cormorant's plumage are softened during the breeding season by the rich reddish brown of the head feathers, which are shaggy like the "fur" of a teddy bear. In flight, its long paddle-like tail sticks out almost as much as its head, so that at times it may look as if this unusual bird is flying backwards.

The Pygmy Cormorant differs from its large relative also in its ecology. Although like most cormorants it is primarily a fish-eater, it seeks its smaller prey in very different surroundings – river backwaters, oxbows, fish ponds, flooded fields, rice paddies, drainage channels and swamps. Here it dives down to about 2.5 metres at most, typically emerging after only five or six seconds and rarely staying under as much as a minute. The other primary need is for shrubs, trees, reeds or other dense emergent vegetation where it can find sanctuary for nesting. Some colonies contain several hundred birds, while smaller ones are often shared with egrets, Night Herons and Glossy Ibises. Here, the Pygmy Cormorants' strange rhythmic, almost gooselike calls can be distinguished from the cries of their neighbours.

BITTERN
Botaurus stellaris

Widespread but rare and patchily distributed throughout W. Europe, owing to drainage and persecution; depends on large reedbeds for breeding; wintering birds can make do with smaller areas of reeds. Conservation initiatives are bearing fruit. In E. Europe (esp. Poland, Russia), numbers are far larger.

For most of us, seeing this extremely secretive bird is a matter of luck, even though a male may be broadcasting his presence with foghorn booms. Days spent at a known site may yield only a brief glimpse of a bird swallowed up by the forest of reed stems. More likely you will see an individual flying from one stand of reeds to another, when it can look like a big owl, until you see the stiletto bill or long green trailing legs.

For those fortunate to see one well, it can look comical when clambering through the reeds, large feet clutching a bunch of swaying stems for support. This behaviour seems surprising for such a large bird unless one realizes that, as with owls and other birds whose thick, loose plumage and big broad wings make them look far bulkier than they really are, the skeleton beneath is surprisingly small and compact.

The Bittern is a consummate shape-shifter, one moment looking plump and compact, the next slender and elongated as it stretches out its neck in response to danger. In the famous "bittern stance" the bird points its bill skywards and its streaky plumage blends into the reeds. It even goes so far as to sway with them when there is a breeze.

Although they can look very clumsy as they flop down after a short escape flight, Bitterns do make far more impressive aerial excursions, as in spring when the polygamous males need to establish territory and the right to mates. Up to half a dozen or more birds may take to the air above the reedbed, circling round and lunging at one another with their fierce bills. On the ground, too, males can be murderously aggressive.

SQUACCO HERON
Ardeola ralloides

Breeds in scattered populations in Europe, around the Mediterranean and the Black Sea (with a sizeable population in the Danube Delta), in Turkey (about 32 percent of the European population), and Russia (35 percent). It winters in northern tropical Africa. The larger African population is mainly resident.

Arguably the most beautifully plumaged of all Europe's herons, the Squacco Heron is one of the pond heron group, whose five other species are found outside Europe, in Africa, Madagascar and Asia. In contrast to most herons, pond herons have a striking seasonal plumage change. With the onset of breeding, the Squacco Heron changes from a dark-streaked fawn bird into a far more handsome creature, sporting rich golden buff breast feathers, and a shimmering violet tinge to the dark tawny back with its long plumes covering the white rump, tail and wings.

Its crowning glory is a long spiky crest of black-bordered white feathers which it erects during courtship displays.

As with other herons, the bare parts of breeding birds change colour in spring. The bill, legs and feet are a dull greenish-yellow for most of the year. In courting birds the bill takes on a bright, pale blue, as does the patch of bare loral skin between bill and eye, while the legs and feet briefly glow coral-red. This is also a bird that transforms itself when it takes wing, from a mainly brown or buff bird to an almost all-white one. The large snowy-coloured wings also makes it look larger than it is.

The English naturalist John Ray referred to the bird by a local Italian name, "Sguacco", in 1678. By 1752 this was being spelled "Squacco" by another naturalist, John Hill. It is most likely to be a reference to the heron's harsh squawking calls, often heard at dusk, especially during the aggressive "forward display" that is part of the bird's ritualized defence of its territory.

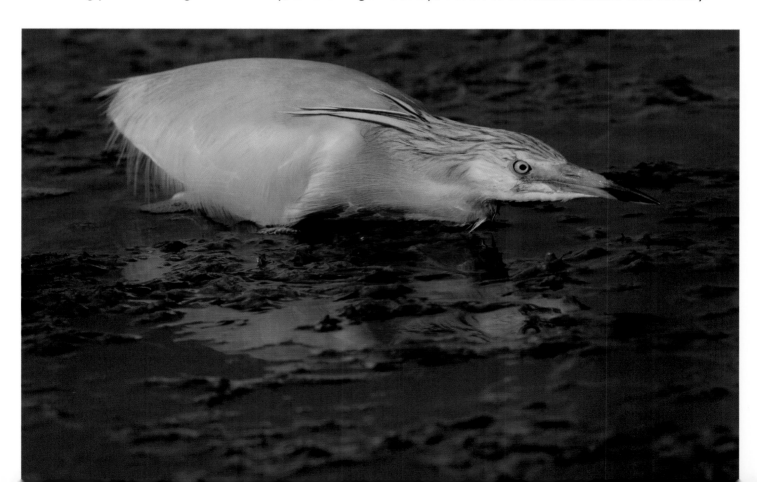

CATTLE EGRET
Bubulcus ibis

Breeds widely in Portugal and in Spain, with small but expanding populations in France and Italy. Northern breeders disperse widely in winter. Outside Europe, it is a widespread resident in Africa, S. and E. Asia north to Japan, Australia, southern USA, and northern and central South America.

This is a bird that is constantly surprising ornithologists and biogeographers by turning up in new places on the edge of its range or, in the case of especially peripatetic pioneers, far away from others of its kind.

Among European egrets this rather dumpy and ungraceful species is an exception in having relatively short legs and a short, heavy bill, suiting it for feeding on dry land. One of the world's most successful birds, the Cattle Egret has evolved a feeding behaviour that is a classic example of commensalism – the relationship between two or more different species of organisms in which one of the partners gains some benefit without harming the other(s). The common names in English and many other European languages celebrate its well-known habit of employing moving cattle as beaters to flush out its prey. But although using cattle for preference, it also makes use of horses, donkeys, goats, sheep and (especially in Africa) large wild grazing mammals, such as African buffalos, elephants and zebras. Elsewhere it may follow deer, camels and even capybaras, and sometimes chickens, geese, cranes or ostriches. All these are creatures that walk at a similar speed to the egret when foraging.

The British ornithologist Derek Goodwin likened the "head sway", that curious waggling of the bird's head as it is about to strike its prey with its bill, to "a golfer addressing the ball". Like a golfer, too, this crow-sized heron prefers relatively short grass or other vegetation – so that it can easily dart out and snap up grasshoppers or other large insects disturbed by its grazing companions.

The secret of its worldwide success is essentially twofold. First is its ability to feed in habitats cleared and improved by humans for grazing livestock. Then there is its willingness to disperse, travelling huge distances over land and sea, and to establish new populations – including those on remote islands, from St Helena or St Peter and St Paul Rocks, way out in the Atlantic, to many small islands studding the vastness of the Pacific.

GREAT EGRET
Ardea alba

Very fragmented breeding range in Europe, and very scarce. Small, growing populations in the Netherlands and France, larger ones from eastern Austria east to the Ukraine. Most of these birds winter in the east Mediterranean/North Africa. Increasing numbers in central and N.W. Europe are resident.

Almost as cosmopolitan as the Cattle Egret, this large, imposing heron ranges across every continent save Antarctica. Its common name is justified by its size, while the specific name celebrates its stunningly white plumage. Only the "egret" part may be misleading: the bird has recently been moved from the genus *Egretta*, the small to medium-sized day-active members of the heron family, to *Ardea*, containing larger species such as the Grey and Purple Herons. The Great Egret shares various features with the latter, although it has egret-like displays.

As big as a Grey Heron, it shares that bird's ponderous wingbeats rather than the faster, more graceful flight of its comparatively diminutive cousin the Little Egret. Although superficially looking like a scaled-up version of the latter, in flight it generally holds its long neck in a far more abrupt and awkwardly angular kink, almost as if it were broken.

The Great Egret is at its most spectacular during spring courtship, when adorned with a frothy filigree of 30–50 finely barbed, lacy display plumes, or aigrettes, cascading from its back far beyond its short tail and extending up to 50 cm. At this time, too, the bare skin of the lores, that area of a bird between bill base and eye, takes on an extraordinary brightness as it changes from pale greenish yellow to a bright pistachio green.

As well as being admired by female egrets, the aigrettes were also coveted by Victorian fashion designers for the plume trade. Wholesale slaughter almost resulted in the extinction of this and other egret species. During the first quarter of 1885, 750,000 bird skins were sold on the London market alone.

PURPLE HERON
Ardea purpurea

Far patchier in its European distribution than the Grey Heron, being dependent on reed beds. Russia and Ukraine hold the largest populations, probably totalling over 80 percent; followed by France, Spain, Italy and Hungary. European birds are migrants, wintering in tropical Africa.

With their rather pterodactyl-like flight silhouettes, herons and egrets, like cormorants, remind one with a jolt that birds are essentially feathered reptiles. However, in the case of the Purple Heron, a better comparison is with a snake, especially when just the long, sinuous neck and head are visible peering cautiously from reeds. That scrawny neck can look little thicker than the leaf-blades of the reeds among which it loves to hide, its thinness emphasized by neck stripes. If it were a super model, it would be deemed anorexic. Its habit of aiming its tapering head and long bayonet bill up at an angle makes it look even more wary than a Grey Heron. What's more, a Purple Heron will sometimes use the same ploy for vanishing as its slightly smaller but stockier relative the Bittern, by pointing neck and head vertically and mimicking the reeds. As a result, this is one of those big birds, like the Bittern, that is far more often seen in flight. Then, the disproportionately big feet are apparent, splayed out behind the bird as an ungainly afterthought.

Thin in appearance and thin on the ground, too, Purple Herons are, in Europe at any rate, tied to dense reedbeds for feeding and largely for breeding as well. Unfortunately, these are severely threatened habitats in most countries. Furthermore, the birds are very sensitive to disturbance. There have been major declines in many places. Losses (especially of first-year birds) also occur on migration, due partly to hunting. Others die as a result of the drying out of their African winter quarters.

BLACK STORK
Ciconia nigra

Western limits are in central Portugal and Spain and France, with far more breeding across central and eastern Europe, from Germany to Russia, and small numbers in N. Greece and Turkey. Most winter in Africa and S. Asia, though Spanish and South African breeders are resident.

Unlike the White Stork, this rarer relative craves solitude, far from human settlement. Darker than the woodland shadows it haunts, the Black Stork is like a photographic negative of its far more familiar cousin, in behaviour as well as appearance. It feeds mainly on fish and amphibians rather than insects, reptiles and small mammals, and so is usually found nearer water. Although it clappers its bill far less often and far more quietly, it has a well developed voice compared with the almost mute White Stork, with a range of whistling, piping and soft hissing calls.

Most nest as solitary pairs, in mature, undisturbed forest. Some, however, breed on crags and cliffs or in caves, as in Spain, the Carpathians, and the Caucasus. Over half the world population of only 16,000–22,000 pairs breed in Europe, where it is vulnerable to deforestation, drainage, illegal hunting and pesticides. Yet there have been increases in many European populations recently, and this striking bird still breeds over a larger global range than any other member of the stork family. The isolated population in South Africa is thought to have originated as a result of migrants from Europe staying in their winter home.

The bird has benefited from what was, for humans, a grim tragedy. Since the world's worst nuclear power station disaster in 1986 at Chernobyl in northern Ukraine, Black Storks have colonized woodland around what was once a bustling city with a human population of some 49,000 people: a sobering example of nature taking advantage of human catastrophe.

WHITE STORK
Ciconia ciconia

Breeds across much of Europe, as far north as St Petersburg (but not Britain). After Poland, largest populations are Spain, Ukraine and Belarus, with smaller but still sizeable numbers in Lithuania, Latvia and Russia. West European breeders winter in western Africa, eastern birds in eastern and southern Africa.

Few birds have such an intimate relationship with humans as do nesting White Storks in countries across Europe as diverse as Germany, Spain, Bulgaria and Poland. Their return from Africa to traditional nest sites on the rooftops of rural towns and villages is as eagerly awaited as that of the Barn Swallow. No other European bird nesting in such close proximity to people is tolerated to the same degree – especially one building such huge nests as the stork's piles of big sticks, up to 3 or even 4 metres high and weighing as much as 2 tonnes.

Nevertheless, as this supposed bringer of babies and good luck entered the 20th century, its own future looked far less promising. Increasingly, it faced problems caused by modern agriculture, especially the destruction and degradation of wet grassland, exacerbated by wetter summers that diminished food supplies. A pair needs at least 75 hectares to keep them and their 2–4 young supplied with grasshoppers and other large insects, small rodents, lizards, frogs, toads and small fish, and when food is scarce they may need to search an area over 40 times greater. Drought in the Sahel, pesticides, collision with power lines and shooting on migration added to the toll. Conservation measures and reintroduction have helped reverse this trend, but today, apart from in Spain, large populations are all in the east, where agricultural modernization remains a threat. Poland, with large expanses of seasonally flooded grasslands, has about a quarter of the European total.

BALD IBIS
Geronticus eremita

The reasons for its virtual extinction are not certain, but probably include habitat destruction and climate change as well as hunting for food. Today, classed as critically endangered, it continues to face threats from hunting on migration as well as from disturbance, habitat loss and DDT poisoning.

Its head looks like a Hallowe'en fright mask, with wrinkled reddish bare skin resembling a photograph in a medical textbook of epidermal diseases. This bizarre visage is surmounted by an unruly crest of black feathers. The rest of the loose, untidy plumage is sepulchral black, enlivened somewhat by patches of green and purple gloss. All in all, this big, scruffy-looking bird is, arguably, the least aesthetically pleasing of all rare birds for whose protection from the effects of modern civilization appeals are made. But as with other supposedly "uncharismatic" endangered animals, from medicinal leech to Balkan mole-rat, looks should be insignificant when assessing a species' right to continue to exist.

Although the Bald Ibis no longer occurs in the wild in Europe, it was widespread and locally common until about 400 years ago, in broad river valleys and open grasslands in the Alps and other mountain areas of central and south-east Europe. Today, a bold project aims to encourage a small captive-bred population in Austria to migrate to Italy by training birds to follow microlight aircraft. The biggest (though still precariously small) wild population in Morocco is heavily protected.

In ancient Egypt, this strange bird was revered, along with the Sacred Ibis. In Islamic tradition it was one of the first birds released from the Ark by Noah and deserves special protection for its role in guiding pilgrims to Mecca. On the other hand, it was regarded in Europe as "impure, uneatable and untouchable" and may even have been persecuted as a witch.

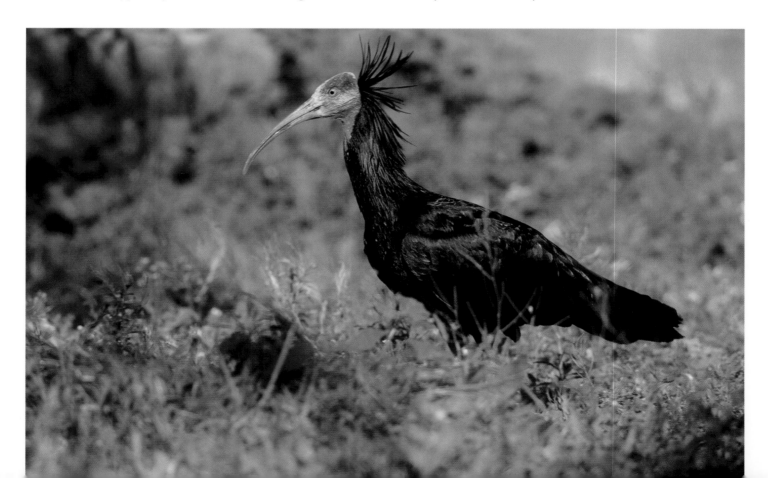

GLOSSY IBIS
Plegadis falcinellus

Mainly small scattered populations in Europe, with a few in the west (most of them in Spain), and most in Romania, Azerbaijan, Russia and Ukraine. To the east, breeds from the River Volga to Kazakhstan. Western populations winter around the south Mediterranean, eastern birds mainly in East Africa.

Many birds have glossy feathers (think of Rooks and a duck's speculum), but there are none in Europe that have more lovely metallic plumage – burnished sooty to coppery brown on the head and body, with wings and tail glossy green shot with magenta and purple. Such finery earns this otherwise rather ungainly-looking bird its name, and accolades from those watching it as the gloss is revealed by a sudden shaft of sunlight.

The Glossy Ibis is the only self-sustaining ibis species now native to Europe. Apart from the odd vagrant, it occurs regularly in western and central Europe only in a few places; most are found in the south-east. Its breeding population is relatively small (fewer than 22,000 pairs), and declining.

The world's 27 species of ibises are classified together with the spoonbills in the family Threskiornithidae. But whereas a spoonbill mainly sieves invertebrates and small fish from the shallows by sweeping its big spatula from side to side, an ibis tends to use its curved bill curlew-style to probe in mud or soil for its food – chiefly insects, molluscs and other invertebrates. Those not familiar with the Glossy Ibis might mistake distant wandering individuals seen outside their normal range for extra-dark Curlews, which are similar in size and bill shape. However, the ibis is bulkier, with a more upright stance, a longer, thinner, more curved neck and longer legs. In flight, with a few rapid wing-beats interspersed with glides, it looks more distinctive still – flat and elongated, its bill and legs drooping slightly.

SPOONBILL

Platalea leucorodia

In W. Europe, most breeders are in the Netherlands and Spain; farther east the main populations are in Hungary, Romania, Russia. With as few as 9,000 breeding pairs, Europe holds slightly over half the world population of these scarce birds. All European breeders migrate to winter in Africa.

The name is inexact: one would get relatively little food in one's mouth using a utensil shaped like this bill, as it has no depression in the end; rather, it closely resembles the shape of a medical spatula – though "Spatulabill" does not have such a ring to it.

Why have these birds evolved such an odd-shaped bill? Of course, it's all tied up with diet and method of feeding. A Spoonbill has a beak whose upper and lower mandibles are both extremely flattened, like a pair of hair tongs. Viewed from above, it becomes waisted towards the centre and then blossoms into a broad oval at its slightly downcurved end.

Instead of probing the mud like waders and its relatives the ibises, a Spoonbill walks about in the shallows to feed. Its long legs enable it to wade into relatively deep water, often up to the waist. As it does so, it swings its head in semicircles from side to side, in a scything motion, sweeping that strange, long bill through the water. It is likely that the expanded tip provides a large area for the concentration of thousands of microscopic touch sensors, housed in minute pits just beneath the surface and linked by nerves to the brain. The bird holds its bill slightly open, so that as soon as any prey touches the tip, the touch sensors react virtually instantly, in as little as 25 milliseconds, and the bill snaps shut. A further adaptation is that the legs are laterally flattened, minimizing resistance as the bird walks through the water. Gregarious when roosting, resting and nesting, Spoonbills also often feed communally. Small, tight-knit groups wade together in the same direction in constant slow movement, snapping up small fish, marine worms, molluscs and crustaceans.

GREATER FLAMINGO

Phoenicopterus ruber

The only European flamingo, it has the widest distribution of any of the world's five flamingos, occurring right across the warmer regions of Old and New Worlds. Colonies of the race *roseus* are dotted across S. Europe, breeding in the Camargue and variably at sites in Spain and Italy; also in Turkey.

Instantly recognizable, flamingos may look awkward – grotesque even – as individuals, standing almost 1.5 m tall, with their elongated necks and little heads that end in the uniquely shaped and oversized bill resembling living hockey sticks. But en masse they produce scenes of immense beauty, as a large flock feeds together, with plumage like rose petals – and of the same delicate pink and deep red hues as roses – or the tutu of a ballet dancer. Indeed, in Spanish the word *flamenco* is used for both the name of the bird and the famous dance of Andalusia.

In flight, too, these unique creatures are a stirring sight, especially when the glorious plumage contrasts with blue water and sky. Their very long, slender necks and equally lengthy and disturbingly thin legs (the longest of any birds' legs in relation to its body) protrude improbably far fore and aft.

The exquisite colours enter the feathers via the birds' stomachs, in the form of carotenoid pigments obtained by feeding on blue-green algae (or, at one remove, from the shrimps that eat the algae).

With its bill underwater and head upside down when feeding, the flamingo can simultaneously look backwards between its legs to scan for danger. In the Camargue this can come from dogs, red foxes, polecats and otters, but especially Yellow-legged Gulls, which have several tricks for getting at eggs or young, including pecking at a sitting parent's legs to make it stand up and expose the eggs, and grasping it by the bill and lifting it.

FROM RAPTORS TO BUSTARDS

HONEY-BUZZARD
Pernis apivorus

Widely spread across Europe and beyond, as far east as W. Siberia. Not necessarily as scarce as it sometimes appears. Populations fluctuate with weather, damp and cool summers reducing vital supply of insects. In Europe, the largest populations are in Russia, France, Sweden, Finland and Germany.

Not a buzzard, and not a great honey eater, the inaptly named Honey-Buzzard has a whole suite of adaptations for finding, exposing and eating its main prey – insects. Exceptionally for a raptor, its diet consists of the larvae and pupae of various social wasps (including hornets) and bees, as well as the combs of their nests and, to a lesser extent, adults.

These adaptations include the bird's horizontal posture on the ground, linked to its ability to walk and run well. The feet are also adapted for digging out the insect's nests from the soil or snatching those hanging from a tree branch or trunk. Relatively straight and blunt claws replace the sharp, curved talons of most other raptors. The legs have extra-strong scales to protect against angry stings, while small, scale-like feathers form a facial armour. The bird has a small, narrow head (giving it a gentle, pigeon-like look) which aids insinuation into the nests. And compared with the typical bird of prey's meat-slicing and tearing implement, the bill is far more dainty, with a small, slender hook at the tip, suited for probing into the combs to pluck out the morsels within. Finally, the nostrils are angled slits so that soil blockage is reduced to a minimum when the bird is busy digging.

The Honey-Buzzard's onslaughts on wasps' nests are an unforgettable sight for those lucky enough to have come across one in the act. Its feet digging furiously, perhaps aided by the bill, the bird may become almost hidden from view as it exposes its living, buzzing lunch container.

BLACK-WINGED KITE

Elanus caeruleus

Locally common and often patchily distributed across Africa south of the Sahara; much scarcer and declining in North Africa. Over the last 40 years, it has colonized Spain (500–1,000 breeding pairs) and Portugal (300–1,000 pairs) and has started breeding in southwestern France (fewer than 20 pairs).

This small, distinctive raptor is now high on the wish-list of many birders visiting the Iberian peninsula, although it did not spread from North Africa until the end of the 1960s, and it is still a rare bird there and even more so in its toehold on France.

As characterful as its almost gull-like pattern of grey, white and black is the large head. This looks remarkably owl-like, thanks to the finely hooked but broad-based bill and the big eyes that look even bigger by virtue of their black pirates' eye-patches. The eyes themselves are especially lovely, and unusually coloured for a raptor, being an intense ruby red (you need a close view to see this). Unlike the two large European kites, it has a tail that is unforked, very short and square-ended. Above all, there is the feature that distinguishes adults instantly: the great black blotches on the lesser and median coverts extending back from the bend of the wing: these account for the alternative name of Black-shouldered Kite. Resembling a rapidly spreading ink-stain, they are impossible to miss even at very long range.

Often active around dawn and dusk, this bird has a flight that recalls a Kestrel or Barn Owl, especially when hovering. With its floating, buoyant action, it can even resemble a Lapwing, a small gull or an oversized Black Tern. At other times, it quarters like a miniature harrier, but with wings raised in a much deeper "V", when it looks like no other raptor. It spends much time perched high on a look-out post, Kestrel-style, until it spots prey and drops on it. Another hunting technique involves hovering in stages, alternating with long glides or steeper drops in which it closes its wings and plummets to its prey.

RED KITE

Milvus milvus

Apart from a few in Morocco, this bird breeds exclusively in Europe. It requires a mosaic of open country such as grassland for hunting and scavenging with woodland edges or clumps of trees (or cliffs) for nesting, and is sensitive to agricultural intensification. The Cape Verde Red Kite is now extinct.

This is one of the most beautiful of all raptors. No other European bird of this size has such a deeply forked tail, while the long, narrow wings are usually held sharply angled so that they form an "M". Once the light is on it and the details of its rich chestnut body, streaked whitish head and tricoloured wings are visible, there can be no doubt that the encounter is with a Red Kite. Seen from below, the longish tail often seems to glow orange-red as it twists this way and that, sometimes even at right angles. The almost constant movements of this supremely effective rudder are one of the secrets behind the bird's graceful, buoyant flight. By contrast, the long, narrow wings seem hardly to move, the flexible "fingers" of the five outer primaries producing lift from the slightest eddies as the Kite glides low over a field or soars to a great height.

Until the end of the 17th century, the Red Kite was common in much of Europe. Although it was persecuted in the country as a chicken-killer, the large numbers that inhabited towns and cities, along with Ravens, were welcomed as scavengers; in places, such as London, they were protected by royal decree. The species began a long decline as improved sanitation reduced the food supply, and it was killed in far greater numbers as guns became widespread. Finally, agribusiness finished off many more.

Today, Red Kites are declining throughout most of their range. Only in Britain (with a very effective reintroduction programme) are numbers increasing significantly. The threat of poisoning, both deliberate and accidental, is particularly serious with a bird that eats so much carrion.

WHITE-TAILED EAGLE
Haliaeetus albicilla

Breeds mainly along sea coasts across N. Europe, from Iceland and Britain (reintroduced in N.W. Scotland and elsewhere) through Scandinavia, Finland, Baltic states, Belarus, Ukraine, Russia, as well as N.E. Germany, Poland, Hungary, Romania, Yugoslavia. Many populations have increased with protection.

This is a huge bird. Apart from the Black Vulture, Lammergeier and Griffon Vulture, no other European raptor exceeds the White-tailed Eagle in bulk and wingspan. Its broad, almost rectangular wings and its combination of massive bill and very short tail make it look front-heavy, like a vulture. Moreover, it is fond of eating carrion – as recorded in early sagas from a time when the species was far more common and a frequent visitor to battlefields, where it would feast on corpses. It is also an accomplished pirate, plundering prey from other birds, such as large gulls and other raptors, particularly Ospreys.

But if necessary, unlike any vulture, it can prove itself a formidable predator. It is capable of seizing and lifting a large fish from the sea or striking down a heavy sea duck such as an Eider and carrying it off to eat onshore, and has been recorded killing adult geese or swans. One has even been seen towing ashore a goose, killed on the water, using its wings as paddles. Pairs will co-operate to harass a swimming bird like wartime aircraft dogging a submarine, forcing it to dive repeatedly until it is exhausted and must remain at the surface where they can pick it off.

Being privy to such natural theatre, let alone the "cartwheeling" display in which rivals lock talons in spinning flight, is generally a matter of luck. And many encounters are rather uninspiring, as these frequently sluggish sea eagles spend time perched for hours on end, especially when digesting a meal.

Among the best places to see them are in their communal winter roosts, in tall trees in mature woodland or on crags.

LAMMERGEIER

Gypaetus barbatus

That hackeneyed phrase "master of all it surveys" fails to do justice to the power and majesty of this unique raptor. One cannot fail to be awed by this huge, magnificent bird that makes such skilful use of updraughts to glide and soar silently for hours on end over mountainside or ravine on slightly bowed, angled wings, with just the occasional deep, slow wingbeat. The great pioneering British bird photographer Eric Hosking compared Lammergeiers to "albatrosses of the land"; and like those of albatrosses, these great vultures' wings are remarkably long and pointed, in the biggest individuals spanning 2.75 m – some 50 cm longer than the maximum for a Golden Eagle.

The silhouette of a flying Lammergeier, with its narrow pointed wings and long wedge-shaped tail, has been likened to that of a titanic falcon, but its generic name *Gypaetus* conflates the Greek words for vulture and eagle. In reality it is in a class of its own. Aptly for such a creature, which looks as though it could have been dreamed up by an illustrator of Tolkienesque

Very small numbers are scattered thinly across S. Europe, including reintroduced pairs (eg in N. Italy), with most in the Pyrenees. Further east are larger totals in Georgia, Russia and Turkey. Elsewhere it ranges across mountains of the Middle East, southern Asia and a few widely separated areas of Africa.

fantasy, it has a bizarre diet, usually feeding largely on bones. Indeed, it is unique among big animals in this respect.

The retention of the common name has been roundly condemned by some, as "Lammergeier" is German for "lamb-vulture" and erroneously suggests a habit of which this bird is completely innocent. Occasionally the sudden appearance of a Lammergeier patrolling a mountainside may so frighten a sheep that it bolts and falls to its death, but there is no evidence that this is intentional. Preferable, then, are the old names of Ossifrage ("bone-breaker") or, most descriptively, Bearded Vulture.

GRIFFON VULTURE
Gyps fulvus

Although this species was until recently rare in Europe, and is still restricted to parts of the south, vultures can, if they get the chance, be among the most successful of all birds of prey. Before extensive persecution and the hygienic practices of modern farming, which often ensures that the carcasses of dead livestock are removed soon after the animals die, vultures in this continent must have been far more abundant.

Numbers have increased in the last 30 years. More than 80 percent of the total European population of about 21,000 breeding pairs live in Spain. There are over 650 pairs in France, and smaller numbers in Portugal, Sardinia, Greece, and various other areas of southern Europe.

Their ability to make use of thermal air currents for soaring at great heights enables them to cover vast areas of terrain in their search for large carcasses. It has been shown that a big vulture like this one uses 30 times less energy in gliding and soaring than another bird might consume by flapping — hardly any more than it would if it were standing on the ground inactive. These are huge birds, with long, upwardly tilted "fingers" ending wings that span up to 2.7 m, and the largest females can weigh over 12 kg. One might think that such a weight would be a disadvantage to a bird that earns its living

by soaring through the air for hours on end with minimum expenditure of energy. The counter-intuitive reality is that the speed such a bird can glide is directly proportionate to its weight — it's the same for gliders, which may carry ballast in the form of water to help them increase their glide speed.

The savannahs of Spain, with scattered trees, gorges and cliffs for nesting, are the European stronghold of this species. One of the first reintroduction programmes has returned birds to the Massif Central of France, from where they had been absent since the 1930s.

BLACK VULTURE

Aegypius monachus

These mighty birds are among the heaviest of all flying birds, with a maximum weight of 12.5 kg – among birds of prey, second only to the great condors of the Americas. With great broad wings spanning up to 2.95 m from tip to tip and a short, slightly wedge-shaped or rounded tail, the Black Vulture has a flight silhouette reminiscent of a White-tailed Eagle, though distinctly larger.

In contrast to the social griffons, which range far afield in their search for carcasses, the Black Vulture is a largely solitary species that spends most of its time within a home range. It is rare to encounter more than a few birds even at a big carcass. Like the Lappet-faced Vulture in Africa, this is a specialist feeder, concentrating on the toughest parts of carcasses that are usually left by other scavengers. Features fitting the birds for this niche include the long head housing powerful jaw muscles and the massively deep bill. This formidable instrument has specially sharp cutting edges that enable it to scissor its way through skin, tendons and sinews.

Rare in Europe, with small (though some slowly recovering) populations in E. Portugal, central and southern mainland Spain, Mallorca, N. Greece, and possibly Macedonia, Turkey, Crimea and the Caucasus. Reintroduced birds occur in the Grande Causses, south of the Massif Central, France.

Black Vultures build huge nests from sizeable branches as well as smaller twigs and line them with wool and assorted rubbish, sometimes siting them in trees as low as 5 m above ground. Like some other large raptors, including sea-eagles, pairs sometimes perform spectacular displays high above the eyrie – these can be exhilarating if dizzying to watch as two great black birds plunge several hundred feet, talons interlocked in a mutual cartwheeling performance worthy of any circus act.

One of the best places to see this spectacular bird is Monfragüe National Park, Extremadura, with almost 150 pairs.

SHORT-TOED EAGLE
Circaetus gallicus

A scattered breeder across southern and central Europe, with the largest populations in France, Spain, Turkey and Russia. It also breeds in North Africa, a few areas of the Middle East, and in central Asia. European and west Asian populations winter in the Sahel and savannah belts of Africa.

The uniqueness of this handsome raptor from the point of view of Europe is intimately bound up with its prey, for this is the continent's only snake-eagle. It is also the only large raptor in the region that usually has a dark head and chest contrasting with coarsely barred but predominantly whitish underparts. This gives it a striking pattern, making it one of the less problematic birds of prey to identify.

The species is relatively easy to find as a result of its frequent habit of prolonged hovering or slow soaring over a warm maquis hillside or patch of scrubby heath when searching for reptiles. A more memorable event is to suddenly round a patch of scrub or top a ridge and come across a bird that has already made a kill, and is swallowing a snake head-first in a series of gulps. Then you notice the big, owl-like head and glaring yellow eyes. Smaller snakes are often carried off in the bill and killed in mid-air by passing them through the clenched claws, like a person feeding a cable through closed hands.

Snakes form about 75 to 100 percent of the prey in western and southern Europe, adults requiring an average of one or two medium-sized snakes daily – more when feeding young. They prefer non-venomous species but will tackle vipers on occasion. Adaptations for dealing with prey include the short but strong toes, which maintain a firm grip on the writhing victim, dense, downy plumage and the armour-plated legs with their tough scales. Pairs often hunt together, sharing catches.

Today, habitat destruction poses the greatest threat, but birds are still shot on migration (particularly in Malta).

MONTAGU'S HARRIER

Circus pygargus

A widespread but patchy breeder across much of Europe, which holds over half the world population. Most abundant in Iberia, France, eastern Europe. The decline seen in the west may be repeated in eastern Europe with agricultural modernization. It winters in tropical and southern Africa.

This is the most lightweight and graceful of all the harriers. The male is one of the world's most beautiful raptors with his pale ash-grey plumage, contrasting with coal-black wingtips and narrow wingbars, and rusty-flecked white belly and underwing coverts. Floating along for hours on end, their long wings raised in a trademark "V" shape, they quarter the ground for prey. This ranges from insects, lizards and voles to hares and also includes birds such as Skylarks, Meadow Pipits and Yellow Wagtails. Relative to its body size, Montagu's Harrier has not only the longest, narrowest wings of any harrier but also the longest wingtips, with three particularly long, notched primaries forming very pronounced "fingers", and the longest tail, too. All this gives it a buoyant flight, and the ability to fly very low over the ground, slowly, without stalling. The long wings make it look bigger than it is: the male is smaller than a crow and less than half the weight.

Traditional breeding sites were hay-meadows, lowland heaths and steppe-like grassland. With the destruction or degradation of such habitats in western Europe, the birds declined and were forced to breed on farmland. Here they often suffer from a decline in breeding success which may include 20–70 percent of nests being destroyed by mechanized harvesting.

In Britain, the country where it was first identified and named, by the eccentric natural historian George Montagu, it was always on the north-western fringe of its range. But until the mid-19th century it did breed regularly, albeit in very small numbers, in parts of southern England until a combination of game preservation, egg-collecting and habitat destruction finished it off. Today it now barely hangs on there, with fewer than 10 pairs depending on intervention from conservationists to survive.

GOSHAWK

Accipiter gentilis

Despite its size – a large female can be bigger than some Buzzards – the Goshawk can be notoriously hard to see. You may catch a flash of a barred tail or white undertail coverts as it weaves between trunks in dense woodland, or a distant silhouette soaring high overhead. Otherwise, one must rely on circumstantial evidence that this charismatic raptor is present – perhaps even watching with its fiercely glowing orange eyes, unseen, from dense foliage. Such signs include the remains of a Wood Pigeon, Pheasant, Jay, red squirrel or other recent kill at a plucking post on a tree stump or large branch, and perhaps the regurgitated pellets of indigestible remains beneath it, although to make sure this was not a Buzzard's meal one needs to find the Goshawk's moulted feathers. Birdwatchers must avoid disturbance during nestbuilding and incubation, or pairs might desert.

There is, though, one time in the year when Goshawks are easier to see, especially from a vantage point that affords a view over a large area of forest. In March and early April, mainly

One of the most widespread of all the world's raptors. In Europe, it breeds from Spain eastwards to the Urals and from the tree line in N. Scandinavia southwards as far as Crete. Still persecuted in some areas and decreasing in places, in many others its populations are stable or increasing.

during fine weather early in the morning, they throw themselves across the sky in the abandonment of courtship – a splendid piece of natural theatre with birds circling high in the air, soaring in tight spirals, very slow flapping and roller-coaster flights by the male and – perhaps as the finale – a sudden plunge on closed wings straight down into the forest.

Surprisingly, Goshawks have shown themselves to be adaptable in breeding in quite small woods and even wooded city parks in some places in central and eastern Europe, such as Munich and Moscow.

SPANISH IMPERIAL EAGLE
Aquila adalberti

Now virtually restricted to central and S.W. Spain (only about 220 pairs, though this an increase from all-time low of 30 pairs in the 1960s). Reintroduction programmes are augmenting these numbers. A very few pairs have recently recolonized the west of Portugal, after ceasing to breed there in 1977.

One of the world's most threatened raptors, this striking bird has suffered in comparison with its relative the Golden Eagle by generally avoiding the remote, sparsely populated mountain terrain that affords the latter a degree of protection. Instead, it chiefly favours low-intensity agricultural land, especially the dehesa – a unique, savannah-type landscape of flower-dotted grasslands with aromatic shrubs and evergreen holm oaks and cork oaks that provide sites for the massive stick nests.

This is a big, powerful eagle, almost as large as a Golden Eagle. But in comparison with its far more abundant relative, which is some 50 times more numerous, it is a rather sluggish hunter, preying mainly on rabbits which it catches after watching from a tree or slowly soaring overhead.

A major threat is deliberate poisoning, particularly in hunting preserves. Many eagles, especially inexperienced juveniles, get electrocuted on power lines. In recent years, the species' main prey has been decimated by rabbit viral haemorrhagic disease and overhunting: when adults are undernourished, the young often starve. Lead poisoning from pellets in rabbits and other shot carcasses has also claimed the lives of many birds.

However, there is hope for the future, with the population more or less stable after long-term declines. Some good conservation measures are in place. A crucial need is to maintain the integrity of the dehesa habitat. Every wine drinker can contribute to the protection of the eagles, and of their rich and beautiful ecosystem, by refusing to buy wine with plastic stoppers or screw tops and thus supporting the cork industry.

GOLDEN EAGLE
Aquila chrysaetos

Although a clear second in size to the White-tailed Eagle, the Golden Eagle is more formidable and more elegant, especially in the air. It combines grace with immense power as it soars in big, lazy spirals, the six long primary feathers at each wingtip upcurled and splayed like fingers, or quarters a mountainside for miles, head down and moving from side to side as it scans every tussock and rock for hidden prey with its proverbially keen eyes. The final drama is enthralling, as the great bird hurtles down on partly closed wings in a long, slanting trajectory to deliver the *coup de grâce*. Unfortunately, however, a birdwatcher's encounters are all too often brief and tantalizing, as a distant silhouette disappears over a mountain ridge or drifts away high in the sky.

This top predator is one of the largest of the 18 species of *Aquila* eagles, with wings that may span over 2 m and a head-to-tail length of up to 90 cm. Over time the encroachment of civilization has driven it farther into the remote enclaves of the wildest country. The species reached its nadir during the 19th

Breeds in Scotland, Norway, Sweden and eastern Europe into Russia, in central France, the Alps, Corsica, Sardinia, Sicily and the Apennine range in Italy and throughout the Balkans; and, as a smaller, darker race, in Spain and Portugal. The largest numbers are in Spain, Norway, Sweden and Scotland.

and early 20th centuries, when game preservation interests and the craze for collecting eggs and stuffed birds threatened populations in many parts of Europe. With legal protection in most countries since the mid-20th century, numbers have built up again to healthy levels in many places. Although never such a widespread lowland bird as the White-tailed Eagle, in early historic times the Golden Eagle was probably was far more widespread, including populations in the lowlands. There have recently been local signs of a return to such tamer, more anthropogenic landscapes, as in southern Sweden and Denmark.

BONELLI'S EAGLE
Aquila fasciata

Generally scarce, and declining; restricted to the Mediterranean region, in areas with a mix of forest, scrub and farmland for hunting and crags and ravines for nesting. Of 1,000 or so pairs on the continent, 75 percent breed in Spain (over 40 percent in Andalusia; rest in Valencia, Extremadura, Castilla La Mancha).

Although undeniably possessing an eagle's power and gravitas, this species has a dash not displayed by its larger relatives. It combines their strength with the speed and maneouvrability of a bird-hunting *Accipiter* hawk. The common name of this splendid raptor (and, at the other end of the scale, the diminunitive leaf-warbler *Phylloscopus bonelli*) commemorates the early 19th-century Italian ornithologist and collector Franco Bonelli, professor of zoology at the University of Turin.

The bird's usual hunting style makes it very difficult to find when it is hidden among the deep shade cast by tree foliage, as it watches upright and alert for any sign of prey. Then, when it launches itself towards its target, it often keeps low and weaves among cover like a big, long-winged Goshawk. At the onset of the breeding season, pairs can be far more evident as they circle high above their nesting territory. Lucky observers may see them performing an undulating sky-dance, hurtling at top speed far down into a deep rocky gorge, then levelling out and letting their momentum carry them upwards before repeating the process. This is usually accompanied by long melodious whistles. They are fierce defenders of their nests, attacking raptors and other intruders much larger than themselves: they have even been known to kill Griffon Vultures.

For much of the year, they are bird-eaters. As reflected in their Spanish name, *Aguila perdicera*, "Partridge Eagle", they concentrate on Red-legged Partridges as their main prey; by contrast, they catch mostly rabbits to feed their young. In the past they were used by falconers to hunt hares and rabbits.

OSPREY
Pandion haliaetus

This splendid raptor is truly unique, the sole member of its family. It has some attributes shared with other birds of prey, but also a distinctive, languid gull-like flight with wings kinked. More than most raptors, it is a real dietary specialist, tied to one class of food all year round – fish. It is adapted to fishing shallow waters, rather than plunge-diving like gannets and terns or chasing its prey underwater like grebes and divers.

The Osprey needs to find water wherever it goes, from the forested lakes or sea by which it breeds to the rivers in which it fishes on passage or the sheltered coastal waters it often haunts in its winter quarters. And it goes far, for it is more widespread than any other raptor save that eponymous wanderer the Peregrine. Thanks to its strong flapping flight, it is not tied to routes over heat-generating land masses like raptors that rely on thermal soaring. Migratory populations breed across northern Eurasia and North America and winter in the tropics; Australasian breeders are largely resident.

A summer visitor to many countries in N. Europe, from Scotland east through Scandinavia and N.E. Germany to Poland, the Baltic republics, and beyond. These populations all winter in Africa. Perhaps around 11,000 pairs breed in Europe, most of them in Sweden, followed by Russia and Finland.

Also, unlike many raptors, such as Buzzards or White-tailed Eagles, which are content to scavenge dead fish if the opportunity presents itself, Ospreys need live fish. They catch them in a dive from the air, either slanting or almost vertical. The plunge of the long extended feet – and sometimes much of the body – in an explosion of spray is beloved of birdwatchers and photographers alike. The final act of the ballet is the muscular swing upwards of the sinewy legs to hoist the fish, gaffed on the long curving butchers' hooks of talons, wriggling and writhing in vain, the whole drama framed in a shower of water droplets.

LESSER KESTREL

Falco naumanni

Although most raptors are solitary hunters, there are a few exceptions. Just about the most communal of all is the Lesser Kestrel, a smaller, brighter-plumaged relative of the Kestrel. Today, perhaps only a third as many pairs of this beautiful little falcon breed in Europe compared with just 20 or so years ago. This huge decline is related to their specialized feeding — they hawk in flocks, like overgrown swallows, for flying insects (grasshoppers, locusts, crickets), and modern farming, particularly pesticide use, has caused serious depletions in this food supply. Also, they suffer from home eviction, as many of the churches, castles and other old buildings they have used for centuries for nesting are renovated or demolished.

The discovery in January 2007 of a huge roost in Senegal has underlined the need for urgent action. The numbers of birds found here are revelatory — an estimated 28,600 wintering Lesser Kestrels as well as over 16,000 African Swallow-tailed

A summer visitor to S. Europe, where its population is small and declining. Over a third of pairs are in Spain, where it has declined from about 100,000 pairs in the early 1960s to 8,000 or fewer pairs today. Elsewhere, across central Asia east to central Mongolia, it seems nowhere to be common.

Kites, making this one of the largest raptor roosts ever recorded. The former are thought to represent more than half the known breeding population of western Europe. Efforts to save the species in France, Spain and elsewhere will be in vain if the African habitat hosting such a large concentration of birds is not protected. It would be sad if the words of the Victorian ornithologist Lord Lilford, "The cry of these pretty birds is as certain to strike the ear in the towns of Andalusia as the twang of the guitar and click of the castanets," were no longer to be true.

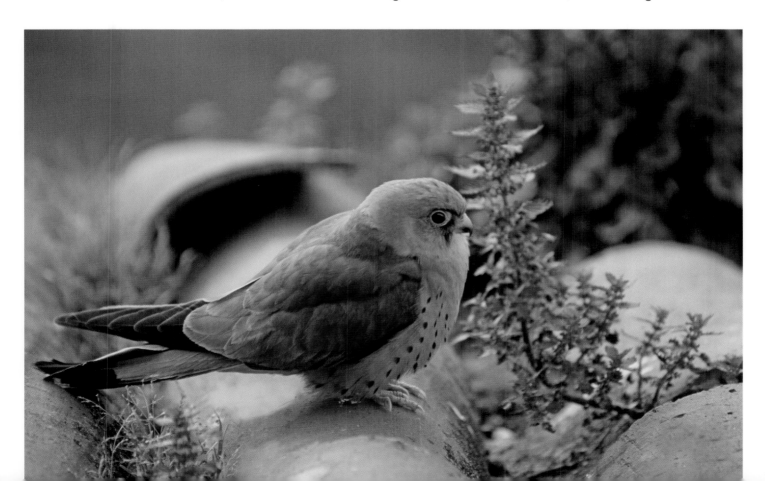

RED-FOOTED FALCON
Falco vespertinus

A declining breeder in steppe-like habitats where insects abound, its main breeding range starts in the far east of Europe, extending east; there are a few strongholds farther west (especially Hungary). It winters in Africa. In periodic irruptions it has nested in Sweden, Germany and France.

The Latin word *vespertinus*, the specific name of this lovely little bird of prey, means "active in the evening". It was chosen by the great 18th-century namer of nature Linnaeus because this is the time when these specialized insect-eaters do much of their hunting. There is also something of the dusk in the plumage of the bird, with its slate-grey upperparts like a darkening sky and the reddish-orange underparts hinting at the setting sun. These are the prettiest of all the European falcons. The male is especially dramatic, the almost sooty grey of head and body contrasting with the glowing chestnut of his "trousers" and undertail. When he flies, the flight feathers gleam paler than the wing coverts with a lovely pearly sheen in good light. The female, though less striking, has a subtle beauty, with her paler, dark-barred upperparts and finely streaked orange-buff underparts. The male lives up to the common name, with bright vermilion legs and feet to match the cere and eye-ring, which stands out against the dark blush around each eye.

The Red-footed Falcon's proportions are between those of a Lesser Kestrel and a Hobby, with long wings that reach the tail tip or even extend beyond it slightly. Like both, but especially the latter, it will also hunt down insects in flight. These falcons take over the old stick nests of other birds, most often Rooks; sometimes large groups evict the rightful owners. They resemble Rooks in being intensely social all year and performing noisy aerobatics over their colonies.

ELEONORA'S FALCON
Falco eleonorae

With a streamlined, scimitar-winged silhouette reminiscent of a giant swift, this rakish falcon is one of the world's most specialized predators. Both common and scientific names commemorate Eleonora d'Arborea (c.1350–1404), a warrior-princess and national heroine of Sardinia, who introduced laws protecting birds of prey, albeit to preserve them for falconry.

This is one of the most striking of all falcons. Although the pale form can be mistaken for a Hobby or even a Red-footed Falcon, it has darker, coffee-brown upperparts, longer, narrower wings and a distinctly longer tail. Dark-phase birds are especially beautiful, very dark all over apart from a little grey at the base of the outer primaries and the contrasting bare skin of the eye-ring and cere, chalky blue in the female, yellowish in the male.

It has an unremarkable insectivorous diet for much of the year, like the Red-footed Falcon and Lesser Kestrel. But autumn brings a change. Unlike any other European bird, it does not start to breed until late summer or autumn. This timing ensures

The entire population breeds on rocky coasts and islands along the Atlantic, in the Canary Is. and Morocco, and in the Mediterranean in Algeria, Tunisia, the Balearics, Sicily, Sardinia, Croatia, the Greek islands (about 80 percent), W. Turkey and Cyprus. Almost all winter on Madagascar and nearby islands.

that the young are in the nest during the peak migration of many millions of birds between Europe and Africa. This abundance of concentrated protein sustains the young – and their parents – until it is time for the predators themselves to migrate south.

Over 100 small to medium-sized species have been recorded as prey. Hunting is mainly by day on the Atlantic coasts of N.W. Africa and the Canaries, but where bird passage is concentrated around dusk and dawn, the falcons are most active then, often continuing to plunder night fliers after dark, in groups of up to 20 falcons working together over the moonlit sea.

GYR FALCON

Falco rusticolus

Breeds in Iceland, Norway, N. Sweden and Finland and Arctic Russia, though Europe forms only a small part of its breeding range, which extends right around the Arctic region. Although there were declines in Russia between 1990 and 2000, populations elsewhere seem to have remained stable.

If the Peregrine is the king of falcons, then its bigger cousin the Gyr, largest and heaviest of them all, is surely the emperor. And this immensely powerful raptor was indeed the "hawk" of choice for emperors, from the great falconer (arguably the first real ornithologist), the Holy Roman Emperor, Frederick II, to the Mongol emperor Kublai Khan, who was reputed to own 200 of these birds. In modern times this is still most highly valued for falconry in the oil-rich sheikdoms of the Arabian Gulf – both legal, captive-reared birds and illegally traded ones taken from wild nests. Some of the most sought-after white individuals have fetched as much as US $100,000.

The Gyr is much bigger than a Peregrine, with a body larger than that of a Buzzard and a wingspan to match that bird. Indeed, it bears a similar relationship to the noble Peregrine as does the Goshawk to the Sparrowhawk. And like the similarly sized Goshawk, it has a combination of deep chest and broad, bulky undertail coverts. Different populations have plumage ranging from blackish, silvery slate-grey or brown to the spectacular almost all-white form, the latter matching the more permanently snowy wastes of the High Arctic where it breeds and the former blending in with a mix of rocks and snow.

Although it lacks the turn of speed for which the Peregrine is renowned, the Gyr is a tireless flier. It rarely stoops from on high, but instead doggedly chases prey in flight for up to 6 miles or more until they tire and it can seize them. A large female is capable of killing even swans, cranes and Snowy Owls. More typical prey are Ptarmigan, Willow Grouse, various ducks, gulls and auks, and Arctic hares. If necessary, these adaptable birds will eat diminutive Arctic Redpolls, voles and lemmings.

PEREGRINE FALCON

Falco peregrinus

The European population occupying a small percentage of its vast worldwide range has increased since its nadir in the 1950s–1970s, when it succumbed to pesticide poisoning. The largest European population is in Spain, then Britain, France and Italy. Many northern birds winter farther south and west.

While one might choose the Gyr Falcon for sheer force and majesty, Eleonora's for streamlined grace and *élan*, and the Lesser Kestrel and Red-footed Falcon for dainty beauty, the ultimate falcon has to be this one. The Peregrine, famous in every book of records as the fastest bird (indeed, animal) on Earth, is one of those birds that exudes power. It is also one of the most widely distributed of all the world's birds, as befits its specific name *peregrinus*, meaning wanderer.

A Peregrine's lightning stoop, when it hurtles at terrifying speeds (sometimes more than 155 mph) onto its prey, is one of the most spectacular performances in all nature. Like lightning itself, it has the power to stop conversation as observers gaze awestruck into the air – and to stop the prey dead as the Peregrine strikes it with the loosely bunched toes of one foot and rakes it with the long middle talon. If the victim isn't killed outright, it is likely to be stunned. It is hardly surprising that the prey's head can be knocked clean off as the falcon strikes.

Stirring words from falconry convey something of this bird's pole position in the food chain. With the panoptic view it gains as it "waits on", circling at heights of up to several hundred metres before taking the destroying plunge, its target must appear as a tiny dot below. If the prey is small enough (a songbird rather than the more typical pigeon, duck, or other larger bird), it may grasp it, or "bind to" in mid-air; otherwise, it will catch it as it falls, or allow it to drop to the ground. Then it does its best to make sure it does not lose its prize to any interloper, however fierce, as it "mantles" its prey with outspread wings.

BAILLON'S CRAKE
Porzana pusilla

Very wide distribution, various races breeding in Eurasia, Africa and Australasia. Northern races winter south of breeding ranges; at least some of the others are resident. Very patchily distributed across much of S. and E. Europe, with tiny breeding populations, mostly in Russia and the Balkans.

Europe's smallest rail, this scarce breeder is little larger than a House Sparrow but creeps along on disproportionately long legs, ending in the outsized feet typical of rails. It looks like a Water Rail in miniature, with the same pattern of warm brown upperparts, blue-grey face and underparts and strongly barred flanks, but has a much shorter, green bill and the barring extends to the often jauntily cocked undertail.

Normally as elusive as most rails, this is a notoriously difficult bird to see in the open, and is not nearly as noisy as the squealing, grunting and shrieking Water Rail. The song of the male is a series of dry, rasping rattles – like the noise of a fingernail drawn across a comb. Each short pulse of sound lasts 2–3 seconds and is repeated for long periods with very brief pauses of only 1–2 seconds between phrases. It is uttered mainly at night, and usually ceases once a pair have mated. Since a single male may alter the pitch between bursts of notes, the listener can be misled into believing there are two or more birds present when there is only one. Also, the sound could be confused with the advertising call of the drake Garganey. All this helps to make this species one of the most difficult of all European birds to census with any degree of accuracy: recent guesstimates vary by a factor of more than four.

Although spending most of its time hidden among dense vegetation, it is not especially shy. Western European populations have declined with the drainage of wetlands.

CORNCRAKE

Crex crex

A widespread breeder over a huge range, from Ireland to W. Siberia; now patchily distributed and scarce or rare, especially in W. and central Europe. E. European populations, though far larger, have declined in recent years. Ongoing conservation programmes centre around changes to mowing regimes.

Some bird songs are memorable for their beauty but the male Corncrake's advertising call is remarkable for its sheer volume and the stamina of the singer. Until the middle of the 19th century, country people all over Europe were often kept awake on spring and early summer nights by the two-note rasping, celebrated in the bird's scientific name, and delivered for hours on end from dusk to dawn. This is still a feature of much of eastern Europe, although even here it is diminishing as the birds become scarcer. In early spring, especially when he is newly arrived after a long flight from the African wintering grounds, the male keeps up the monotonous barrage of sound during the day as well, to deter rivals as much as attract a mate.

Today, in western Europe, this unforgettable sound is heard only in the quieter oases that have retained some traditional farmland and where the relentless march of intensive agriculture has yet to make a real impact. The huge declines over the past 150 years, massively accelerated from the 1950s, were due largely to tractors and mechanized mowing, and the taking of repeated cuts of grass for silage throughout the birds' breeding season. These gave the birds no chance to breed before the blades bore down on nests of eggs or flightless fleeing chicks.

Seeing these birds presents a challenge to most birdwatchers. Signs of the bird's presence in an area include the little pellets formed of compressed wing-cases and other hard parts of the beetles, earwigs, grasshoppers and other insects that form much of their diet, regurgitated via the bill.

PURPLE SWAMPHEN
Porphyrio porphyrio

A very widespread species, divided into up to 13 races, distinguished by plumage colour and pattern. The European race *porphyrio* has the most homogeneous colouring, its body almost entirely bright violet-blue, darker above. It occurs in Portugal, Spain, southern France, Sardinia and North Africa.

This is one of those birds that resembles a caricature dreamed up by a cartoon animator. Looking like a gargantuan, bright purplish-blue Moorhen with a monstrous triangular red lump of a bill, it is by far Europe's largest rail. Despite its size, it can clamber about among reeds by holding onto the stems with its great feet, in much the same, surprising way as that even larger reedbed-dweller, the Bittern. Where it is used to being watched, it may stand, swaying with the plants, near the top of a tall reed stem before taking off and flying low with its sturdy legs and feet trailing. Birds also build mini-roof-gardens of vegetation high in the reeds on which to feed, roost and sunbathe.

Like most rails, these are garrulous birds, with a large and complex range of vocalizations. Many of these are loud and harsh, and variously described in the literature as trumpeting, crowing, cackling, squawking, shrieking, grunting, groaning, wailing, hooting and humming. Often, choruses of loud calls resound across the water at night as well as by day; some calls, by contrast, are much softer, especially those of females.

When feeding, the birds use their huge bills like knives, secateurs, pliers, wire-strippers or spades, often grasping and manipulating plant stems in one of their big but dextrous feet. They sometimes snatch small fish in their gaudy, capacious bills and, if they get the chance, will steal eggs from the nests of other waterbirds or even seize an unwary duckling.

The Romans kept these big, showy birds as living ornaments to grace their villas. Since purple denoted nobility, their appearance may have saved them from the pot.

DEMOISELLE CRANE

Anthropoides virgo

Breeds in S.E. Russia and Ukraine. Occasionally occurs in W. Europe as an escape. In Europe, seen on passage regularly only in Cyprus, south to winter quarters in Africa in Aug and early Sep, a month earlier than Common Crane, and north back to the breeding areas from end of Mar to mid-Apr.

Compared with the larger Common Crane, which in Europe breeds widely if sparingly across the north, this smaller relative is a rare speciality. It nests in far smaller numbers, to the north of the Black Sea in the Crimea. Small as it is, the European breeding population is important on a world scale, amounting to almost a fifth of the global total.

Although it is the smallest of all the world's 15 crane species, almost 20 percent smaller than the Common Crane, at about a metre long this is still a very big bird, and has the combination of wild grandeur, stately beauty and scarcity that makes all cranes special. Striding across the steppe or in majestic flight, it can be hard to separate from its commoner relative at a distance. What distinguishes a Demoiselle at closer range is its purer grey upperparts with long, narrow tertial feathers tapering into neat spikes (instead of the bustle of the Common Crane), its luxurious long white ear-tufts and the elongation of its black foreneck feathers into a wispy scarf. The common name may be an allusion to its loveliness, from the French *demoiselle* for a young unmarried lady, although it is also said to have been given to the species by Marie Antoinette, who admired its maidenly gracefulness when it was brought to the royal gardens of France from the Russian steppes.

As more and more of the steppes in central and eastern Europe fell under the plough in the late 19th and early 20th centuries, the bird dwindled. Today, the trend is more hopeful. The European population seems to be at least stable or even increasing: since the 1980s it has started to adapt to agricultural areas.

COMMON CRANE

Grus grus

A widespread summer visitor that breeds across much of N. Europe, from Scandinavia to the E. border. Largest populations are in Russia, Finland, Sweden, Poland. Breeding populations farther south are smaller; a sizeable one in Germany. Largest wintering numbers: Spain, then France.

Great in every sense, this is one of the most spectacular as well as one of the largest of all European birds. It is certainly the tallest in this continent: adults stand up to 1.3 m high. The metaphoric use of the name "crane" for the long-armed machine dates back to the 13th century. Crane mythology is far more ancient, and as widespread as the birds themselves, from North America to Japan and Australia.

Like all cranes, Common Cranes perform unique dancing displays, not just during the breeding season but on many occasions when they are interacting socially. These are as complex as any ballet, and the basic movements include striding about with legs held stiffly, pirouetting, running, sudden dramatic stops and starts, bowing, throwing the head back and pointing the dagger-like bill skyward, tossing twigs into the air, and spectacular leaps with beating wings – all accompanied by wonderfully wild-sounding, ecstatic, bugling calls. What's more, the birds look as if they are wearing a costume like a ballerina, with a big bustle of bushy, elongated plumes spreading out to cover the tail and the rear of the body.

Crane-dancing rituals feature in many cultures and may date back far into antiquity. Today, the most famous in Europe is at Lake Hornborgasjön, in southern Sweden. Some 200,000 people from all over Europe and beyond gather together and dance along with thousands of the cranes when more than 10,000 of these great birds visit this major staging post between mid-March and mid-April on their way back from Spain to breed in northern Sweden. Crane dancing is contagious.

GREAT BUSTARD
Otis tarda

Globally threatened. Breeds from Iberia east to Mongolia, but in the west of this vast area its range is highly fragmented. After benefiting from forest clearance in Europe creating the open steppes it prefers, it declined from the late 18th century. Large numbers remain only in Iberia, Hungary, Russia, Ukraine.

One of the world's heaviest flying birds, the Great Bustard lives up to its name. Standing over a metre tall, the larger males regularly weigh up to 10 kg, and some have reached 18 kg. This puts them virtually on a par with the Kori Bustard of Africa as the heaviest of all flying birds. An assembly of males viewed from a distance can resemble a flock of sheep or goats because of their size, and the dense, almost woolly-looking plumage, in particular the rusty red and white feathers on the thick neck, is reminiscent of a llama's fleece. Appropriately, the old collective noun for a group of these gregarious birds is "a drove". The display of the males at their non-territorial lek is one of the most bizarre sights in nature, as each bird inflates his neck sac and then appears to turn his plumage inside out so that he resembles a giant white powder-puff, visible at several miles' range.

Like grazing mammals, Great Bustards stride across extensive grasslands in search of food. Their diet ranges from grasses, thistles and clover to large insects such as grasshoppers and beetles, and now and then a small mammal or nestling bird. They have a slow, stately gait and a habit of raising the head at an angle as if haughtily surveying their territory.

Being so big and tasting so good when roasted, they were inevitably a major target for hunters. Iconic in heraldry, they appear on the crests or other insignia of various European families. They are the national bird of Hungary, though now sadly depleted there, as they are everywhere else within their vast range.

LITTLE BUSTARD
Tetrax tetrax

This is the smaller of Europe's two species of bustard – less than half as long and only one-fifth to one-tenth as heavy as the Great Bustard, it is about the size of a female Pheasant. It appears more like a gamebird than does its huge relative, taking off noisily. Its fast, shallow, whirring wing-beats alternate with brief glides on rather arched, broad, rounded wings, looking like a big partridge or a grouse. Opening its wings transforms this mainly brown bird into a strikingly patterned one, as the large white and smaller black and brown areas on the wings are revealed.

This is a denizen of steppes, stony plains, cereal fields or similar habitats where vegetation grows tall enough to provide cover. It often shares them with its larger relative but does not associate with it. Here, in spring, mainly at dawn and dusk, the males perform one of the strangest displays to claim a territory and attract a mate. It consists of three elements, performed by the male in various combinations or separately. The first involves him stamping hard on the ground with his strong feet, surprisingly

Europe contains over 75 percent of its fragmented global range, which extends across central Asia. Spain, with 100,000–250,000 breeding pairs, has 10 times as many birds as Portugal. In Russia, it has increased over the last 15 years. France and Italy are home to over 2,500 and 1,000 pairs respectively.

loudly. The second is a lightning toss of the head followed by raising and lowering the feathers on a swollen collar of skin at the back of his neck, while uttering a harsh "snort", with a flapping of the wings to show the striking pattern. Most spectacular is the sudden vertical leap into the air, wings flapping, lifting the bird above the concealing vegetation. The flapping creates a sibilant titter, more like the song of a Cirl Bunting than anything else, but with a pulsing rhythm like a steam locomotive. This wonderful natural theatre is, regrettably, becoming rarer as many populations decline, including that in its Spanish stronghold.

FROM WADERS TO SANDGROUSE

BLACK-WINGED STILT
Himantopus himantopus

A widespread breeder in S. Europe, with a few breeding sporadically farther north, exceptionally as far as Norway, Sweden and Finland. A few reach Britain, almost annually. Populations generally are stable and those in their stronghold of Spain are increasing. Globally, the species has a vast range.

Proportionate to its size, this striking wader has the longest legs of any bird in the world. Combined with the long neck and bill, they give their owner an advantage in being able to feed on invertebrates by striding, often belly deep, into deeper water than most other waders. The word "stilt" is first recorded being applied to animals, especially birds, in 1597, some 150 years after its first use to describe the long wooden props used to elevate people. The combination of phenomenally long, brilliant cerise-pink legs allied to the little head, needle bill and small body should make this a bizarre, unattractive creature, but oddly the whole is in harmony. In fact, this is one of the most graceful looking of all waders – arguably even more debonair than its relative the Avocet, since its plumage pattern is simpler, with all-black wings contrasting sharply like the tails of an evening suit with the starched white shirt of the body.

The Stilt's elegance also comes from its neat, dainty movements as it tilts its body and darts its bill forward to snatch an aquatic insect. It looks ungainly only in other circumstances – in flight, when its great long legs trail far behind; as it lies down to incubate eggs or brood young chicks, when the bird folds them awkwardly beneath its body; or when a copulating male teeters on his mate's back before resting there briefly on his long tarsi.

The calls, mostly as thin as the legs and the bill – harsh, incessant mobbing cries when a predator approaches, and sharp, Coot-like notes or grating, gull-like notes during courtship – are as much a part of the soundscape of southern European wetlands as those of a Hoopoe or Scops Owl on dry land.

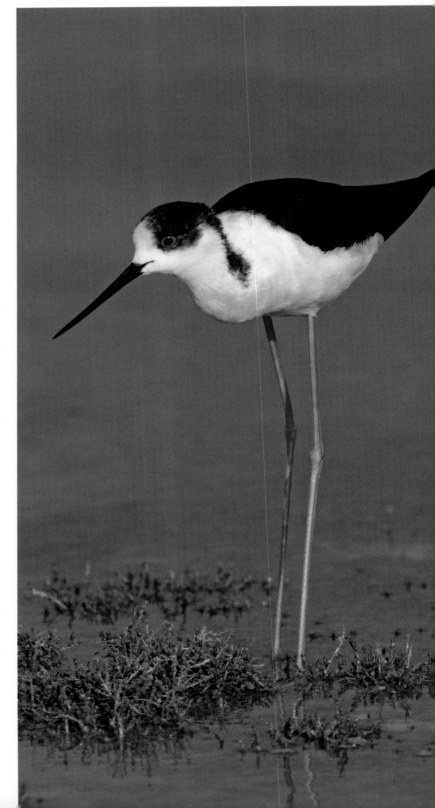

AVOCET
Recurvirostra avosetta

Two-thirds of the European population are in the Netherlands, Spain, N. Germany and Denmark. It breeds patchily from S. Sweden south to S. Iberia and around the Mediterranean, Baltic, Black and Caspian Seas; also in east and southern Africa. Most populations have increased over the past 30 years.

Given a flexible plastic model of a Black-winged Stilt, one could fashion a likeness of an Avocet – by bending the long needle bill upwards, adding white patches to the black wings and back, and shortening and darkening the legs. This is not surprising, since the two species are members of the same small family.

It is not just the shape of the Avocet's bill, with its sudden upturn towards the tip, that distinguishes it from that of the Stilt's. It is in fact a specialized apparatus, containing a complex arrangement of comblike lamellae, lacking in its close relative. The Avocet uses these to filter out small worms and other invertebrates as it sweeps its bill sideways at a shallow angle through water or liquid mud. The trapped prey can then be flipped back into the mouth by the big fleshy tongue.

The dazzling whiteness of these handsome waders (more striking than any gull), coupled with their general jizz, can help one identify them at a remarkably long range. The combination of bold pattern and instant recognizability has made them popular as logos – most famously, following their restoration as breeding birds (after a century's extinction) in England, it led to their adoption as the symbol of the RSPB.

Avocets swim ably, thanks to the small but distinct webbing extending half-way between their toes, a feature not shared with the stilts, which rarely swim. As well as sailing along like strange wildfowl, they will often up-end like dabbling ducks. At nesting colonies, they are often heard before they are seen. Their loud *klute, klute* calls, sweet and melodious when relaxed, are cranked up to a strident frenzy when a pair is alarmed.

STONE-CURLEW

Burhinus oedicnemus

Widespead but patchy, mainly in south Europe, in semi-desert, heathland, steppe and dry farmland fields; declining in most places, including its Spanish stronghold; now rare in S. England. Most in the Mediterranean area are resident, others are summer migrants. Also breeds Canaries, N. Africa and Asia.

The big yellow eyes, set in dark sockets beneath beetling white eyebrows, impart a fierce, glaring look to this odd bird – more suggestive of an owl or raptor than a wader. They help it find ground beetles, crickets and other large insect food in the near darkness of a starry night or by the light of the moon.

Stone-curlews, or thick-knees, are probably most closely related to the plovers. Among the evidence for this kinship is the pebbledash pattern of buff, white and black down in the chicks, which renders them almost invisible against sandy, stony and sparsely vegetated soils: when alerted by their parents' warning calls, they will stretch out prone on the ground motionless and undetected. If the threat is more serious, the adults will lead them away: they have sometimes been seen to run off carrying chicks under their wings for short distances.

Mainly crepuscular and nocturnal, these wary birds spend much of the day inactive, sitting on the ground or standing motionless, often with an ungainly posture that makes them look broken in some way. Another odd sight occurs when a pair in courtship stand close together with necks arched and bills pointing down at the ground. Even more bizarre are the aggressive displays of pairs as they join to repel intruding rivals, erecting themselves until almost vertical, folded wings held away from the body. At such times, and especially at twilight and after dark, their eerie calls work up into a crescendo. These include higher-pitched, harsher versions of the call of the unrelated Curlew.

COLLARED PRATINCOLE
Glareola pratincola

Encountered by a novice, a flock at rest can cause puzzlement. With their short legs and streamlined shape tapering to a narrow rear, they resemble strange, short-billed, mainly earth-brown terns. But then they start to run, twinkling across the ground at high speed, and we think of some odd plover. This supposition too is dashed when the flock takes flight, their forked tails and dark underwings contrasting with white bellies making them look like giant swallows. (A reflection of such confusion lies in an old English name for the group: plover-swallows.)

Seen properly, these birds are never forgotten. In contrast to their relatives the coursers, which are long-legged, highly terrestrial runners, pratincoles spend much time in the air, especially when hawking for insects. They often feed at dawn and dusk, and sometimes by moonlight. Like swallows and terns, they are graceful in flight, twisting and turning in their pursuit. As they swoop and climb overhead, they present a subtly

A widespread but patchily distributed migrant breeder in Europe, where it has long been declining. Largest populations: Spain and Turkey; others with over 500 breeding pairs include Portugal, Greece, Romania, Russia. On migration and as vagrants they often turn up at lakes, reservoirs and flooded fields.

beautiful plumage pattern, the dark chestnut of the underwing coverts contrasting with the surrounding black bands, the white trailing edge of the wings and the flash of white rumps above. However, when they land, their dull-coloured upperparts make them very hard to see against the ground.

With their long wings and powerful flight, pratincoles are well equipped for long migrations. All those breeding in Europe and Asia spend winter in the vast semi-desert area along the southern fringes of the Sahara.

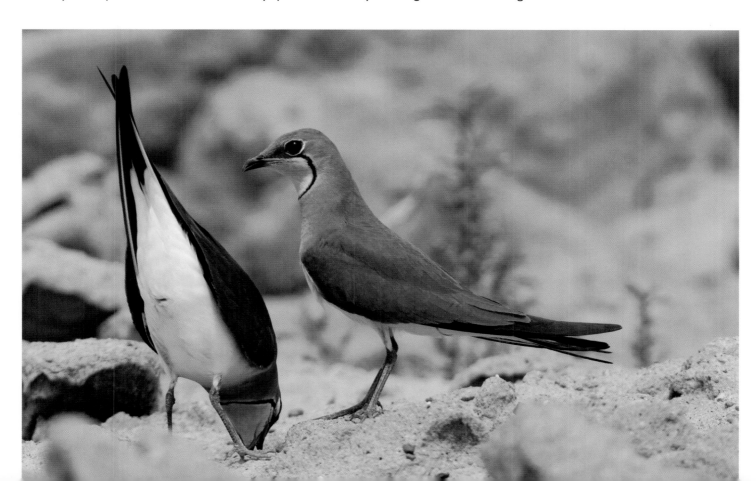

KENTISH PLOVER
Charadrius alexandrinus

In Europe, largest populations are Mediterranean; it is a scarce or rare breeder and a scarce passage migrant in N.W. Europe. Although migrants occasionally turn up inland, this is essentially a bird of coasts, breeding around lagoons, deltas, saltpans, sandy beaches. Many populations are declining.

This is smaller, daintier and more subtly patterned than its close relative, the far more abundant Ringed Plover. Its bigger head has a simpler pattern of bands and the breast band is never complete in any plumage. These markings make the bird look as if a painter had started work on the design but left it unfinished. It is the fastest runner of a fast-running family, dashing along at times as rapidly as a Sanderling. When disturbed, it usually runs rather than taking wing. On landing, it often runs immediately on touching the ground.

The paleness of the plumage is referenced in the bird's American name, Snowy Plover. Another reason that this is a more apt name than its parochial-sounding British one is that it is a truly cosmopolitan bird, found in the Americas as well as Eurasia and Africa. "Kentish" was applied because it was a bird shot by a doctor near Sandwich, Kent, that was scientifically described in 1801 by another doctor and ornithologist, Dr John Latham. Until the 1840s it remained quite common along the coasts of Kent and Sussex; by the early 20th century it was virtually extinct as a British breeder, a victim of specimen and egg collectors. Although making a partial recovery after receiving belated protection, the Kentish Plover had vanished completely from Britain by 1931 owing to disturbance. This is still a major problem over much of its huge range, greatly increasing the chances of predation of eggs and chicks or their exposure to the cold while the parents are kept away.

DOTTEREL

Charadrius morinellus

One of the most colourful of all waders, this little plover is, like the equally delicate little flowers beloved of rock gardeners, an Arctic-Alpine specialist. Although it is still a widespread breeder in the far north of Scandinavia, a glance at the map farther south betrays the relict status of its present-day distribution. Global warming poses a long-term threat.

The species' western outpost is the great stone-strewn, whale-backed tops of Scotland's Cairngorm massif, where it is one of the very few specialists to nest in these bleak remote places, among the few really wild areas of Britain.

On migration, small parties, usually comprising single figures only, halt for rest, recuperation and refuelling at traditional stopover sites. Such a flock is still known by the old name of "trip", a word maybe related to "troop" that has also been used in the past to refer to groups of goats, sheep, hares, wildfowl and other creatures.

Most by far of the European population breed on tundra fellsides in Norway and Sweden; some in Finland. In the south of its range Dotterel occur in pockets only, on the higher peaks – eg E. Pyrenees, Maiella mountains of Italy, Austrian Alps, Romanian Carpathians. It winters in Spain and N. Africa.

The Dotterel is an example of the phenomenon, rare in birds, of sex-role reversal: the female, not the male, is the brighter-plumaged sex, and takes the lead in courtship. After mating, she usually leaves the male to incubate the eggs alone (this is one of only 20–odd species of birds in the world where this happens), although she may share the incubation of a second clutch. Another well-known trait is the bird's tameness: Dotterel have allowed themselves to be picked up and stroked, and there are records of males incubating eggs on people's hands.

GOLDEN PLOVER
Pluvialis apricaria

The northern breeding strongholds are in Iceland (the largest population), Norway, Sweden, Finland, Russia. In Britain, the breeding population in the north and west uplands has declined, owing to afforestation and drainage. "Improvement" of pasture has affected wintering flocks.

Its melancholy piping alarm calls are among the iconic sounds of the northern moors. Often, a sentinel parent bird, posted on a boulder or other look-out, will give this call and then fly on to another perch, leading the intruder far from eggs or chicks.

In much of Europe, this richly plumaged wader is seen mainly as a passage migrant and winter visitor. Farther north, it is more abundant – indeed, it is one of the most widespread of all tundra birds in northern Europe, occurring throughout Scandinavia and Finland.

In many parts of its breeding range, the Golden Plover may be associated with Dunlin in a relationship that long ago earned the latter the Scottish folk name "Plover's Page". One or more Dunlin follow the plovers as assiduously as a little dog trotting at the heel of its master, but their attendance is not one of subservience. Instead, the benefit seems to be all the other way, with the smaller waders using the plover as an early warning system alerting them to predators, so they can feed without pausing to look around constantly. Golden Plovers also form joint winter flocks with Lapwings, which often feed in the same fields as Black-headed Gulls: the gulls steal the earthworms caught by both plover species, but in return warn them of predators.

In flight, the Golden Plovers form a more compact and coherent mass than their cousins the Lapwings, moving faster. On migration, they may travel at speeds up to 60 mph.

SOCIABLE LAPWING

Vanellus gregarius

Formerly known as the Sociable Plover, this subtly handsome wader is listed as Critically Endangered on the Red List of the World Conservation Union. It breeds only in northern and central Kazakhstan and (in far smaller numbers) in southern Russia, with a tiny proportion of the total in Europe.

    This is a big plover, only slightly smaller than the Lapwing, but longer-legged. Although it lacks the latter's unique wispy crest, it has an equally bold head pattern, with a brilliant white supercilium sandwiched between a black crown and narrower black eyestripe, and delicately apricot-buff cheeks. In the breeding season, the soft pinkish grey to greyish buff body is suffused with black on the upper belly, which merges into a chestnut patch behind.

    In the 19th century this was still a common migrant to south-east Europe and until the early 20th century was breeding as far west as Ukraine. In northern Kazakhstan between 1930

It breeds in steppe country (mostly in Kazakhstan, also in Russia). Small numbers nest in grassland between sand dunes, semi-desert, or meadows and pastures. All migrate via south-west Asia, including Turkey, to winter mainly perhaps in Syria, Iraq or as far away as East Africa.

and 2004 the population seems to have declined by over 95 percent, comprising as few as 200 pairs. The prospects looked grim. But spring 2007 saw the discovery of at least 4,000 birds in Kazakhstan, at migratory stopover sites in Turkey, and in Syria. In October 2007, 3,000 were found in Turkey alone. Satellite tagging should teach us about where they spend the winter. Many of the "new" birds have been found breeding on land grazed by cattle, so perhaps the threat of habitat destruction has been somewhat exaggerated.

LAPWING

Vanellus vanellus

A very widespread breeder across most of Europe; less abundant in the south, where it is mainly a winter visitor. Up to 90 percent of the breeding population occurs in relatively few countries; and in at least three (Russia, Netherlands, UK) there have been serious declines related to intensified agriculture.

Many country folk will have powerful childhood memories of this large, boldly patterned plover – the wild tumbling spring displays of the male throwing himself about the sky on strangely humming wings, or the long, twinkling black-and-white procession of a big ragged winter flock against a leaden winter sky, evading the grip of a sudden freeze.

Lapwing flocks of up to a thousand or more birds may move long distances cross-country in their urgent search for unfrozen ground. Often a flock will overshoot land and travel far over the sea, some individuals on rare occasions even reaching the east coast of America. In Spain, where it is far more familiar as a winter visitor than as a scarce breeder, the common name is *ave fria*, the "bird of the cold".

One of the best-loved of all European birds, and one of the easiest to identify at a glance, the Lapwing has several features unique among the waders of this continent: the long, upswept, wispy crest, especially impressive on males; the distinctive paddle-shaped wings, with the hand broader than the arm and very rounded at the tips; and the cinnamon undertail patch, important in ritual courtship.

In contrast to their boldly pied appearance in the sky, a feeding flock on farmland can be very hard to make out as it blends into the background. But when detected, a good view in sunlight reveals just how handsome these most lovely of plovers are, with their dark green upperparts shot with iridescent patches scintillating in tones of purple, magenta, rich blue and bronze, depending on the angle of the light.

KNOT
Calidris canutus

Although this stocky, compact, short-necked wader breeds no nearer to us than Greenland and Siberia, it visits this continent in huge numbers as a passage migrant and winter visitor.

Among the most well-travelled migrants of all smaller waders. Those nesting in E. Canada winter in N.W. Europe. Largest numbers are in the Waddenzee, the Netherlands; next largest concentration is on the Wash estuary in E. England. Birds from Siberia fly to western Europe before moving on to Africa.

This is one of the less graceful of the waders as an individual, but its impact *en masse* is sensational. Among the greatest of all natural spectacles on the estuaries of the British Isles and other parts of north-west Europe are the vast assemblies that build up at peak passage periods, when blizzards of birds pack tightly into high-tide roosts or perform their dramatic aerial maneouvres as they arrive or leave. In the air a big flock appears in the distance like smoke drifting across the estuary, its form changing constantly as the waders rise and fall and turn to left or right. Together with the flashing white undersides of the birds as they bank and climb, this produces a dizzying op-art effect.

As wave after wave of birds land at a roost, they soon fill up every available inch of space; sometimes, the later arrivals are forced to stand on the birds that have already touched down. One huge roost in the Wash was estimated at 200,000 birds. The combined sound of their individually rather subdued, gruff *knut* calls – a more likely explanation of their name than the legend of King Canute (Knut) attemping to turn back the waves – creates a roar that may drown conversation.

This is one of the most northerly of all breeding waders. It nests in the High Arctic, and may telescope its entire breeding cycle into just the two brief months of June and July.

SANDERLING

Calidris alba

In Europe, Sanderling breed only in tiny numbers on Spitsbergen, Norway; elsewhere, spread around the High Arctic, Siberia, N. Canada and Greenland. They winter from north-west Europe to S. Africa. Probably the most wide-ranging shorebird in the world, on all continents except Antarctica.

During the breeding season, this little member of the group of *Calidris* sandpipers looks like many of its compatriots in the far northern breeding grounds – a confection of chestnut, brown, buff, grey and black feathers above and at the front end, and white beneath. The intricate pattern camouflages them well against the barren stony tundra where they breed, hiding them from the prying eyes of Arctic foxes and Ravens.

In autumn, they moult and start to move south and west on their vast migrations. They now look like different birds, palest of all their tribe, delicate pearl grey above and pure white below. This paleness is relieved only by the very fine black streaks that are the shafts of their crown, nape and upperpart feathers, the short, thick-based black bill and the short black legs – and, when not hidden by breast feathers, by the small black smudges on the shoulders, formed by the upper lesser wing coverts. These look as if someone had caught and grasped the bird on either side with ink-stained fingers. Sanderling are among the easiest of all waders to identify on jizz alone, as small or larger flocks career along the edge of the waves at breakneck speed like a toyshop full of clockwork birds, legs a blur, darting out now and then from the straggling line of the race to snap up sandhoppers or other small morsels of prey from the surf. A really close telescope view reveals that they differ from all other small *Calidris* waders in having no hind toes – probably an adaptation to help them run faster over flat ground.

TEMMINCK'S STINT

Calidris temminckii

Compared to its close relative the Little Stint, this tiny wader is drabber and far shorter-legged, with a plumage pattern that makes it look rather like a diminutive Common Sandpiper, though with a mouselike, shuffling jizz. For the many birders living far from its breeding range, this is much more of an inland bird. In contrast to many coast-hugging or sea-crossing waders, it flies mainly overland on its long migration from the northern European breeding grounds to winter in West Africa.

Although quieter than the Little Stint on passage, it is very vocal when breeding. The male song includes a ringing trill, like tiny tinkling bells, that is not typical of a wader: indeed, it resembles the song of the Grasshopper Warbler, though less mechanical and often interspersed with sweeter, longer notes. The male delivers this in a dramatic display flight, fluttering his wings like a huge moth, often hovering in the wind.

This bird has an unconventional mating system, whose intricacies were unravelled by a Finnish ornithologist, Olavi

Far more widespread as a breeding bird in northern Europe than Little Stint, nesting not only in Russia and extreme N. Norway like the latter but also extensively in Finland and Sweden and, more locally, down much of W. Norway. It breeds in many habitats – dunes, saltmarsh, river banks, lakes, mountain fells.

Hildén, in the 1970s. Typically a female mates with a male and lays her first clutch. Within a week, she leaves him to incubate the eggs and takes another mate. She then incubates her second clutch, from this new pairing, in a different nest some distance away. Meanwhile, the first male mates with a second female, who may have already laid a clutch fathered by a third male – and so on. This bilateral bigamy doubles the number of young – a useful adaptation where the time for breeding is short. Many clutches or young birds fall victim to Arctic foxes, Common Gulls, and, in one Finnish study, other waders such as Ruddy Turnstones.

CURLEW SANDPIPER
Calidris ferruginea

Breeds on the tundra of north-central Siberia; also a few times to the west, within Europe, on Vaygach Island to the west of the Urals and far to the east in Alaska. Migrates to winter over a vast, mainly coastal range, from Iberia and Africa to the Indian Ocean coasts, Australia and New Zealand.

This handsome sandpiper breeds far to the east of our continent, but the long south-westerly migration route followed by birds flying to Africa in autumn takes them across central and western Europe. In spring, by contrast, Curlew Sandpipers are very scarce on passage in western Europe, because they take a more direct route through eastern Europe, to reach their breeding grounds in time for the start of the brief Arctic summer.

Slightly larger than the Dunlin, its more common close relative, this is a more elegant, attenuated bird, with wings projecting beyond the longer tail; it stands taller on its distinctly longer legs. The "curlew" part of the name alludes to the bill. This is generally rather longer and more downcurved than that of Dunlin — although there is some overlap between the bills of male Curlew Sandpipers and those of females of long-billed races of Dunlin. Such differences are hard to judge, but the bold white rump is a certain recognition feature in all plumages, including juveniles. The specific name *ferruginea* refers to the bright rust-red underparts of adults in the breeding season, contrasting with grey and black-chequered upperparts — a striking pattern shared with the bigger, sturdier, shorter-billed Knot.

These waders are generally far tamer than most others. They spend a good deal of time feeding, with remarkable single-mindedness, especially on passage and in winter, their longer legs allowing them to wade in deeper water than Dunlin usually do, and probe rather more deeply with their longer bills.

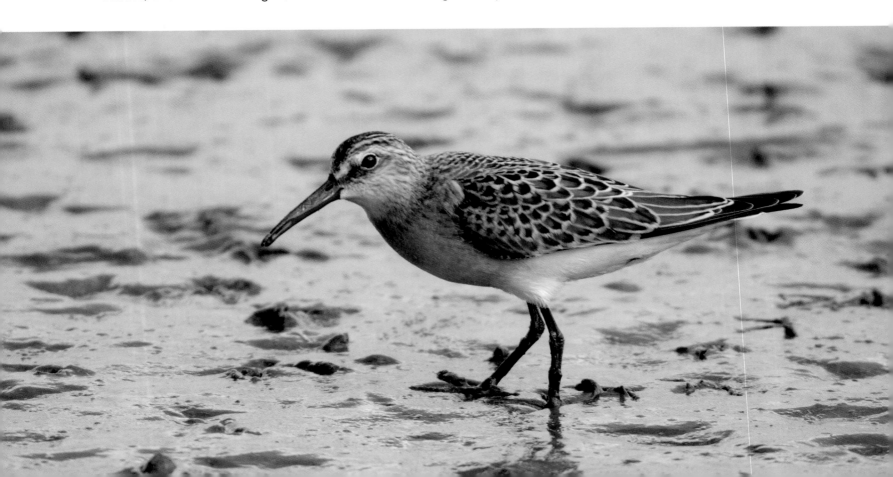

RUFF

Philomachus pugnax

Breeds across N. Europe and Asia, with a tiny outlying population in eastern England. By far the largest numbers of breeding birds in Europe are in N. Russia, but more accessible sites exist in many places in the Netherlands, Scandinavia and Poland. Ruff migrate vast distances to winter in tropical Africa.

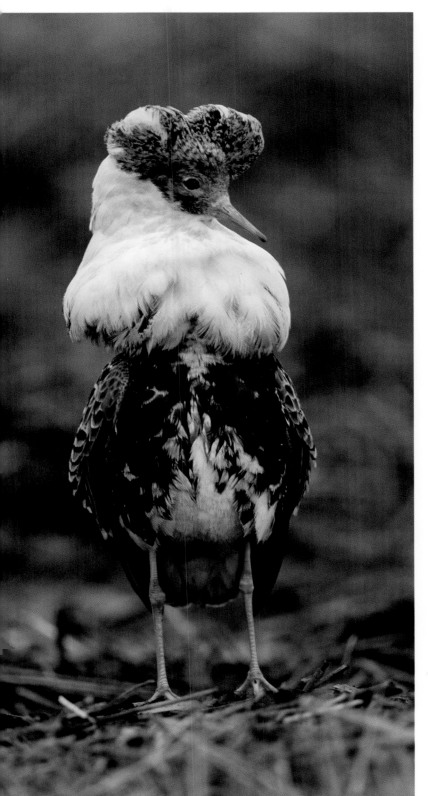

For extravagance in appearance no wader can match the male Ruff in his "supplementary" plumage – developed from April when he returns to northern Eurasia to breed. This dandy's name celebrates the singular spread of feathers girdling his neck. Thanks to the permutations of colours and patterns on the ruff and ear tufts, no two males appear quite the same. No other bird in the world shows such a degree of individual variation.

At the leks (or "hills") where they gather to compete for females, each male takes up position on a display "court". He erects his long ear tufts and expands his ruff like a feathery umbrella framing a wizened-looking head. In contrast to many waders, the Ruff is remarkably silent. The lek is conducted without a sound, apart from the eerie rustling of feathers as competing males leap and joust, aiming kicks at one another's heads. This aggressiveness is referred to in the specific name *pugnax* and in vernacular names, such as the French *Chevalier combattant*, Polish *Battalion*, or Welsh *Paffiwr*, meaning "Boxer".

Their mating is highly complex. Most males are "independent" (or "resident"): with mainly black and chestnut-red or orange adornments, they are the aggressive, territorial ones. The rest, dubbed "satellite" males, have pale, mottled or white ruffs and do not own territories, but will sneak onto a court and mate. The satellites are tolerated by the independents since they attract more females than the latter would alone. A recent discovery is that about one percent of males are runtish individuals, which mimic females. As the real females crouch, indicating readiness to mate, they quickly mount them and copulate.

GREAT SNIPE

Gallinago media

A scattered breeder in N. Europe, mainly on boggy mountainsides around the tree-line, also lowland marshes and forests in E. Europe. Most in Norway, Belarus and Russia, some in N. Sweden, Poland, Baltic, Ukraine. Hunting has caused recent declines, in E. Europe and in the African wintering grounds.

The Great Snipe has the distinction of having much of its breeding distribution in Europe. It breeds in treeless tundra bogs and marshes, as well as in wooded areas that also host that dedicated woodland breeder, its relative the Woodcock. Like the Woodcock, it feeds mainly on earthworms.

Instead of the aerial display flight of other snipe, this species gathers at traditional leks in late spring and early summer to perform a communal display, usually around dusk, continuing well into the night. Up to a hundred or more males have been recorded at some sites, but far smaller assemblies are more usual. The males typically take up position in hollows and on their "mounds" – often clumps of sphagnum moss. They extend their wings and fan their tails, so that the white wingbars and large area of white at each side of the tail gleam in the dark. Every now and then, they leap into the air with wings fluttering, or give voice with neck stretched back so far the head is almost resting on the back. The song is strange and complex. It begins with sounds remarkably like a warbler singing ("bibbling"), and others like those made by rapidly clicking your tongue against your teeth or by a fast-bouncing table-tennis ball, and ending with a strange whizzing. During the show, the birds may become ridiculously tame. In places such as the Biebrza marshes in Poland, the displaying males may be hidden among dense vegetation; in Scandinavia it is often easier to see a lek, as it takes place on more open ground and starts in daylight.

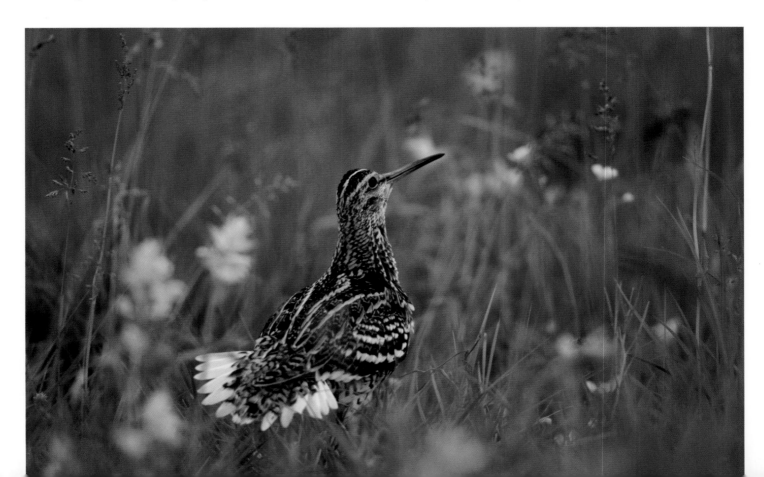

WOODCOCK
Scolopax rusticola

This is a truly odd bird – a wader that lives in the woods all year. Its cryptic plumage, a tapestry of russet, brown, buff, grey and black mottling, marbling and barring, allows it to vanish against the woodland floor. The usual experience is to suddenly put one up when almost trodden on; then it dashes off with the fast, jinking flight that makes the species such a challenge to shooters. One possibility of connecting with this elusive bird is to find out where it comes to feed, in places where it can probe for earthworms: in spring and summer a damp area of woodland and in autumn and winter fields next to woodland or scrub. Its big eyes, set near the top of the narrow head, give it all-round vision so that as it thrusts its long bill into the soft soil it can avoid being taken unawares by a creeping fox or a hurtling Goshawk.

A more reliable Woodcock-watching time is during the dusk or dawn "roding" display flight of the male, when the plump-bodied bird appears silhouetted in the darkening sky. As

Breeds from Norway to N. Spain and across much of Europe (not far south) into Russia, in damp woodland and in the north in upland birchwoods. Northern and eastern populations migrate, wintering to the S. and W. Largest populations in France, Scandinavia, Finland, Estonia, Belarus and especially Russia.

he patrols above the trees with slow wingbeats, his croaking and sneezing courtship calls drift down to a waiting female on the woodland floor. When she responds with a softer version of his sneeze, he drops like a stone to display and then mate with her.

Alarmed on the nest, the female will clatter off with loud wingbeats, capable of momentarily fazing a predator – often adding a Jay-like scream. At times, she will remove a chick from danger by flying off with it slung beneath her body and gripped between her thighs, or even transport one in her bill.

BLACK-TAILED GODWIT

Limosa limosa

Many waders are honoured with the epithet "elegant": none deserve the title more than this. The sumptuous pinkish-chestnut and black-scalloped pattern of its breeding dress, its erect, leggy beauty and small, perfect head with the dark eyes set off by white lids, recall a svelte, high-stepping fashion model on a catwalk. Were it not for the length of those steel grey legs, the long bodkin of a bill would look top-heavy, but they create a pleasing balance. This species is able to venture into deeper water than the shorter-legged Bar-tailed Godwit, and it often feeds wading into the shallows until the water laps its belly feathers.

The time-shifting potential of cine-film has revealed that while the Black-tail is a more leisurely prober than some other waders, it still thrusts that great beak into the mud and wet sand vertically close to its toes at a rate of up to 36 times a minute. Sometimes, a godwit will turn, describing a circle, all the while probing vigorously – perhaps to increase the area of search for the buried worm or mollusc or even to "fence it in".

The Netherlands is the most important breeding area in the world; elsewhere in Europe it breeds in large numbers only in Iceland (as a darker, shorter-billed and shorter-legged race), Germany, Poland, Belarus, Ukraine, Russia. European birds winter from Britain to the Middle East and Africa.

The curious word "godwit" seems to be devoid of apparent religious connotation. The first part may be a corruption of "good", referring to the esteem in which they were held as gourmet food. Although they must rarely be eaten these days, migrants are still hunted in parts of their European range and this adds to the much greater toll resulting from wetland drainage and intensification of agriculture. Indeed, habitat loss has already caused these magnificent creatures to vanish from many parts of their Netherlands stronghold, and is also starting to have an impact in eastern Europe.

CURLEW
Numenius arquata

Europe's largest wader, the Curlew is also among its most distinctive. The only other likely contender among larger |waders with decurved bills is the Whimbrel, whose striped head and shorter, more abruptly bent bill and shorter legs usually soon reveal it as this handsome but rather less elegant relative. It is easily found: one or more Curlews often form a static or slowly moving background to the livelier or downright frenetic activity of smaller waders feeding on a winter estuary.

When at its breeding ground on moorland, marsh or meadow, the great bill, longest in females, is often used like a pair of super-tweezers to deftly pluck an insect from the vegetation or even to snap at flying insects. By contrast, on the coast, hunting is mainly by touch, the bird often making a series of shallow test probes as it walks forward slowly and deliberately. In an analogous way to the annular shape of a metal detector, the long curve of the Curlew's bill ensures that it covers the maximum area when probing for its own, living, hidden treasure. Watching a Curlew when it makes contact with deeply buried prey is always fascinating, as the bird is suddenly transformed into energetic action, shaking its head vigorously to wrench the animal from its burrow. Marine worms are often broken by this treatment and have to be removed piecemeal. Even more lively is a chase after a large crab, which involves a tussle before the crustacean is subdued; often this is achieved only when it has been shaken and dropped on the ground, but it is surprising how big specimens can be swallowed whole.

The Curlew has one of the most poignant, melancholy voices: even a recording has the power to transport us back to a lonely estuary or moor, as is well-known to producers of radio and TV programmes. On the breeding grounds the effect is even more dramatic as the males perform their song flights. They fill the air with a series of rising *cooour-lee* notes that build up into the ecstatic crescendo of rhythmic bubbling trills — surely among the most beautiful sounds produced by any bird.

Breeds across N. Eurasia, from Ireland to Siberia, with probably over 75 percent in Europe. Excluding Russia, where the large population is not accurately censused, over 60 percent of Europe's population occurs in Finland, UK, Sweden, Ireland and Norway; these key populations are declining.

SPOTTED REDSHANK
Tringa erythropus

Breeds in shrubby tundra and swampy open birch or conifer forest, from N. Norway, Sweden and Finland across N. Russia. European breeders winter in Africa, with smaller numbers along the coasts of Britain and other W. European countries and the Mediterranean. Numbers have declined in recent years.

At all times of year, this is one of Europe's handsomest and most distinctive waders, but at none more so than during spring and summer. Then the adults are unmistakable in their sooty black plumage set off to perfection by the constellation of tiny white flecks on the mantle and upperwings, the white eye-ring, and the delicate white barring on the flanks and undertail, especially in the female. A birdwatcher's first sighting is unforgettable whatever the plumage, as the bird is clearly more elegant than the everyday Common Redshank – distinctly longer and slimmer, with a longer neck, longer bill and longer legs. The densely barred rather than sparsely streaked underparts distinguish the juveniles, while the pale silvery-grey and white winter adults have a ghostly beauty all of their own. The half-way house of a bird moulting into or out of breeding plumage is, as with the Ruff, an odd sight, patchy black and white.

The peculiar little downward kink of the mainly dusky bill, due to a slight droop in the tip of the upper mandible, is a feature that can be appreciated at close range. Perhaps it provides an adaptive advantage in dealing with particular prey, such as small fish. These are generally much livelier feeders than Common Redshank, often pursuing active prey with short dashes hither and thither, swishing their bills from side to side in the shallows like mini-Avocets, swimming and upending like dabbling ducks, or even zigzagging and leaping after flying insects.

The usual brief *chewit* flight call, while lacking the plaintive melancholy of the Common Redshank's contact call, has a cheerful, almost chirping sweetness of its own. On its far northern breeding grounds, this bird often utters a very different call when alarmed or excited – a chattering *tack tack tack* that sounds like it should come from a Fieldfare or other thrush rather than a wader. The male ascends on his song-flight during the half-light of the high-latitude summer, often around midnight. His song is a repetition of brief phrases with a strange buzzing quality, mixed with short trills and the chattering alarm notes.

GREENSHANK

Tringa nebularia

This elegant wader is one of the two largest of the subgroup of tringine sandpipers popularly known as "shanks". The structurally similar Greater Yellowlegs of North America, seen in Europe only as a rare vagrant, is about the same size or slightly smaller. As the common name indicates, the Greenshank has olive green legs, their greater length elevating the slender body higher than the less spectacular Redshank.

In most of Europe, Greenshanks are familiar only as birds of passage and, in smaller numbers, as winter visitors. Often they are encountered singly, but small flocks also occur, particularly when on migration. As they come into land, individuals or small parties of Greenshank sometimes "whiffle" like geese, twisting erratically from side to side. The usual alarm call – a loud, ringing, usually triple volley of *tyew* notes – is both highly distinctive and evocative of the lonely estuaries and lake or reservoir shores where this bird is often seen.

It is a very active feeder, probing deep into wet mud with the long, slightly upturned bill or using it as a precision tool for snapping up invertebrates from the surface or, in the case of flying insects, from the air. At other times, it sweeps the bill from side to side or chases after small fish in the shallows, where its long legs put it at an advantage compared to most other medium-sized waders. It may immerse itself almost completely.

On their breeding grounds, against the wild backdrop of the northern forest marshes or (as in Scotland's Flow Country) on the great treeless expanse of blanket bog, the male performs a spectacular song-flight. He ascends to a great height, and often embarks on a switchback course, delivering his rich, melodic fluting song on each downward phase of his undulating path, so that it drifts down to the female just as he himself planes earthwards. Sometimes she will join him in a spectacular duet. Often, before the young can fly, one adult, usually the female, leaves them, embarking on her southward migration alone. The young typically follow, chaperoned by their father, about a month later.

Breeds widely in N. Europe, from Scotland and Scandinavia to Finland, Baltic states, Belarus and across Russia; most in Scandinavia, Finland and Russia. Farther afield, most breed right across Siberia to Kamchatka and N.E. China. European breeders winter mainly in central and southern Africa.

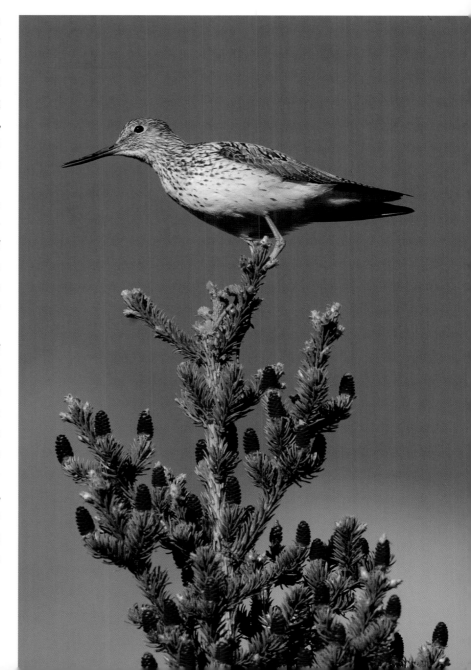

TEREK SANDPIPER
Xenus cinereus

To most European birders, this unusual wader is just an enticing entry in a field guide. Aptly given the generic name *Xenus*, from the Greek for "stranger" or "foreigner", it is a rare vagrant to the continent, except in Russia, Latvia, Belarus and Ukraine, where it breeds mainly on river and lake shores within the vast belt of taiga forest that rolls eastwards into Siberia. It has also expanded its range westward over the past century to Finland, where it is now a rare but regular breeder, as far west as the north-east Baltic coast. Here, it chooses to nest on dry, relatively treeless islands and also on landfill sites, industrial "wasteland" and other man-made habitats.

Although it is of a similar size to the *Tringa* sandpipers, especially Green Sandpiper, its long, gently but distinctly upswept bill, longer neck and relatively short legs give it a very different, odd appearance. Probing and surface-picking are the main methods it uses to catch fly larvae and other invertebrates in the breeding season. After removing buried prey, it often runs to the water's edge to wash the mud off its catch. On migration and in winter, its specialized diet is small burrowing crabs. They try to escape by tunnelling deeper, out of the bill's reach, but have to emerge to feed and mate; it is then the bird catches them after a short sprint. Dashing about, it makes abrupt turns and frequent stops, head down and tail up, as it snaps up the scuttling prey.

The Terek is a very noisy bird, not just on the breeding grounds, as with many waders, but also at other times of year. Its usual contact and flight call, a series of rapid, rather doleful, melodious whistling sounds, has been likened to a cross between the cries of a Whimbrel and a Redshank. Its song, too, recalls a Whimbrel's, but with a harder, more strongly rippling or rolling middle section to each phrase, more like a Stone-curlew's.

This bird is an impressive traveller. It migrates from its Finnish and Russian breeding grounds to winter quarters in Africa across the twin barriers of the Mediterranean and the more daunting Sahara, apparently in a single flight.

Breeds mainly in the Russian taiga. Small numbers nest farther west, with 500 or so pairs in Ukraine, fewer in Belarus, a handful in Latvia and Finland. Western breeders winter in coastal lagoons, saltmarshes and beaches in southern and eastern Africa and Middle East; vagrants turn up in similar habitats.

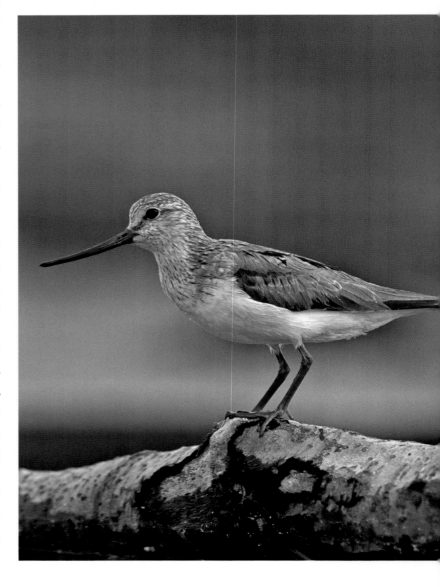

RED-NECKED PHALAROPE
Phalaropus lobatus

This is the daintiest member of the subfamily of three species of waders called phalaropes (from the Greek for "coot-footed", referring to their lobed toes). With its exquisite plumage of blue-grey, russet, grey and white, it is also a little beauty.

As with the other phalaropes, its breeding biology is remarkable. Like a few other birds, such as the Dotterel, it indulges in sexual role reversal and polyandry. The brighter-plumaged, higher-testosterone females take the lead in courting and aggression. After egg-laying they leave incubation and chick rearing to the males, which are often astoundingly tame.

These diminutive birds, with a body scarcely longer and heavier than a sparrow's, are as ocean-going as any seabird, spending up to nine months far out to sea, often in flocks, travelling huge distances to winter in tropical waters. The lobes on their toes, together with the small webs between them and the laterally compressed tarsi, make them excellent swimmers.

Very common worldwide (4 million), right around the Arctic; but scarce for most birders, owing to high-latitude breeding range and pelagic habits when not breeding. It breeds widely across northernmost Europe – mostly Iceland, Russia, Sweden, Finland, Norway; few in Shetland and Hebrides.

They have a Moorhen-like habit of nodding in time with the swimming action of their legs, and with their necks angled forward resemble a miniature Black-headed Gull when wearing their grey and white winter plumage. Even when they come ashore to breed, they sleep at sea like divers or auks.

At sea, phalarope have a distinctive way of feeding. Spinning in tight circles ("pirouetting") creates a vortex that brings tiny invertebrates within reach of the needle bill. Sometimes they immerse the whole head or even upend like miniature ducks.

LONG-TAILED SKUA

Stercorarius longicaudus

This is the slightest, smallest and most elegant of the skuas, with a head and body the size of a Black-headed Gull's. The spiky elongated central tail feathers of the adults can add an extra 20 cm or so. At least twice the length of those on an Arctic Skua, they add to this bird's graceful tern-like appearance in flight.

Long-tails breed in the Arctic, mainly along the coastal tundra. In Scandinavia, their range extends inland up onto the mountain plains and stony, heathy fells, to about 1,300 m. Here, they feed themselves and their chicks mainly on lemmings and voles; but they take a wider variety of prey than other skuas, including shrews, birds such as Snow Buntings and young waders, and birds' eggs, as well as insects and berries.

Like other skuas, they resemble a cross between a gull and a falcon, with strong, hooked bills and small but sharp talons on webbed feet – though, unlike raptors, they never use these to kill or hold prey. This means that both parents must co-operate to tear up larger prey such as lemmings or birds by a tug-of-war

Breeds in the Arctic – on Svalbard, in Norway, Sweden and Finland; and in northern Russia, which holds most of Europe's population. Elsewhere, breeds across Siberia, down the east coast of Russia, and from Alaska to Greenland. An impressive migrant, wintering in the Atlantic, Indian and Pacific Oceans.

technique, bills firmly clamped onto the prey and pulling in opposite directions. As the chicks grow older, they will take the place of an adult in this strange ritual. They usually hunt lemmings by hovering, Kestrel-style, before plunging for the kill.

Migrating birds, especially juveniles, may rest in places as far removed in wildness from their breeding grounds as ploughed fields or golf courses, where they find voles or other prey to refuel them on their voyages south. At sea Long-tails are less likely than other skuas to pirate food from other seabirds: they feed mainly by swimming and dipping for prey from the surface.

GREAT BLACK-HEADED GULL

Larus ichthyaetus

This very large, strong-billed gull is also known as Pallas's Gull, after the German Peter Simon Pallas (1741–1811), the explorer-naturalist who spent much of his life in Russia, where the main breeding populations are located. The shape and plumage of the head give it a very different appearance from its slightly larger, better-known relative, the Great Black-backed Gull. The forehead slopes up gently to a very shallow curve on the crown ending in an abrupt angle at the top of the neck, making the head almost triangular. As the name indicates, this is one of those gulls that acquire a dark hood in its breeding plumage; no other gull so large has this feature. The white eyelids contrast with the velvety black hood and red and yellow bill. Its wings are very long and narrow with more pointed tips than those of other large gulls; together with its more streamlined appearance, this adds elegance to the impression of power. It normally has a slow, ponderous flight, reminiscent of a Grey Heron or even an eagle.

In Europe, breeds only in Russia (over 90 percent of Europe's total), and in small numbers in the Ukraine. Colonies undergo year-to-year fluctuations. European breeders migrate to the Middle East and the Caspian Sea, with smaller numbers in the east Mediterranean. A rare wanderer to S.E. Europe.

The specific name *ichthyaetus* (from the Greek for "fish eagle") refers to its preference for fish (often dead or sickly). It also takes crustaceans, small mammals, reptiles, birds and their eggs, and swarming insects; and it has been observed indulging in piracy, robbing other gulls, grebes and Coots of food. Its colonies of several hundred pairs or more usually maintain a discreet distance from other gulls using the same site. Though loud, the deeply pitched calls, some goose-like, others reminiscent of a Raven, can have a curiously strangled quality.

SLENDER-BILLED GULL

Larus genei

The European population forms between a quarter and a half of total world numbers. Biggest populations are in Ukraine, Italy, Turkey, Russia, Spain and France, with the number of breeding pairs ranging from 25,000 to 40,000 in Ukraine, 4,000 in Italy, down to 1,000 in Spain and 900 or so in France.

This very attractive gull is an oddity within its family. It could clearly be regarded as one of the "white-headed" group that also includes Common, Herring and Lesser Black-backed Gulls, but has various features — especially its repertoire of displays — in common with the small "black-hooded" gulls. In plumage, too, it resembles the slightly smaller Black-headed Gull. However, its general jizz is more reminiscent of one of the white-headed gulls, particularly Caspian. It has a smaller head, a flatter crown and a narrower, more sloping forehead than Black-headed, which combined with the bill gives it a much more rakish appearance. In its lazier, stiffer-winged flight, too, it appears more like a larger gull than a Black-headed. And though it has a similar repertoire of calls, they are delivered less harshly and at a lower pitch, and have a mellower, throatier quality. The species is misnamed, for its bill is not particularly slender. It is, however, long — and this length is exaggerated further by the long gape line at the base. The most beautiful — though not constant — feature of this gull is the lovely rosy tinge to the body plumage of adults, especially in summer but also sometimes in winter. This is acknowledged in the Italians' common name for the bird, *Gabbiano roseo*.

Numbers nesting in Russia have declined in recent years, but populations elsewhere in Europe have remained stable or shown increases, especially in France. It is still a scarce bird, though, and the fact that 90 percent of the European population breeds at just 10 sites makes its future somewhat uncertain.

AUDOUIN'S GULL

Larus audouinii

Named for a 19th-century French naturalist, Jean Victoire Audouin, this handsome pale pearl-grey and white gull was once one of the rarest of the world's 50-odd species of gulls. It is special in being the only gull restricted to the Mediterranean basin as a breeding bird, although it is increasingly recorded elsewhere as a vagrant.

The rich crimson of the chunky, deep bill can appear blackish at a distance, emphasizing its size on the slender head. There is a black vertical bar near the tip but this is hard to see. Unlike any other large gull, Audouin's has dark legs at all ages. The black wedge at the wingtips is adorned only by little white spots, like a short string of pearls, rather than big white "mirrors" as in most other large gulls. Also in contrast to many of the larger gulls, which obtain a good deal of food by scavenging, this is a specialist fish-eater, concentrating mainly on small fish such as sardines and anchovies, and sometimes feeding at night.

Spain has almost 90 percent of the world population, most at the Islas Chafarinas (very near Morocco) and the Ebro Delta, the latter holding 65 percent of the global total. Three other countries have more than 500 breeding pairs: Greece, Italy, Algeria. Winters in southern Mediterranean and N.W. Africa.

With over 90 percent of the European population at just 10 sites, a catastrophe affecting a major breeding colony would have serious implications for the entire population, especially if the probably unsustainable fishery at the Ebro Delta collapsed, causing mass starvation. As well as overfishing, a serious threat comes in the shape of another, far commoner gull: the Yellow-legged Gull plunders its smaller congener's nests of eggs and chicks, and competes with it for nest sites. Other hazards include entanglement with fishing nets and snaring by baited hooks.

GLAUCOUS GULL

Larus hyperboreus

Along with the rather smaller Iceland Gull, this ghostly pale Arctic breeder is the only large gull with almost white primary wing feathers rather than the usual black with white "mirrors", and the grey of the back is extremely pale, almost white in strong light. The whitest plumages of all are those of first-winter birds, which can appear all-white with plumage wear. In winter, the head, nape and upper breast of adults becomes suffused with dark brown streaks, so that the bird looks as if it is wearing a loose-knit stocking pulled down over its head and shoulders. Distinguishing this species from its smaller, scarcer relative, the Iceland Gull, is a challenge for seabird watchers. Compared with the rather gentle "expression" of the Iceland, a Glaucous has a very fierce-looking appearance, befitting its reputation as a predator and pirate as well as a scavenger. This is emphasized by its small, beady eyes with their cold pale yellow irides.

Although some individuals travel far to winter to the south of their Arctic breeding range, especially around Shetland

Breeds on Svalbard, in Iceland and Arctic Russia, with 10,000 or so pairs in each of these areas. Beyond Europe, its range extends along the Arctic coasts of Siberia and N. America to Greenland. Winter visitors to N.W. Europe include birds from Greenland as well as from Iceland and areas east.

and other parts of northern Scotland, many see out the bitter cold of the winter in the far north. The species' typical gull family adaptability regarding its diet helps it survive – on anything from seaweed, seeds and starfishes to sand-eels and seal carcasses. They may in the same day use their powerful, strongly hooked bills to delicately pluck a berry or tweezer a fly larva from among driftwood, then to slice like a scalpel into the corpse of a whale or hack an unfortunate auk or wader to death. Sometimes they will not only drive off their own kind, but also other large gulls, even the king of all gulls, the mighty Great Black-backed.

ROSS'S GULL

Rhodostethia rosea

Regarded by many birders as the most beautiful of all its family, this small, High Arctic seabird is among the most sought-after birds by twitchers when it makes one of its rare appearances outside its remote northern breeding range.

Breeds only in north-east of Siberia (main population), Canada and Greenland. A few recorded annually in N. Europe, in Iceland, Scandinavia, Finland and the Netherlands, and especially in the British Isles. It is an even rarer wanderer to most other European countries, south as far as Spain and Italy.

Like the Roseate Tern, this is one of the very few seabirds that have coloured plumage in addition to the white, grey and black feathers typical of almost all marine species. As with the tern, its underparts are suffused with pink in the breeding season, in this case set off from the white of the head by a neat black neck ring.

The gently rounded head, delicate little bill and short legs make Ross's Gull look like a strange marine dove when it is on the ground. On migration or at other times when flying far and strongly, it beats its wings quickly, with deep downstrokes, again reminding us of a small pigeon. The usual flight, though, is more tern-like, airier and buoyant, with shallower wingbeats. The wedge shape of the long tail, unique among gulls, is often hard to make out, and in a brief view, perhaps in windy weather with poor visibility, there is a risk of this exciting wanderer being passed off as just another Little Gull by all but the more experienced seabird afficionado. Such vagrants include a total of 80-odd to date in the British Isles since the first certain record there, of an immature bird found sick or exhausted in Shetland in 1936.

As well as its great beauty, this species is invested with the additional cachet of mystery. It was not known to ornithologists until 1823, when the English naval explorer James Clark Ross first encountered some – and shot one to take back to Britain – on his last attempt to find the North-west Passage. Even more remarkably, the breeding grounds were totally unknown until the early 20th century. Although an isolated nest was found in Greenland in 1885, it was 1905 before the first colonies were discovered by the Russian explorer Alexandrovitch Biturlin in north-eastern Siberia among low scrub in boggy river valleys.

IVORY GULL

Pagophila eburnea

Along with the lovely little Ross's and Sabine's Gulls, this striking gull inhabits the far northern regions right around the Pole. Indeed, it breeds farther north than any other bird. The adult is the only completely white-plumaged gull – the word "Ivory", though more romantic than "White", does not really do it justice. Juveniles, by contrast, have their upperparts peppered with blackish spots and a variable scruffy smudge of dark feathers on the face.

These incredibly hardy birds face extreme stress from the fearsome cold they endure in the High Arctic climate. Part of their capacity for survival is due to their relative inactivity for much of the time, to avoid wasting precious energy. Also vital is their ability to take advantage of limited food supplies, especially in winter. Earning the old soubriquet "Vulture of the Arctic", this gull behaves like other, even odder, all-white seabirds, the sheathbills of Antarctica, in feeding on excrement, in this case that of polar bears and seals: indeed, its jaw structure may be adapted

Relatively scarce: at most there are 25,000 breeding pairs worldwide, but the true number is likely to be 9,000 pairs, only a third of them in Europe, where it breeds on Svalbard and Novaya Zemlya. Planes and other disturbance can interfere with breeding. Global warming is also a problem.

for feeding on frozen faeces. Also like the sheathbills, it takes advantage of female seals giving birth by feasting on their nutrient-rich afterbirths, as well as devouring refuse discarded from ships or by humans on the ice or land and carrion from carcasses of mammals and birds. At such times, the pristine white of the adults' plumage is often sullied with blood on the head. Such exotic tastes are most important in winter; during the breeding season the Ivory Gull feeds mainly on crustaceans, midge larvae and other invertebrates as well as smallish fish, such as young cod, and this is what they feed to their young.

KITTIWAKE
Rissa tridactyla

In Europe, most breed in Iceland, Faeroe Is., Spitsbergen, Bear Island, Norway, Finland, Russia and Scotland, with small numbers south as far as France and Spain. Elsewhere, breeds on islands off Siberia and along coasts of E. Russia, Alaska and N.W. Canada, in N.E. Canada and USA, and in Greenland.

This comely seabird is by far Europe's and the world's most numerous gull, with maybe more than six million breeding pairs. These are real seagulls: they winter far out in the ocean, and are seen inshore only when driven there by especially foul weather.

The dark brown eyes give the bird a gentle "expression" that adds to its soft blue-grey and pure white plumage to make it one of the prettiest of all gulls. The wings extend well beyond the tail when closed, their neat, all-black "dipped-in-ink" tips a distinctive feature, except during the moult into winter plumage. When opened, the pale lemon bill, often with a tinge of green, reveals a startlingly bright orange-red mouth. This is a frequent sight at colonies, as the birds keep up a deafening cacophony of the strident calls celebrated by their common name.

Kittiwakes are superb fliers, able to use the air currents around their nesting cliffs with consummate skill, seemingly allowing themselves to be blown about like snowflakes, but always in control. At sea, in calmer conditions, they have a light, almost tern-like flight, with pulses of quick beats of stiffly held wings. When the wind picks up, the wing-beats become deeper and the flight more powerful. In a real blow, they switch to a shearwater-style action, bounding along in great arcs.

Most breed on perilously narrow sea cliff ledges, often at dizzying heights. Here their untidy nests of grass and seaweed seem precarious, though cemented with mud and droppings. As colonies expand, they take to lower cliff ledges. Adventur-ous pairs have colonized man-made structures, from ledges on warehouses to piers, bridges, even a nuclear power station.

CASPIAN TERN

Hydroprogne caspia

While it has bags of character, this remarkable tern scores low on elegance, the huge brilliant scarlet bill and large head combining with the extremely short, shallowly forked tail to give a bizarre front-heavy appearance. Its very purposeful, direct flight and slow, relaxed wingbeats make for a far more stately progress than that of smaller terns – more like a large gull. Largest of all terns at up to 55 cm long, it is almost as big as a Herring Gull. Extending below the eyes is a rakish black cap, which shows pepper and salt streaking for much of the year and ends in a short-spiked crest. And to underline its difference from its relatives, it utters un-ternlike deep, hoarse, angry-sounding calls reminiscent of a Grey Heron or an amplified Jay.

Almost cosmopolitan in warmer parts of the world except for South America, this mega-tern formerly bred, albeit often sporadically and in very small numbers, in various countries to the west and south of its current limited breeding range on this continent, including Denmark, Germany and Italy. It

Breeds around the Baltic in Sweden, Finland and Estonia, and farther south at a few sites in Turkey, and around the Black and Caspian Seas, in Ukraine, Russia and Azerbaijan. Most European breeders winter in tropical West Africa, with small numbers in the Mediterranean basin. Breeds widely outside Europe.

has undergone a sustained decline in Europe over the past 100 or so years, with its ephemeral colonies at risk from flooding, burial by wind-blown sand, disturbance, predation and food shortages due to human overfishing. Despite an encouraging increase between 1990 and 2000, it remains a very scarce bird, with a total European population of fewer than 10,000 breeding pairs.

It is a rare but regular wanderer to many parts of western Europe, including Britain. Most of these vagrants are likely to be from the European breeding populations, but ringing has shown that some have travelled much farther.

WHITE-WINGED BLACK TERN

Chlidonias leucopterus

This rarer, more easterly breeding relative of the Black Tern and the Whiskered Tern is one of the most beautiful of all terns – some would say *the* most beautiful. This assessment is not based on its shape, for it lacks the long, sinuous tail streamers of such species as Roseate and Arctic Terns. In fact, it has the least forked tail of any of the European terns: it ends in barely a notch, and can often look square when fully spread. Although less streamlined than the Black Tern, with a stubbier bill and more compact, sturdier body, reminiscent of a Little Gull, it has an even more striking plumage. At rest, the silvery white wing coverts stand out dramatically against the grey back and glossy black head and body. In the air, a group of these terns rising and falling as they dip down to the water surface to feed creates a dazzling impression, with the twinkling effect of the three-tone upperwings and the two-tone underwings, on which the black extends onto the coverts.

A widespread but localized visitor to eastern Europe; major populations in Russia, Ukraine, Belarus and Azerbaijan, smaller ones in Hungary, Poland and Latvia. Despite declines in Romania and Turkey between 1990 and 2000, the species is generally stable or fluctuating over much of its range.

Compared to the two other marsh terns, it has a much more restricted range, being found only in central and eastern Europe and as two discontinuous populations in Asia. The species is restricted to shallow seasonal marshes and other wetlands, with major colonies at sites such as Hortobágy (Hungary) and the Biebrza Marshes (Poland). Here, White-winged Terns are often seen feeding with Black Terns, when their swifter, more agile flight is noticeable. The chicks, their cinnamon-orange down marked with black and white, are as attractive as the adults.

ROSEATE TERN
Sterna dougallii

Rarest by far of European breeding terns, this especially lovely bird in a family of lovely birds is honoured with the longest tail streamers of any of the world's 44 species.

Up to 20 cm long, these are very flexible and float or whip about behind the bird as if invested with a life of their own. In spring the breast acquires a delicate rose-pink flush that is celebrated in the common names in many European languages as well as English. This is often so subtle that it may be hard to make out at all, and it is always the palest of all European terns, pale pearl grey above and dazzlingly white below. Its calls includes a short *chew-it* sound, like a cross between a Sandwich Tern and a Spotted Redshank with a sore throat.

Although they nest over a huge range, from Europe, Africa and Asia to New Guinea, Australia, Fiji and the Americas, Roseates are nowhere common, and in many countries their breeding colonies are few and small. During the 19th century,

The breeding population in Ireland is by far the most important in Europe. Concentrated at tiny Rockabill Island, off Dublin, numbers there have almost doubled over the past 20 years. Small numbers breed in France, in Brittany, and at a few sites in Britain, including Coquet Island, off Northumberland.

they were almost wiped out in Britain and Ireland, the birds being slaughtered to supply the millinery trade, but they recovered during the 20th century to reach a peak of about 3,500 breeding pairs in the 1960s. Then storm damage to nests in Ireland, predation and trapping, often by children, in Africa took a serious toll, and by the late 1980s there may have been as few as 450 breeding pairs in Europe. Conservation measures, and an education programme in Ghana, have helped turned things round. Today, the European population approaches 2,000 pairs.

ARCTIC TERN
Sterna paradisaea

With a star billing in every book of avian superlatives, this svelte, delicate-looking seabird, weighing about the same as a Blackbird, makes the longest annual migrations of any wild animal. Each year it covers a minimum of 21,750 miles in the round trip, with some following longer routes than others and probably making journeys of up to 31,000 miles. Over their lifetime, a few long-lived individuals, aged 25 years or more, clock up a distance greater than that involved in flying to the Moon three times.

Although a good many breed farther south, most Arctic Terns live up to their name by nesting around the fringes of the Arctic Ocean. The northernmost colonies are perched at the very top of the globe at the far tip of Greenland, which apart from one nearby offshore island is the world's most northerly land. Arctic Terns spend most of their lives in the air, and see more daylight than any other bird because each year they live through two entire high-latitude summers. They are only likely to experience long periods of darkness while transiting the

The largest European population by far is in Iceland, with other sizeable ones in Britain, Norway and Finland. Elsewhere they breed across Siberia, Alaska, Canada and Greenland. They migrate south to winter off the pack ice of Antarctica, and some may circumnavigate the globe.

tropics. In contrast to their light, buoyant flight when feeding, they travel fast with flexed wings and shallow wingbeats.

The slender spike of the bill is entirely blood-red during the breeding season — an appropriate colour for its use as a needle-sharp defensive weapon when the birds feel threatened by human visitors to their teeming colonies. They are infamous for launching screaming, diving attacks in which they may draw blood from the scalps of those who come hatless.

Overfishing of sand-eels by factory ships (for cattle feed) is the most serious threat faced by these remarkable birds.

BRÜNNICH'S GUILLEMOT
Uria lomvia

This is an example of one of a pair of species that has a greater cachet for most birders because it takes more effort to see, being a truly Arctic seabird. Its range overlaps widely with the northernmost populations of its closest relative the Common Guillemot, but also extends much farther north. Brünnich's Guillemots "fly" underwater to find their food with flicks of their narrow wings to depths of about 10–70 m in dives that last from half a minute to just over a minute. On occasion, though, they may stay under for over four minutes and they have been recorded – usually trapped in fishing nets – at up to 200 m. Hunting in the freezing Arctic waters, they often swim beneath the ice.

At their huge noisy sea-cliff colonies, or loomeries, Brünnich's Guillemots often use narrower ledges than their Common relatives. Birds flying in from fishing expeditions perform amazing feats as they land with only inches to aim at among the shuffling ranks of adults and, later, young as well. On

In Europe breeds on islands and precipitous sea cliffs in Iceland, N. Norway and other northern regions. Some birds stay close to their breeding cliffs all year; many move out to sea in autumn, wintering as far south as 62°N in Norway. Many vagrants that turn up farther south are found dead or dying.

these cold, bare, exposed rocky shelves, often far above the crashing waves, the birds often lean forward facing into the cliff to support themselves. As with Common Guillemots, their single eggs have a pyriform shape that helps them to roll in circles rather than off the nest ledge if accidentally knocked. The eggs also have a unique pattern so that the parents can recognize them. Individual birds distinguish each other by voice. The tiny, still partially down-clad, flightless chick swimming far out to sea with its father is one of the most poignant sights in all nature.

LITTLE AUK
Alle alle

Encounters with these delightful little seabirds are a scarce event for most European birders, as they turn up south of their Arctic range in fair numbers only in years when driven onshore by storms during so-called "wrecks". Though exciting for their watchers, these usually spell disaster for the birds, as they are frequently blown far inland, where the exhausted, emaciated individuals often fall victim to cars, and to cats, crows or other predators, or die of starvation.

This aptly named seabird is the smallest European auk: an adult is only the size of a Starling, and half that of an adult Puffin. A good view of a bird bobbing about on the water reveals a compact, plump little body and often a squat, short-necked profile, with the wide gape of the tiny stubby bill imparting a curiously frog-like appearance to the rounded head.

Their flight is surprisingly agile. Although they have the same whirring wing action, they can take off without the lengthy foot-splashing taxiing across the water of the larger auks. In

A very numerous and difficult to census seabird, with a world population of possibly up to 100 million breeding pairs. Up to 3m may breed on Svalbard; a further 100–500k on islands off European Russia. Elsewhere there are huge colonies on Siberian islands and off Arctic N. America and Greenland.

flight, the long, narrow wings and short body and the fast, fluid wing-beats can make them look like waders at long range.

Little Auks breed in immense numbers on Arctic islands, in colonies of up to a million individuals. They nest up to 5 miles inland on steep slopes of coastal mountains, in narrow crevices among the cliffs or in the dark sanctuaries beneath boulders on scree slopes. Birds that have fed and are speeding back to hungry young can be identified by their bulging throat pouches. They often run the gauntlet of Glaucous Gulls and Ravens, but a greater threat is posed by oil spills and global warming.

PUFFIN

Fratercula arctica

With its pied plumage and huge, multicoloured bill, this stout little seabird is one of those birds, like penguins and owls, whose appearance strikes an anthropomorphic chord with people. Even its scientific name reflects its image as a miniature human, for it means "little Arctic brother" – the noun being a reference to its plumage, as sober as a monk's habit.

Puffins are best appreciated at one of their big clifftop colonies, as the birds stand outside their burrows that honey-comb the green turf, or flotillas rest offshore, bobbing like little brightly painted toy ships. Most spectacular is the sight of a huge "wheel" of Puffins milling round in the sky, with birds dropping out as they pass over their particular place in the colony.

A "triphibious" bird, the Puffin, like all other members of the auk family, is clumsy on land and in the air but superbly at home on – and especially *in* – the sea. Here, where it winters farther out than any auk except the Little Auk, it can ride out all but the roughest seas. Diving beneath the surface it

Breeds widely in the colder parts of the North Atlantic. Colonies are scattered across coastal N.W. Europe, with over 90 percent of world population. Outside Europe, breeds in Greenland and N.E. North America. All disperse over a huge area of ocean in winter. Has declined over the last 30 years.

becomes a fast if portly missile. Hooks on the roof of mouth enable it to catch and hold many fish in one dive. Record catches have exceeded 60 sand eels. Nevertheless, such a haul is actually not such a surfeit for the young as it might seem, but an indication that the surrounding sea area has been fished out by trawlers, and all that remains are the tiny immature fish that can fit into the bill in such numbers. On the other hand, despite the problems posed by overfishing, as well as oil slicks, fishing nets and global warming, these are long-lived birds, the record being held by a bird from Iceland, at 33 years.

PIN-TAILED SANDGROUSE

Pterocles alchata

The 16 species of sandgrouse comprise an unusual family of birds that live in open, dry habitats in warmer parts of the Old World. Just two species breed in Europe, this one and the Black-bellied. Both are found in Iberia.

On the ground where they spend most of their time, sandgrouse look pigeon-like or partridge-like as they shuffle along picking up seeds. Indeed, they were often regarded as being most closely related to the pigeons and sometimes to gamebirds. But the consensus nowadays leans towards their being part of the Charadriiformes, the great order containing the waders, gulls and their relatives.

As its name suggests, this bird has elongated central tail feathers. It is one of the handsomest members of the family. Males are particularly splendid, with a complex pattern of chestnut, bright golden green, yellowish spots, black, and white. Females have a similar though somewhat duller appearance,

Breeds on dry plains, dried-out lake beds and marshes and other arid habitats. In Europe 98 percent of the population are confined to central and southern Spain; maybe a few pairs in eastern Portugal; in France there is a small population restricted to La Crau, Camargue. Declining in most areas.

and like their partners have gleaming white bellies, which help distinguish the species from a distance when seen flying noisily overhead. Looking rather like large plovers with their long pointed wings and strong, rapid flight, big flocks make often lengthy journeys each day to tumble down and drink at fresh or brackish water sources – vital to slake the thirst of the adults whose dry seed diet contains virtually no water. These flights usually occur in the early morning, but in very hot weather they may take place shortly before dusk.

FROM PIGEONS TO WOODPECKERS

TURTLE DOVE

Streptopelia turtur

Breeds in much of Europe but patchily distributed in places. Outside Europe, breeds in N. Africa, parts of the Sahara and the Middle East and across south-east and central Asia as far eastwards as Mongolia. All except the scattered Sahara populations are migratory, wintering in tropical Africa.

Of all the sounds of high summer, none is more evocative than that of the exquisite little Turtle Dove. The male's soporific, throaty, purring song seems to emanate from the hot air itself – as much a vibration as a sound. It has a distinctly ventriloquial quality, so that it is hard to pinpoint the source. It is for this song that the bird was given its specific name, which is approximately onomatopoeic. The English common name is a corruption of the more accurately imitative French *Tourterelle*. It is pure coincidence that the boldly chequered bright chestnut and black upperparts resemble the shells of turtles such as the hawksbill.

Although it loves to hide in dense cover when singing and sites its nest well within a bush or tree, it is also fond of perching out in the open, especially on overhead wires, and finds its diet of weed seeds on the ground, mainly in fields. Its relatively long, pointed wings speed it on its long migratory journey, flicked backwards in an abrupt, jerky action. It has a curious habit of tilting its body from side to side during the brief glides in between bursts of wing-beats.

These monogamous birds have been an icon of tenderness and marital fidelity for centuries, yet slaughter by humankind has all too often been their reward. Huge numbers of migrants – 2–4 million birds – are blasted out of the sky by Mediterranean hunters each autumn. In addition, Cyprus has flouted the ban under EC law on spring shooting. An even greater threat comes from loss of food and habitat, in both its breeding and wintering ranges. It is hardly surprising that European populations have declined by up to 80 percent.

GREAT SPOTTED CUCKOO

Clamator glandarius

The largest numbers are in southern Spain. It also breeds in small numbers in Portugal, S. France, N.W. Italy, Croatia, Albania, Greece, Bulgaria, Cyprus. Most populations are increasing and the range is expanding. Almost all European breeders winter in Africa, a few in southern Spain.

This striking, long-tailed, crested bird is essentially an African species living in Europe on the northern fringe of its range. No other European species looks like the Great Spotted Cuckoo. With a body slightly smaller than a Magpie's and a tail almost as long, it has an intimate relationship with that species of crow. Like the far more widespread Cuckoo, the Great Spotted Cuckoo is an "obligate brood parasite" – that is, it always lays its eggs in the nest of another bird, which incubates them and rears its young. In contrast to its smaller relative, which has been recorded parasitizing over a hundred host species, the Great Spotted Cuckoo usually targets the Magpie (though occasionally Carrion Crow, Raven, Azure-winged Magpie or Jay). Unlike the Cuckoo, the usurper chick does not heave the host's eggs or very young nestlings overboard, but sometimes it tramples the smaller, weaker Magpie chicks underfoot. Often it competes so effectively for the food their parents bring to the nest that they simply starve. This is achieved by its imitating the food-begging calls of the host chicks and its possession of a gape similar in colour to theirs but even more vivid: this serves as a "super-stimulus" so that the parents cannot resist feeding it first and most.

These birds may be running an avian "protection racket". The "Mafia hypothesis" suggests that the hosts are allowed to keep their eggs or young if they accept the cuckoo's egg, but if they reject it, their own eggs or chicks are destroyed by the female when she pays her next visit.

CUCKOO

Cuculus canorus

Breeds across Europe; vast range of habitats. Females belong to different groups, each specializing in one host, from Chiffchaff to Red-backed Shrike. Has declined in many parts of W. Europe, esp. France and Britain. European birds winter in central and southern Africa. Elsewhere, breeds as far east as Japan.

This is a bird with a contradictory profile: it is both one of Europe's most familiar birds and one of its least known. The familiarity comes from the universally recognized song, responsible for one of the most onomatopoeic names of any bird in the world. This far-carrying two-note announcement symbolizes the return of spring, as celebrated in folklore, song and poetry. Simple but sublime, the sound often has a dreamy, ventriloquial quality as it carries through the air on a still spring morning. Far less well known are the bird's other calls. These include the strange "bubbling-water" call of the female and a variety of chuckling, choking, growling, hissing and mewing sounds. In addition, the pitch of each of the song's syllables may differ considerably between individual males, and more than two may be uttered, or sometimes the first note be left hanging without its usual partner. The quality, too, varies: birds at the end of the breeding season can sound hoarse and even out of tune.

The unfamiliarity is, however, mainly with the look of the bird. When a Cuckoo does emerge, flying low – perhaps a female on her way to lay an egg in the hosts' nest while they are away feeding – its camouflaging plumage and its fast, low flight may suggest a male Sparrowhawk's. This may be due to convergent evolution of the same features for different purposes – rapidly approaching prey unawares; quickly sneaking up to nests. Or it may be a case of the Cuckoo mimicking the hawk, to avoid predation or to encourage the hosts to fly out and attack it, giving away the position of their nest – and the eggs or chicks that will soon be usurped by the Cuckoo's bulky nestling.

BARN OWL
Tyto alba

Great variation in abundance across a huge range. Declining in many parts of Europe. Spain and France hold about two-thirds of the European population and 90 percent of the race *alba*. Not globally threatened. Has seriously declined in the UK, often with large fluctuations between years.

Arguably the most beautiful of all European owls, the Barn Owl is simply heartstopping in its impact. With its graceful, aerobatic, floating hunting flight, it has a ghostly white appearance as it searches for rodents by quartering up and down just a metre or so above a patch of rough grassland; perched on a post on a winter evening, the grey-and-white-flecked golden colour of the upperparts glows in the setting sun.

Although Barn Owls usually spot most of their prey on the wing, they use a more energy-efficient perch-and-pounce technique quite often in the cold winters of temperate Europe, especially at times of food scarcity.

This is one of the world's six most widely distributed landbirds, breeding on every continent except for Antarctica. Conquering such a vast range has led to the evolution of many different races: currently 32 are generally recognized. Some are restricted to just a few islands such as Corsica and Sardinia, others extend over thousands of miles.

Much of the species' decline in western Europe is due to the obsessive tidying-up of the open farming landscape. This has deprived the owl not only of suitable areas of rough grassland for hunting but also of the sheltered nest sites it requires, as old barns are destroyed or converted into dwellings for affluent commuters. The felling of old trees with deep hollows carved out by wood-rotting fungi removes more sites.

Barn Owls are most easily seen in summer when they need extra food for their young and in winter when food is scarce – at these times they often hunt well before dusk.

SCOPS OWL
Otus scops

Breeds across S. and E. Europe, preferring hot summers and plenty of insect food, and extending as far north as the Loire in the west and S. Russia in the east. Can thrive in tree-lined streets, but has declined in many places. Most winter in Africa; southernmost ones are resident or partially migratory.

The song of the Scops Owl has been heard on summer nights by so many tourists throughout the Mediterranean who have no idea that these notes come from a bird. The penetrating, deep, fluty whistle is variously transcribed as *pew*, *chook* or a more disyllabic *kiup* or *tyuh*. It can sound rather like the song of a Pygmy Owl, and there is overlap between two species in a few parts of central and eastern Europe, but the little thrush-sized Scops Owl is a bird of lightly wooded habitats, especially those established by man, while the even smaller Pygmy Owl favours dense conifer forests. Scops Owl song is slower and resembles more closely still the mating call of the midwife toad. Often it is hard to say whether the fluting is a single slurred sound or two syllables, but frequently a performance consists mainly of a single-syllabled note, with occasional switching to two syllables, in which the second element is higher-pitched. What is only too clear is the fact that it is repeated monotonously every two to three seconds, for up to 40 minutes on end without interruption. Often, a female will duet in response to the male's pipings with similar but softer and higher-pitched notes.

While the Scops Owl's song is only too obvious, its appearance is another matter. Extremely nocturnal, it can be very hard to see, unless one is lucky to trace the source of the sound to a bird that has taken up a station somewhere it can hawk for moths or drop down to catch some other large insect. During the day, its black-streaked, mottled grey (or rufous) brown and cream plumage, like that of many owls, usually renders it invisible on its roosting perch against a gnarled tree-trunk.

EAGLE OWL

Bubo bubo

This is one of the world's biggest owls, much larger than a Buzzard. An immensely imposing bird with long ear-tufts and burning orange eyes, it is capable of striking down and killing prey as large and formidable as fully grown red foxes, young badgers and adult Grey Herons. Avian prey also include many raptors and other owls, including such fierce or aggressive species as Goshawks, Peregrines and Tawny Owls – although it usually eats them, the Eagle Owl's motivation for killing them may be largely to remove competition for food. Ironically, the male's deep, throaty calls can sound like the cooing of some imaginary giant dove, that supreme symbol of peace.

Received wisdom used to be that this mighty predator epitomizes wilderness and is being driven out to the nether reaches by encroaching civilization. The reality today is more complex. While most Eagle Owls do inhabit wonderfully wild landscapes, some are invading manmade habitats. In parts of Europe, including the Low Countries, Sweden and at least one

Although widely distributed in a variety of climates and habitats, this is a rare and localized bird, facing a range of threats. Where it is protected, there have been recent increases due to both reintroduction and birds escaped from captivity. Outside Europe it occupies a vast range across Asia.

site in England, they have taken to breeding in quarries – and not just deserted ones. In Sweden, some urban invaders rear their big woolly owlets amid city garbage dumps, where prey is plentiful in the shape of scurrying, squeaking colonies of an infinitely commoner and more successful invader, the brown rat.

Conservation bodies now face a dilemma over these huge owls. Although some concentrate their killing power on rabbits, they may pose a threat locally to declining or rare birds, especially where rabbits have been largely eliminated – not to mention causing alarm to owners of cats and small dogs.

SNOWY OWL

Bubo scandiacus

Almost all 1,500–6,000 pairs are in Russia. A few breed some years in N. Finland and in Sweden or Norway, one or two in Iceland. In its periodic irruptions, it may visit open country. Outside Europe, more numerous across the tundra zone of N. Siberia, Alaska and Canada. At risk from global warming.

All owls command attention. It's in the eyes, as with a cat's stare – unsettling yet compelling. And of all owls, this great white one looks most cat-like, as it crouches on the ground and regards you with its big yellow eyes. No other owl is as white, especially the smaller male, whose meagre scattering of tiny dark spots is visible only at close range. With her heavy barring and spotting, the female is hard to find against the Arctic tundra – which serves her well when incubating eggs or brooding owlets.

At such times, the male spends much time perched on a lookout rock or ridge. An Arctic fox or a human invader is often submitted to a fierce aerial attack as the great owl swoops down and buffets the intruder's head with his wings and strikes out with closed feet or sharp talons. Snowy Owls have been known to attack people up to half a mile from the nest.

Some individuals remain on territory all year, able to endure bitter cold and deep snow, thanks to dense plumage which almost covers the bill and extends to their feet and toes. The feathers contain many air cells that provide effective insulation – second only to that of the Adélie Penguin of Antarctica. But after a peak in the numbers of voles and lemmings, their staple prey, encouraging the owls to raise many young, the increased population may find there is not enough food to go round. Many, especially younger birds, disperse south or west. In most years, they get no farther than Iceland or southern Scandinavia, Finland and Russia. But when the rodent population experiences one of its periodic "crashes", the owls erupt in greater numbers and reach farther, including Britain, France and central Europe.

GREAT GREY OWL

Strix nebulosa

Breeds in northern conifer forests. Pairs reach double figures in Norway, more in Sweden (hundreds), up to about 1,500 in Finland, up to 100 in Belarus and Ukraine, 1,500–4,500 in Russia. Most remain in their home range all winter. Far greater numbers in Siberia, and northern North America.

This sombre giant of the northern forests is one of the world's largest and most imposing owls. The round head, as big as a small child's, looks like a section through a tree trunk, with the dark concentric rings of stiff feathers that form the facial disc resembling the wood's growth rings. The biggest facial disc of any owl, it serves as a powerful parabolic reflector to focus sound into the huge, complex ear openings that give its owner incredibly acute hearing. With their eye-shadow-like black edging bordered by large white crescents, the piercing yellow eyes, though small for an owl, give it an air of dignified intensity.

The bird is rare and sparsely distributed, and often elusive or unobtrusive. Even the deep, Bittern-like booming that is the male's song is audible only at quite close range.

One time when it may become bolder is when defending its owlets from intruders near the nest site hidden in a disused raptor's nest. Anyone unwise enough to approach unprotected by helmet and face-mask is at risk, as the huge bird swoops down to strike. Sometimes, a particularly angry owl will break facial bones, inflict deep gashes or even rip out an eye.

Great Greys can survive harsh winters, breaking through the snow crust to reach voles hidden deep below. From a perch or hovering, a hunting owl listens for the sound made by the prey as it moves or as its tiny teeth gnaw a seed. When precisely over the target, as much as 45 cm below the surface, the owl plunges in, often headfirst. It may almost vanish from sight and row with outstretched wings for balance as it feels for the rodent and inflicts the death grip with widespread talons.

HAWK OWL

Surnia ulula

An owl that thinks it's a hawk – that's how many people familiar with this northern speciality would sum up its character, expressed in its common name. The broad face, flattened head and rounded facial disc clearly say "owl", but the long tail, dashing flight and diurnal hunting speak more of a hawk. This is the only Hawk Owl species in the northern hemisphere – the southern hemisphere has a score of species, all within a different genus.

Most birders who come to seek this owl in its breeding range – the great boreal forests of the far north of Scandinavia, Finland and Russia – are well aware that a good way to pick it out, even at long range, is from its habit of perching right at the top of a conifer, surveying its hunting domain. Less well known is the way in which occasionally it will hover like a Kestrel when searching for voles, its staple prey.

A vagrant Hawk Owl is an exciting find for any birder in temperate Europe – only in certain years do good numbers of

Breeds regularly only in northern half of Norway, Sweden, Finland and (by far the largest population) Russia. Best western sites include Abisko NP, Sweden; good sites in Finland and Kola Peninsula, Russia. Numbers fluctuate year to year. May have declined over last 100 years, but some local recoveries.

individuals chance their luck farther south, forced by periodic crashes in the vole populations over a large area.

Any brave souls who have a license to photograph this owl may find that the harsh expression of its facial disc (resulting from the glaring yellow eyes combined with "frowning" white eyebrows) is matched by its ferocity in defending its eggs or young at the nest site: it can launch a swooping attack with formidable talons – the male tending to pose the greater threat. Caution, and a crash helmet, are the order of the day.

PYGMY OWL

Glaucidium passerinum

Its stronghold is conifer and mixed forests in W. and S. Norway, southern half of Sweden, S. Finland and farther east across the Baltic states and Russia to the Urals. Occurs in smaller numbers south of these countries, in forests clothing high mountains, such as the Alps, Jura, Carpathians and Transylvanian Alps.

By far the smallest of European owls, about the size of a Ringed Plover or a Quail, and weighing considerably less than the latter, its rounded wings have a span about the same as a Blackbird's.

The facial disk is poorly defined and the small yellow eyes set closely together on the small, flattish head. Its "expression" is fierce and frowning beneath white eyebrows. Although also adopting the archetypal upright owl pose, it often perches at an angle when it may cock its strongly barred tail, which is relatively long as owls' tails go. A restless bird, it will fidget and may flick or swing its tail from side to side like a shrike.

Much of its large repertoire of calls sounds distinctly un-owl-like. The male's territorial song is a sequence of repeated *peeu* notes rather like a Bullfinch's contact call, to which his mate may respond with a high-pitched *seeee* like the warning calls of various passerines. The owls' own anxiety or alarm call is a high-pitched two-note affair recalling the song of the Chiffchaff.

These miniature predators have a strength and ferocity out of all proportion to their size. They supplement their main diet of voles with small mammals such as mice and shrews, and also birds. These, taken mainly in winter, are mostly smaller songbirds, but occasionally larger ones such as Song Thrush and Great Spotted Woodpecker. Most hunting is done around dawn and dusk, although in winter the owl may be active all day. Then it often hunts near settlements, even in gardens, adopting look-out posts on small conifers and chasing songbirds in fast, agile, whirring flight. It regularly caches prey in old woodpecker holes or nestboxes, which it also uses for nesting.

TENGMALM'S OWL
Aegolius funereus

Widely distributed over northern conifer forests of Asia, Europe, N. America. In Europe, occurs in Scandinavia and through Finland, the Baltic, Belarus, Ukraine, Russia. Some isolated populations in central Europe; largest numbers in Romania, France, Italy, Germany, Austria, Switzerland, Czech Republic, Poland.

This is one of the most attractive of all European owls. The generally flat-topped rectangular shape of its head, with the yellow eyes set in a neat black-edged white facial disc and frosted black crown, are reminiscent of the Hawk-Owl. But this bird, besides being a good deal smaller (the size of a Little Owl) and shorter-tailed, has a very different facial expression – in contrast to the Hawk-Owl's forbidding glare, a look of perpetual astonishment, thanks to the white eyebrows, raised in a surprised "V", and the two small downward-pointing smudges of black at their sides.

It is a strictly nocturnal owl that feeds mainly on voles. These it detects with pinpoint accuracy using extraordinarily acute hearing, aided by very large, strikingly asymmetrical ears. Although it is distinctive in a good view, its nocturnal habits mean that often it is only glimpsed flying in the light from the moon, a torch or headlamps. At such times, it can resemble a Little Owl or Pygmy Owl. It is worth remembering that it flies with a level, rather wavering flap-glide action, distinct from the Little Owl's bounding progress or the Pygmy Owl's dashing flight.

On late winter and early spring nights males broadcast their presence with a rapid sequence of brief repeated *poop* notes, which rise slightly in pitch at the end, or rise and then fall again. At first, you can count about a dozen or more (up to 25) units in each song-phrase, but soon the bird typically settles down to just five to eight. These have a soft, mellow, flutelike quality, rather like a Hoopoe with more to say than usual. The announcements can carry up to 3 km or more on a windless night. Unpaired males may keep up a barrage of calls all night.

LONG-EARED OWL
Asio otus

Widely but patchily distributed across Europe. Northern and eastern birds migrate south for winter. Outside Europe, occurs in N. Africa and Canary Is, extending across Middle East and Turkey through the centre of Asia to easternmost China; widespread across southern Canada and northern USA.

This is one of the world's most beautiful owls, with richly patterned cryptic plumage to conceal it against bark and lichen, glowing orange eyes, and the dramatic ear-tufts that earn it its common name. Because it is strictly nocturnal, except in very cold weather or on migration, it is not nearly so easy to find as some other European owls – including its closest relative here, the diurnal Short-eared Owl. Although, like that species, it hunts over open country, it breeds and roosts along the edges of coniferous and mixed woods and forests, and in copses and other islands of cover, where it is hard to see. It is easily overlooked, and censuses tend to underestimate its numbers.

Many are not familiar with its voice, in contrast to that of the well-known Tawny Owl. The adults have a wide vocabulary, including the soft, moaning hoots of the male's song, like the noise made by blowing over the open top of a bottle, the strange "comb-and-paper" buzzing call of the female and various barking, yelping, mewing and twittering sounds. The often incessant food-begging calls of the hungry owlets, like the sound of a swinging gate with rusty hinges, provide evidence of breeding.

These owls are most easily observed at their communal winter roosts. There they can be surprisingly confiding during the day, when you can enjoy the sight of their shape-shifting from a relaxed ball of feathers to an alert bird, a long, slim cylinder with ear-tufts erected like feathery antennae. Avoid repeated or intrusive visits, as the birds are vulnerable to disturbance. Versatile predators, they are themselves predated by Goshawks, Tawny Owls and Eagle Owls.

NIGHTJAR
Caprimulgus europaeus

The word "crepuscular" could have been invented to describe this wonderful and mysterious bird's habits. It is often possible to set your watch by its first appearance on a summer heath soon after sunset. Early risers may catch sight of a pre-dawn hunter as it pursues moths across the lightening sky. Soon it will retire to roost for the day, perched lengthwise along a tree branch or on the ground among heather twigs and leaves. Here, its invisibility cloak of soft, intricately mottled and barred plumage ensures it will be ignored by all but the keenest eyes.

Its excellent vision in dim light, its light, agile and silent flight and the huge gape of its tiny, weak-looking bill fit the Nightjar perfectly for its niche as a nocturnal eater of moths and large beetles: it is the avian equivalent of a bat. It selects individual insects to snap up, the stiff bristles surrounding the bill reducing their chance of escape. The half-imagined, shadowy shape of the bird, with its remarkably long wings and tail, looks larger than it really is as it floats past with sudden changes of

Breeds across Europe (not treeless areas, dense forests, highlands or tundra), where 95 percent are concentrated in the south (apart from southern Spain, where it is replaced by Red-necked Nightjar) and east. Beyond Europe, breeds in N.W. Africa and across Asia. European nightjars winter in Africa.

speed and direction, maybe pausing to hover briefly before side-slipping off again. Equally thrilling are the male's courtship and territorial defence flights, in which he glides with wings raised in a "V" and tail fanned to show off their almost luminous white spots. The silence of his flight is frequently interrupted as he gives sharp, penetrating *coo-ic* calls, and smartly slaps his long wings together above his back to produce a loud clapping sound.

Most magical on a summer's evening is the male's ventri-loquial, rhythmic churring song, often likened to the noise of a distant motorbike, with its subtle changes of pitch and volume.

SWIFT

Apus apus

Abundant in most of Europe; absent from Iceland and other parts of the far north. Nests in small colonies beneath roof tiles, in church towers and other such sites. Still nests in woodpecker holes in a few remote forests of northern or eastern Europe. Winters in tropical and southern Africa.

This is truly a bird of superlatives — as well as being the most aerial landbird, spending up to three years in the sky without landing, it is the smallest of all soaring birds. It not only catches all its food on the wing, but also drinks and bathes in flight, garners nest material among the aerial flotsam, and even sleeps in the air. Some pairs mate in mid-air rather than in the relative safety of their nest cavity. In an average lifespan of seven years, a Swift might have flown almost 1.28 million miles; for the oldest known individual, a 21-year-old ringed bird, the total may be 3.8 million miles, equivalent to flying to the Moon and back eight times!

Supreme in the air, Swifts are virtual cripples on land owing to their tiny feet. These are, however, strong for their size and furnished with very sharp claws, for clinging onto vertical surfaces at their nest sites, now almost entirely on buildings. Once these birds were believed to be footless — a myth celebrated in their scientific name. The "martlet" of heraldry is in reality a swift *sans* feet. Early naturalists classified swifts with swallows and martins, on the basis of purely superficial similarities. More recently, their affinity has been recognized with the exclusively New World hummingbirds.

The arrival of Swifts, later in spring than most other migrants, is a momentous event in the ornithological calendar, for the joy it brings when you see the first flickering, sickle-shaped silhouette or hear again that shrill, penetrating scream. Their early departure in autumn brings sudden quiet and the sad realization that we have to wait over seven months for these fabulous birds to return.

ALPINE SWIFT

Apus melba

Of all the birds that epitomize the special avifauna of the more mountainous parts of Europe, this is one of the most engaging. It is a giant among European swifts, and one of the largest in the world. At first glance or at long range high overhead it can easily be mistaken for a small falcon. With a thickset body and a bill-to-tail measurement of up to 23 cm, it is in fact only 2 cm shorter than a small male Merlin, and its wingspan of up to 58 cm can even exceed the same measurement in that falcon. The relatively slow, deep beats of these long wings can give an illusion of leisurely progress but this is deceptive, for its flight is usually far faster than that of its European congeners. It generally flies very high and may cover astonishing distances in search of its aerial insect prey – up to 300 or even 600 miles in a day.

Its combination of plumage and size makes it so distinctive that its identity is not normally in doubt. Upperparts, wings, breast band and hind quarters are the shade of loam rather than soot as in the Common or Pallid Swift. A good

A widespread but localized summer visitor to S. Europe, from Iberia to S. Russia, wintering in northern tropical Africa. A vagrant to the rest of Europe, including Britain, where it is annual, and Sweden, where it is almost so. Restricted mainly to mountains, though occurs in some coastal towns and cities.

view of the pattern of the white-throated and white-bellied underparts, on a bird resembling a gigantic Sand Martin with double-length wings, usually enables quick identification.

The high-pitched trills that are their usual calls have a dramatic rising and falling pitch. They have been compared with the trilling elements of Canary song, but can also suggest the distant call of a small falcon such as a Hobby or, incongruously, a Little Grebe. It is a stirring sound when given in chorus by a gang of these gregarious avian tearaways as they streak past through a mountain pass, or above the streets of an upland town.

KINGFISHER
Alcedo atthis

A widespread breeder by fresh waters across most of Europe. Depends on both water quality, ensuring a plentiful supply of small fish, and soft vertical banks alongside for digging out its nest burrow. Largest populations are in Russia, Romania, Portugal, Spain, France, Poland, Italy and the UK.

Often, a Kingfisher may be perched and surprisingly hard to make out against a backdrop of foliage or water. At other times, it is glimpsed in high-voltage action with a power that matches the electric blue and green blur of its upperparts as it zips along low and straight on short whirring wings, on one of its regular patrols of hard-won territory. Usually preceding this vision — often by a tantalizingly long time — are the shrill, insistent warning whistles of this tenacious guarder of fishing rights. Often, as the little bird bullets into view, these sharp calls continue to knife the air, as if cleaving a path for its progress.

It is one of the unwritten rules of nature that rivals — whether males disputing rights to a mate or, as in the case of Kingfishers, both sexes defending feeding territory — go to considerable lengths to avoid serious conflict that could end in damage or even death. But, like Robins and that other European waterbird that defends a linear territory along a stretch of river, the Dipper, the Kingfisher is a remarkably pugnacious bird, and posturing sometimes escalates into sparring and occasionally spearing with those daggerlike bills. Grappling rivals have ended up falling into the water and drowning. Dulled by being waterlogged, the sodden little piles of feathers are a tragic reminder of such a grim struggle. Whether a rare sighting like this or the more common one of a bird stricken by starvation in a hard winter, a Kingfisher corpse is always an especially poignant find, of a bird that in life was so full of glittering energy.

Pairs can thrive in surprisingly unidyllic surroundings, such as unpolluted canals and ditches in big cities.

BEE-EATER
Merops apiaster

A widespread but local breeder across S. Europe. Strongholds include Iberia, S. France, Bulgaria, Romania, Ukraine. Small numbers in N. France, Germany, Denmark. Overshooting migrants are found in N. Europe, where they occasionally breed. Outside Europe, found across Asia; also breeds in N. Africa.

One of a suite of tropical-looking European migrants associated especially with the Mediterranean, the Bee-eater is the most exotic and gaudy of them all. This is among the most elegant and distinctive of all European birds in shape, too, with its streamlined body, smoothly curving spike of a bill, long triangular wings and often-fanned tail with its short, sharp central spike.

The Bee-eater spends a great deal of time in the air, both when hawking for insects and on long migrations to and from its wintering quarters in tropical Africa, when it can fly up to 300 miles each day. From its vantage point on a telephone wire or other perch, or during continuous food-searching flight, martin-style, a Bee-eater can spot an insect up to about 100 m away. Few must escape their agile swooping and gliding advance, and the moment of capture is marked by an audible snap of the bill. When breeding, each bird consumes about 400 honey bees or insects of comparable size per day. The diet includes a very wide range of flying insects, but bees and wasps predominate. A fondness for eating honey bees has earned them the wrath of apiarists, even though the birds' destruction of wasps and other predators of the bees mitigates the harm they cause.

These are voluble as well as gregarious birds for much of the time, often calling ceaselessly in concert, with soft but far-carrying liquid, rippling notes in a pleasingly rising and falling rhythm. This makes it easy to detect an approaching flock when it is still some way off, although the exact position can be difficult to pinpoint as the gentle lilting chorus drifts down from on high.

HOOPOE
Upupa epops

At all times, this is one of Europe's most unmistakable birds, whether shuffling rather crouch-backed across a patch of grass or soil, pausing now and then to probe deeply for insect grubs with its long, slightly downcurved bill, perched by its nest hole in a tree or on a wall, or in lazy flight across a sun-burned olive grove. When it takes to the air, it becomes transformed as the black and white markings on the broad, rounded wings flicker in and out, alternately opening and being held closed against the body – a flitting action which, added to the shape and pattern, makes the bird resemble a huge butterfly.

Contrasting with the species' delightful appearance is its foul smell. Both the nest and the birds themselves take on a powerful stench, especially the brooding females and nestlings. This is in part due to changes in the make-up of the preen oil secreted by the gland at the base of the tail, but the droppings of the young also make a contribution. Presumably this evolved as an anti-predator strategy (along with the loud hissing of the nestlings) against snakes and mammals.

One of the quintessential sounds of spring mornings in the Mediterranean countryside is the pure-toned mellow hooting call of the male Hoopoe, which can be imitated by blowing across the top of a bottle. Although sometimes described as monotonous, this is a subtle and beautiful sound when heard from a bird at some distance. Then, like the song of the Eurasian Cuckoo, it forms a backdrop to other southern European sounds such as the buzzing of insects, the songs of warblers or the bleating of goats. Each phrase is typically of three notes, but the units may instead be double (like the onomatopoeic common and generic names), quadruple or, on rare occasion, quintuple or single. As the bird calls, at the rate of up to 30 or more notes a minute, it bows its neck so that the bill is pointing vertically down, and at the same time inflates its neck. This presumably increases the volume of air passing over the voice-box, amplifying the sound.

Breeds widely and commonly across southern Europe; also in much smaller numbers in central and N. Europe, from Germany to Estonia. Spain may contain half Europe's total. Range extends across S. Russia and Ukraine eastwards into central and S. Asia. It also breeds in Africa, where European birds winter.

ROLLER
Coracias garrulus

This bird gladdens the heart when it flashes chestnut and blue through a pine wood or along the tree-lined bank of a dried-out river. The only member of its family to occur in Europe, it may not be quite as stunning as some of its relatives from Africa, but it is certainly one of the most colourful of European birds. In silhouette, this sturdy, compact, strong-billed bird has a Jackdaw-like jizz in flight. But as soon as it emerges into the sunlight, the glowing rich chestnut back, the pale azure to powder blue of the body and wings and the dazzling deep violet-blue of the carpals and flight feathers of the underwing are instantly distinctive.

Although the Roller is not related to crows, its raucous voice has a distinctly corvine sound, reminding one of several species – sometimes within a single call variant, as with the addition of a Jay-like screech to the angry-sounding *rrrak-rrrak-rrrrak* notes, which recall both a wooden football-fan's rattle and the call given by a Carrion Crow when mobbing a raptor.

The territorial display that accounts for the common

A locally fairly common breeder in dry, lowland open country with some trees, especially oak or pine, across most of S. and E. Europe. Most in Russia, Romania, Ukraine, Bulgaria, Cyprus and Spain. Many populations are declining and those in the north-west have disappeared. It winters in Africa.

name of this and other species of roller involves the male rocking his body from side to side as he dives in vigorous half-rolls, like the performance of a displaying Lapwing. The belief that a Roller can flip right round in a complete 360° roll and, more dramatically, perform somersaults, is apocryphal.

It is surprising that the bird has no distinct cultural status in Europe considering its brilliant plumage, loud voice and familiarity to rural folk. But it does feature disproportionately in Renaiassance paintings containing birds, no doubt to show off the skill in representing such scintillant plumage in paint.

WRYNECK

Jynx torquilla

A widespread but often scarce and patchy breeder. Migrates to winter in Africa south of the Sahara. Over the last 100 years, has suffered huge declines almost throughout Europe; since 2003 effectively extinct in Britain. Decline of its ant prey owing to modern farming is likely to be a major factor.

Only a little larger than a House Sparrow, this odd and intriguing bird often looks more like a long-tailed miniature thrush than the aberrant woodpecker it really is. The Wryneck is most easily seen hopping with tail raised on the ground, where it finds almost all its food. A dedicated ant-eater, it has the longest tongue in relation to its body size of any bird in the world.

At a distance, the plumage looks simply dull grey-brown but seen closer to, this resolves into an intricate mosaic camouflage, which like a Nightjar's is highly effective against tree bark.

Its common name refers to the extraordinarily mobile neck, capable of extreme contortion, as if made of rubber; as does the specific name *torquilla* ("little twister"). When a Wryneck is disturbed at its nest hole, it stretches its neck, erects its crown feathers and writhes its head, in imitation of a menacing snake. It may reinforce this mimicry by opening its pink mouth and hissing or sticking out its long tongue. If picked up by a persistent pursuer, it often feigns death. These apparently magical deceptions led to the Wryneck's use in ancient Greece and Rome in rites aimed at charming a desired or faithless partner: a captured bird was tied to a revolving wheel called an Inyx (giving rise to our word "jinx", a curse or an agent of bad luck).

The Wryneck relies on existing holes for nesting, and may eject Redstarts, Spotted Flycatchers, Nuthatches, even Starlings and Great Spotted Woodpeckers. In the process it may turf out any eggs or chicks and eat them or feed them to its nestlings.

GREY-HEADED WOODPECKER

Picus canus

Smaller-headed, slighter-billed and about 20 percent of the size of the Green Woodpecker, this species has a less flamboyant plumage. The head, neck and shoulders are pale ash-grey, the rest of the upperparts duller green and the rump greenish rather than brilliant tropical yellow. The head pattern is much simpler, with a red patch on the forehead of the male only. In the Green Woodpecker the black mask encircling its staring eye gives the bird a fiercer mien compared with the gentler Grey-headed, whose black markings are reduced to two thin stripes, one from bill to eye and the other a curving pencil "moustache". Unlike its close relative, it often drums, with a louder sound and in rapid bursts, and its main call is a pleasant series of fluting notes, more musical than the harsh, almost manic "yaffle" of the Green.

Its distribution in Europe overlaps the central part of the Green Woodpecker's range. But the latter is far more numerous, with a more uniform distribution. As often, teasing out reasons for a species' presence or absence is laden with contradictions.

The heart of its European range is the more mountainous areas of central and E. Europe, but it occurs in forested or lightly wooded habitats down to sea-level. Absent from Britain, parts of N.W. Europe, most of S. Europe and N. Scandinavia and Russia. Beyond Europe, its range extends right across Eurasia.

Although the Green is more sedentary than the Grey-headed, and is declining in many parts of Europe, it has achieved an expansion in Britain that now takes it well into northern Scotland.

With its smaller bill, the Grey-headed Woodpecker faces a greater problem than the Green during winters with heavy snow in gaining access to ants' nests. It is often forced to fall back on a commensal relationship with the Black Woodpecker for survival: having spotted the bigger bird uncovering and hacking open an ants' nest, it waits for it to finish feasting on the insects and fly off, then flies down to exploit the nest-finder's efforts.

BLACK WOODPECKER
Dryocopus martius

Fairly common in many types of mature forest over much of Europe. The largest numbers are in Russia, Belarus, Poland, Germany, Romania, Sweden, Finland, France. The only woodpecker that has increased much in range and numbers in W. Europe (N. France, Low Countries; not yet Britain).

By far the largest of all European woodpeckers, this splendid creature is as big as a crow. Indeed, an earlier alternative common name was Great Black Woodpecker. It is also as black as a crow, apart from the pale bone-coloured bill and the pale staring eye – and its crowning glory, the brilliant all-red patch on the head. Extending from forehead to nape on the male, but restricted to the hindcrown in the female, this badge of sexuality develops early, and is recognizable in young birds before they leave the nest hole.

The Black Woodpecker has a distinctive jizz on the wing. The broad, rounded wings have strongly "fingered" primaries reminiscent of a raptor. In contrast to the smoothly bounding flight of most other European woodpeckers, it has an awkward-looking, floppy, Jay-like flight action, with occasional stiff downward wingbeats, the head held up on the long, slim neck.

Given its size and big, powerful bill, it is not surprising that this bird leaves dramatic signs of its feeding as it excavates huge areas of soft conifer wood in its search for tree-dwelling ants. It is the noisiest of all the European woodpeckers, especially in spring; calls include a more manic, evenly pitched, unaccelerating version of the Green Woodpecker's "yaffle", a high-pitched, loud trilling flight call like the sound that might come from a giant grasshopper, and long, shrill, mournful wails. Its bursts of springtime drumming ring out like machine-gun fire, carrying up to 2½ miles.

The expansion of the species' range over the past 50 years or more is important to a whole suite of birds that use its abandoned big nest holes. These include Tengmalm's Owl, whose distribution in managed forests where natural holes are lacking may depend entirely on the presence of the woodpecker, as well as Goldeneye, Stock Dove and Jackdaw. This unwitting benison is greatest in large forests containing only dense stands of conifers, because of the relative scarcity of holes created by rotting after branches fall off the trunks.

WHITE-BACKED WOODPECKER

Dendrocopos leucotos

This is the scarcest of all Europe's woodpeckers. The largest and longest-billed of all the pied woodpecker group, it is easily distinguished from medium-sized Great Spotted, Middle Spotted and Syrian Woodpeckers, since it lacks the prominent white shoulder patches that are a feature of those birds in all plumages. The only woodpecker of the region that shares its ladder-backed pattern is the tiny Lesser Spotted, little more than half its size. The feature that gives the bird its common name is not always easy to see, certainly not compared to the long white blaze on the northern race of the Three-toed Woodpecker – which also has a distinctive head pattern and far less white barring.

More than any other European woodpecker, the White-backed needs mature, old-growth broadleaved or mixed woodland with plenty of standing rotten or dead trees. The decaying wood is not only ideal for boring new nest holes each spring, but also contains a year-round supply of the timber-boring beetle larvae that form the major part of these almost exclusively insectivorous birds' diet. Each pair needs a large territory, typically about 100 hectares, in which to find food for themselves and their young. Such an area may support up to ten pairs of Great Spots. Although the birds are still widespread in some eastern areas where forest management has been minimal, such as parts of Transylvania, Latvia, Poland and Belarus, in many other places they are scarce, if not downright rare. Declines have been severe in much of their Scandinavian range. In Finland, the situation is critical, although a rescue plan is underway.

Southern birds in upland Mediterranean forests (Pyrenees, Apennines, Balkans) belong to the race *lilfordi*. Slightly larger, they have a longer post-auricular stripe on the head, heavier streaking below, and lack the unmarked white lower back and upper rump patch of the nominate race. Some ornithologists have regarded them as constituting a separate species: Lilford's Woodpecker. Its fate may be even more compromised than that of the nominate race, by fragmentation and in-breeding.

This increasingly scarce species is nowadays most common by far in E. Europe. In Scandinavia and Finland, huge declines show damage done to old-growth forest ecosystems by invasive forestry and acid rain; the species is reasonably abundant there only in western Norway. Outside Europe its range is huge.

LESSER SPOTTED WOODPECKER
Dendrocopos minor

Over much of its range this species occurs in a wide variety of wooded habitats, including forests, parkland, old orchards, tall hedgerows with trees, trees lining rivers and large gardens. It prefers woodland with old, native broadleaved trees and abundant dead wood, a declining resource in many places.

The smallest of all European woodpeckers, the "Lesser Spot" is even smaller than that oddball of the family, the Wryneck. Only fractionally longer than a Nuthatch, this dwarf is often hard to find – not so much because of its size but because it spends much of its time high in the crowns of trees. Admittedly, it is easier to see in winter, when it joins roving flocks of tits, with sometimes one or more Treecreepers or Nuthatches tagging along as well. With luck, you might be privileged to watch the male's floating, butterfly-like display flight from tree to tree in spring.

Although easily overlooked, the bird does frequently advertise its presence to those familiar with its voice. Its *tchick* call is quiet and does not carry far. Louder and more distinctive is the song, a *pee-pee-pee-pee-pee-pee*, reminiscent of the Wryneck, and confusable with the calls of a distant Kestrel, but curiously flat-sounding, with all notes at the same high pitch. Drumming is very fast and light, higher-pitched, less powerful and more brittle-sounding compared with bigger woodpeckers.

Feeding mainly by gleaning insects from the surface of branches, twigs, leaves and trunks, this little bird is light and agile enough to hang upside down, titlike, on the thinnest branches and twigs. Another technique is to fly out to snap up an aerial insect, though without a flycatcher's finesse.

The nest holes made by a pair each year have a tiny entrance, just 3–3.5 cm in diameter, little bigger than a Blue Tit's. The Great Spotted Woodpecker is a threat to the young.

THREE-TOED WOODPECKER

Picoides tridactylus

One of a small number of birds with one fewer than the usual number of toes, this is the only European woodpecker to have this feature. The toe lost through evolution is the first and smallest, known as the hallux, and is not of great use for climbing.

This distinction is not in fact of much use for identifying the bird in the field. Instead, the features to look for are the broad white blaze down the back, strongly barred flanks and a head pattern of white stripes on a black background rather than the reverse as in other European pied woodpeckers. Males also have a unique yellow crown patch. The southern race *alpinus* differs mainly in that most adults have a dark-barred white back panel. Superimposed on this racial division there is much individual variation, and where the two races occur together, as in Poland, it is often difficult to assign birds to subspecies.

The Three-toed Woodpecker is relatively quiet and unobtrusive. It finds most of its food by boring, more so than

In the north of its range, widespread in mature forests of conifers, esp. Norway spruce. Extends far beyond Europe across Asia to the Pacific, with three non-European races. Farther south, a more fragmented distribution, in mixed spruce, pine and fir forests, in the mountains of central and eastern Europe.

any other European woodpecker. It eats very little plant matter, concentrating on the larvae of bark-beetles, although in some areas it supplements this with tree sap which it obtains by bark-ringing in spring. Males are dominant when feeding at prime sites, which they do mainly by scaling the bark on thick lower trunks methodically with their longer bills; they also have a relatively short tail to provide a firm prop. Females feed more by gleaning, higher on the trunk and on branches, for which their longer tails serve as an effective counterbalance.

FROM LARKS TO CRESTS

DUPONT'S LARK

Chersophilus duponti

This unusual lark is a scarce and fast-declining resident breeder in much of its relatively small, fragmented range in Spain and North Africa. In Spain it is nowadays a very local nester in areas of flat or rolling upland steppe with short grass, low scattered shrubs and at least some bare ground.

It is the only member of its genus, although it bears a superficial resemblance to the much larger, desert-dwelling Hoopoe Lark which occurs in south-east Europe only as an exceptionally rare vagrant (except on Malta). Dupont's is a medium-sized lark, a little smaller than a Skylark. The short tail and long neck make its body look bulky. Its most distinctive structural feature is the rather slender, long, slightly decurved bill.

This is one of those legendary hide-and-seek species, with a reputation for being one of the most frustratingly difficult of all European birds to see. Like a rail, it spends much time hidden, superbly camouflaged among grass tussocks and scrub,

In Spain, breeds on shrubby steppe, esp. with feather-grass *Stipa* and mugwort (*Artemisia*), chiefly at 1,000–1,400 m. Most in Castilla and middle Ebro Valley. Outside breeding season, feeds amid cereals, especially oats, barley. Has declined dramatically in Spain, and in North Africa, owing to land use change, wind farms.

and, if it needs to flee, it prefers to escape by running off on its strong legs rather than taking wing.

Even when a male is located by his twittering and buzzing song, tracking him down is a challenge, owing to the sound's ventriloquial quality. Like other larks, Dupont's delivers its song in a song flight, up to 150 m or so, and remains aloft singing continuously, for half an hour or more. Added drama is provided by the timing, as the protagonist does not usually ascend the aerial stage until after dusk under a star-studded or moonlit sky.

THEKLA LARK
Galerida theklae

Widespread but patchily distributed across most of Iberia; also breeds in Balearic Islands (where Crested Lark does not occur) and in extreme S.W. France. Outside Europe, breeds across N.W. Africa, N.W. Egypt and N.E. Africa, from Somalia to northern Kenya. Resident and generally very sedentary.

With the Crested Lark, this bird forms one of those species pairs whose identification challenge is notorious. Although restricted in Europe to Iberia, the Balearics and a very small part of southern France, it is catholic in its choice of habitat. Like the Crested Lark, it occurs mainly in dry open country with sparse vegetation, but this encompasses steppe-like grassland, cultivated land, coastal dunes and open woodland. It tends to breed at higher altitudes than its close relative, on rocky, scrubby hillsides. It also prefers to have different parts of its habitat within a relatively small territory — for example, a roadside separated from a cornfield by a stone wall, or a mix of bare soil and areas of dense cover. Such "in-between" landscapes are often naturally impermanent, or vulnerable to development, and the Thekla Lark has suffered declines in Europe as a result.

There are also subtle differences in structure, plumage and behaviour. These include the Thekla's less hunched shape, shorter bill and more fan-shaped raised crest, and its more strongly streaked breast, far less rufous underwing and orange-sided tail, as well as its habit of perching in bushes, rarely shared by the Crested Lark. There are also differences in the songs. That of the Thekla is often simpler, but like other features of both species, it varies between individuals and perhaps regionally. Like the Crested Lark, this bird is an accomplished mimic.

The German ornithologist and Lutheran minister Christian Ludwig Brehm wrote the first scientific description of the species in 1858, naming it for his adored only daughter Thekla who had died of heart disease the previous year, aged just 24.

WOODLARK
Lullula arborea

Prefers warmer climates, so absent as a breeder from the extremes of N.W. Europe (apart from S. England) and from the far north. Iberia has 75 percent of Europe's total. Birds in the west and south are resident; those in central Europe and farther north winter to the south of their breeding range.

In polls of great avian singers, this small, streaky passerine often makes the top 20, along with far more famous performers such as the Nightingale, Blackbird, and its close relative the Skylark. The male's song is a rich medley of varied repeated phrases including fluty, almost yodelling *loo-loo-loo* notes which have given the Woodlark one of the most onomatopoeic scientific names of any bird: *Lullula*.

The song is delivered dramatically in a slowly rising and spiralling flight that may carry the performer up to 100 m above the ground. The exaggerated fluttering action typical of many larks is sometimes interspersed with direct forward plunges with wings closed. The whole act takes the bird, pouring out a constant stream of sound, over a wide area. But it will also proclaim its presence from a perch, and occasionally from the ground – sometimes as it wanders about snapping up beetles, flies or other insects. The Woodlark often sings on warm, windless moonlit nights when there is less competition from other sounds, and a reduced chance of predation.

One of the daintiest larks, its most diagnostic plumage feature is a subtle insignia – a small white-dark-white patch on the fore-edge of the wing. This can be seen both on the closed wing and during the bird's bounding, floppy flight on broad rounded wings that emphasize the extreme shortness of its tail.

Although its names rather overstate its association with woods, this is one of very few larks that perches in trees and shrubs. It also needs very short vegetation for finding food and longer vegetation for nesting.

SKYLARK

Alauda arvensis

Once almost ubiquitous in Europe, but numbers are much depleted in many places. Even so, still breeds in every country except Iceland in a huge range of open habitats. Northern and eastern populations are migratory; those of western and southern Europe normally make only local movements.

Thanks to its literally heavenly song, this unspectacular-looking streaky brown bird is second only to the Nightingale in inspiring its human admirers to write poetry, prose and music in its praise. Shelley, in his famous poem "To a Skylark", written in 1820, described the song as "harmonious madness", which captures its unique blend of control and abandon. No sound produced by any creature is more evocative of the freedom of the open countryside. Heard for most of the year, its glorious synthesis of warbles, trills, flutings and whistles is delivered without a break from shortly after taking off in a slow spiralling ascent, through the hovering phase and in the circling descent, until it folds its wings to drop like a stone back to land. Most songs last from two to five minutes without a break but exceptional performances of over an hour have been heard. More than any other bird, it uses the sky as a perch from which to broadcast its message of territorial ownership and eagerness to mate.

The Skylark spends a great deal of its time on the ground, where it finds all its food, roosts, performs most of its displays, mates and builds its well-hidden nest in a sea of grass or crops.

Although this is one of the birds that has benefited most from deforestation to create open landscapes over many centuries, it is ironically farming that has been its downfall. Most populations have suffered declines, especially severe in the past 25 years. These have been most extreme in those countries where agricultural intensification has been greatest. Populations have plummeted by 60 percent or more. In Britain alone the decline is equivalent to the loss of 100 pairs each day.

HORNED LARK

Eremophila alpestris

Breeds sparsely and locally in mountains of Scandinavia, Finland and Russia (declining); and in the Carpathians, Balkans and Caucasus (increasing). Wintering range extends from Britain and N. France to Germany, Denmark and E. Europe. Outside Europe, breeds in North Africa, Asia and the Americas.

This characterful and brightly patterned lark is often known by its old English name of Shore Lark; indeed, some books still refer to it thus. In Europe, only those who venture to the mountains of Scandinavia and south-east Europe, or the bleak rocky tundra coasts of north-east Russia, stand a chance of seeing them on their breeding grounds. Hence, "Shore Lark" is accurate in describing its habitat, for most birders on this continent encounter it only as a coastal passage migrant or winter visitor to salt marshes, dunes, sandy or shingly shores and nearby stubble fields. Even then, in western Europe it is localized, essentially restricted to North Sea coasts; farther east it occurs inland as well as along Baltic shores. In North America, by contrast it is found across most of Canada and the United States in sparsely vegetated or barren open habitats, from tundra and desert to grazed farmland and mown grass at airports.

On a north European seashore, in places such as the north Norfolk coast in England or Texel in the Netherlands, small flocks of these spry, comely little birds delight the eye when they appear on a winter's day to fuel themselves on strandline seeds or forage among the marram grass on a sand dune. Although often easy to approach, they may be hard to find, their streaky brown backs and broken face pattern well camouflaged against sand and pebbles. The "horns" are tufts of stiff, curving feathers that continue the black crown-band. These are poorly developed and hard to see in autumn or early winter, when the black and yellow markings are at their dullest. Later in the season, they become more prominent, especially in the males.

CRAG MARTIN

Ptyonoprogne rupestris

Breeds widely across S. Europe, and northward as far as Switzerland and Romania. Large populations in Portugal, Spain, Italy, Greece. Found in mountains to 2,500 m; some occur at lower altitudes, including coastal cliffs. More northerly birds winter in Africa. Also breeds in N. Africa and Asia.

Distinctly bigger than the far more common and widespread Sand Martin, this is a plainer, more subtly patterned bird, more greyish brown above and pale dusky greyish buff below, and without its smaller relative's breast band. As it wheels and turns, you can make out the diffuse dark streaking on the paler throat and, when the bird fans its virtually unforked tail, the neat row of little white spots on the tail's underside.

Although they may roost in large assemblages, Crag Martins lack the intensely sociable nature of Sand Martins, which seem to do almost everything in concert. They often nest alone or in small discrete groups of just a few pairs, rarely over a dozen. The nests are usually at least 3–4 m apart, and at some sites the average distance between a nest and its nearest neighbours is about 30 m. This accords with the birds' belligerent nature at their breeding sites. Territory holders will dive on intruding rivals with bills open, accompanying their chase with short angry rattling calls. They have a wide vocabulary, including a hurried, squeaky, twittering song that was memorably described by the Cambridge animal behaviourist Joan Hall-Craggs as sounding like "a bicycle in which all moving parts are in need of oil".

Although not as graceful and handsome as the streamer-tailed Barn Swallow or as dapper as the House Martin, the Crag Martin has an understated appeal of its own. This robust and powerful hirundine adds interest to any stay in a southern European mountain town or village as it zooms around the streets or flies up to feed its young, crammed into its big quarter-sphere mud nest on a church or castle or under the eaves of an old house. It is not just such venerable structures that are used as a substitute for the cliff crevices or overhanging rocks that were the natural nest sites for millennia before the appearance of mankind. In some places, these avian alpinists are colonizing new areas by nesting on, for example, motorway bridges. Even so, this is the only European species among the hirundines that still nests mainly in natural sites.

RED-RUMPED SWALLOW

Cecropis daurica

Widespread but local summer visitor to S. Europe, expanding north-west. Most in Iberia and Balkans; small but growing numbers France, Italy. Widespread in Mediterranean as passage migrant; vagrant over much of the rest of Europe. European breeders winter in Africa. Also breeds in Africa and Asia.

This attractive swallow was originally a bird of tropical Africa and Asia that has colonized North Africa and southern Europe relatively recently. It is conquering new territory as the climate warms. In the south-east it advanced north-westwards from the Middle East through the Balkans into Italy. South-western Europe witnessed a similar expansion. Until 1929 it bred only in the south of Spain but by 1951 had reached the central part of that country and by 1960 was approaching the French border.

Its presence also helped with the expansion of another, much rarer, European bird, the White-rumped Swift. This small swift is a bird that adopts the nest of another species, in this case that of various swallows or the Little Swift. White-rumped Swifts are birds of tropical Africa, so when four pairs were discovered in 1966 nesting in disused nests of Red-rumped Swallows in south-western Spain, it caused a stir in the world of ornithology. Since then, although it is still rare, the species has spread elsewhere in southern Spain and has even started breeding farther north in Extremadura. All pairs breed in swallows' nests.

The north-westward spread of the Red-rumped Swallow is reflected in the number of vagrant individuals turning up in north-west Europe, where it has even reached Iceland. In the British Isles, for example, 1987 brought a remarkable 61 individuals, compared with 39 birds between 1957 and 1976.

Although not as vocal as Swallows, small flocks on migration can instantly be distinguished from that species and other hirundines by their long chirping contact calls, which have an oddly complaining sound, rather like a peevish sparrow.

RED-THROATED PIPIT

Anthus cervinus

In Europe, breeds in extreme northern Norway and Sweden (where it also extends quite a way south), Finland (major range contractions in 1974–1978 and 1986–1989, for reasons that are unclear) and Russia. Beyond, its range extends right across Siberia and just into Alaska.

To casual birdwatchers, pipits are a bewilderingly similar group of LBJs – not ex-presidents of the United States, but "Little Brown Jobs": small, dull, streaky brown and buff songbirds. Experienced birders may feel the task of distinguishing them a bit more of a challenge than a bewilderment, but still find many species maddeningly similar. These include many of the Red-throated Pipits encountered in Europe on passage from their far northern breeding grounds, which are first-winter birds. But if you are fortunate enough to get a good view of an adult – especially a spring migrant in breeding plumage –

there will be little doubt about its identity. The gorgeous rich salmon-pink to almost brick-red face and throat, brightest in the male, is unique, and makes the bird in this plumage the most colourful of all the *Anthus* pipits (though some females are much duller). Even in autumn and winter, adults are still quite striking, even with the head colouring toned down to a rich orange-buff. At its opposite end, too, the bird is distinctive, having a rump that is much more strongly streaked than other confusable pipits such as Meadow, Tree or Olive-backed.

Of all the pipits breeding in Europe, this species has the northernmost range; indeed, it is one of the most northerly of all the world's songbirds, spending summer almost entirely within the Arctic Circle. It has one of the longest migrations of any pipit: European breeders winter mainly on the east side of tropical Africa. Some, though, end up in the Near East and North Africa, while a few remain in Europe, and can be found with good fortune in south-east Italy and southern Greece.

WATER PIPIT
Anthus spinoletta

Breeds high in mountains of central and S. Europe, from Spain through central and S. France, Alps and Apennines to central and S.E. Europe, Caucasus, and beyond. Winters lower in the same area, or in coastal areas farther north. On passage and through the winter in W. Europe, occurs by water.

This is one of those birds, like the Marsh Tit and Willow Tit, that has been saddled with an inappropriate common name – at least during the breeding season. At this time, Water Pipits live in mountains. They usually stay well above the tree line and the range of Meadow and Tree Pipits. Although a pair may choose a damp alpine meadow for their territory, or search for food among the rocks in a fast-flowing stream, they are not by any means invariably associated with water. It has been suggested that a more suitable name would be the Mountain Pipit but this is equally misleading during the non-breeding season when the species forsakes higher altitudes.

In its breeding plumage the contrast between the delicate pale apricot-buff to peach-pink blush of the throat and breast with the bluish grey head and nape, bold white supercilium and belly and rich brown upperparts makes a particularly lovely combination reminiscent of the delicacy of alpine flowers. No other European pipit has such mainly unstreaked white lower underparts – a feature that stands out on flying birds at long range. This handsome plumage can be seen on passage birds in spring, although it is rather more muted in females.

Although not unduly shy when breeding in the mountains, Water Pipits are often extremely wary on passage and in their winter quarters. They tend to check for danger frequently, and at the first sign take off and tower high into the air, sometimes flying as far as half a mile before settling.

CITRINE WAGTAIL
Motacilla citreola

Breeds from Russia eastwards as far as N.W. Manchuria and southwards to the northern flanks of the Himalayas; a very common breeder in the tundra belt of N. Russia; less abundant to the south. Passage birds regular on some Greek islands, and in Cyprus and Georgia. Winters in India and S.E. Asia.

With its dazzling yellow head and body, a male in breeding plumage is a stunning sight. The grey back and black wings with two large, boldly contrasting white wingbars, like a smart White Wagtail, give it a far more dramatic appearance than the mainly olive-toned upperparts of the Yellow Wagtail; moreover, the yellow is unbroken from the bill base to the whitish undertail.

Even more than Yellow Wagtail, this is essentially a bird of wetlands. Its core breeding area is the heart of Siberia, from where tongues of summer distribution extend in all directions.

In the nominate subspecies, breeding from northern Russia eastwards, the brilliant yellow of the male is edged by a narrow "scarf" of black feathers on the lower hindneck and upper mantle. This is the race that is pushing in from westernmost Russia across the border into Finland. A more southerly-breeding race, *werae*, is the one that is penetrating the southern Baltic states and eastern Poland; it is purer grey and paler yellow. (Most stunning of all three subspecies is *calcarata*, but its breeding grounds reach no nearer Europe than eastern Afghanistan.)

In contrast to the declines undergone by its relative in many parts of Europe over the past quarter of a century, the Citrine Wagtail is expanding its range westwards. After colonizing Ukraine from 1976 and Belarus from 1982, it now breeds in small numbers in Finland, Poland and on occasion farther west – for example, in Switzerland, the former Czechoslovakia, Germany and even Britain.

WAXWING
Bombycilla garrulus

Russia has over 75 percent of the European population of 100,000–500,000 breeding pairs, Finland about 23 percent, Sweden 1–7 percent and Norway usually less than 1 percent. Irruptions into W. Europe vary in size, but have become more frequent recently. Small flocks have reached the Mediterranean.

The word "irruption" might conjure up images of skin infection, but to birders it may speak of delights to come in the shape of a visit from a flock of these extraordinarily handsome birds.

Although a flock silhouetted in flight could be mistaken for Starlings, once they grace a tree or bush there is no mistaking them, with their jaunty crests and silk-soft, immaculate plumage in shades of pinkish brown, fox red, fawn and grey. The peculiar brilliant red waxlike tips to their secondary feathers are not in fact made of wax. Shaped like elongated teardrops, each one develops as an extension of the feather. The likely function of these odd appendages is as badges denoting age and sex — males and older birds have more and longer tips than females and younger individuals. This helps in the choice of suitable partners.

At least some birds make more local migrations, but the mass eruptions that see huge numbers leaving to winter much farther south occur only at irregular intervals. These follow a spurt in population, when birds soon use up local supplies of their staple diet of berries. Flocks roam, exhausting the supply in one area before moving on to find another. At such times, Waxwings become fearless of humans, as they strip trees and shrubs planted by city roads and in parks and gardens. They stuff the plump red berries into their wide gapes at rates that may equal up to three a minute before taking a break to digest — and produce a constant shower of droppings in which the undigested seeds are wrapped in a gelatinous coating like strings of pearls.

DIPPER
Cinclus cinclus

As tied to water as treecreepers are to trees or swifts to the air, the Dipper of Eurasia and its four similar relatives in Asia and the Americas are the only passerines that are truly aquatic: they regularly swim, dive and walk underwater in search of their prey, aquatic invertebrates and small fish. Numerous adaptations include sturdy legs and feet powered by extra strong muscles; toes equipped with very sharp curved claws, for holding fast to rocks on the riverbed; sealable nostrils; and long, soft body feathers over a thick insulating layer of down – but not webbed feet, since they use their stubby wings to propel them through water. They favour fast-flowing streams, mostly in upland areas.

Built like an oversized Wren, the Dipper frequently cocks its short tail like that bird, and, most characteristically, bobs its body up and down as if its legs were springs. At the same time, it flicks the tail downwards and blinks its conspicuous white eyelids. This dipping action, accounting for the common name, is a signal to a potential predator that the bird has noticed it and is fit and healthy; it probably also sends the same message to other Dippers during courtship displays and territorial disputes.

The song, of rich warbling phrases intermingled with harsher, explosive notes, is loud and sustained, so that it can be heard above the sound of rushing water. Both males and females sing for much of the year, especially from January to April, when establishing breeding territories, and in winter, when securing winter feeding territories. These exclusive domains follow the course of the waterway, which one or other partner patrols regularly, zipping along on short fast-whirring wings low over the water and warning of its approach with equally penetrating, staccato *zit zit zit* calls.

The big, untidy domed nest of moss and grass is often sited in a hole in a river bank, but the birds also make use of bridges and walls, which are more rarely prone to flooding. Some pairs position their nests under the overhang behind a waterfall, which must render them almost immune from predation.

Largest population by far is in Romania; other major ones in Norway, Sweden, France, UK, Russia and Germany. Many birds remain on their waters in winter but icing over can force them to move to lowland rivers, lakes and even estuaries. Outside Europe they live in North Africa and parts of Asia.

WREN

Troglodytes troglodytes

Almost ubiquitous and very numerous in Europe except N. Scandinavia, Finland and Russia. Populations can be cut by up to 75 percent in hard winters, but the species soon bounces back. Northern races are migratory, wintering farther south in Europe. Elsewhere, found in North Africa and right across Asia.

This tiny bird is the sole Old World representative of the wren family, almost all of the other 75 or so species being restricted to Latin America. The wrens are presumed to have evolved in the New World, where "our" species lives in North America. There it is known as the Winter Wren, to distinguish it from eight other species there and since it occurs in the US mainly as a winter visitor. The bird is renowned for its extraordinarily loud and spirited song. This barrage of sweet warbling notes mixed with hard rattling trills is one of the loudest songs relative to the singer's size of any of the world's birds.

Although not quite as small as the smallest European bird, the Goldcrest, the Wren is the shortest when, as it often does, it jauntily cocks up its tail. This tiny, stumpy bird is full of vitality, of necessity, for like the equally insectivorous shrews among the mammals, it must spend much of its time feeding to maintain its high-energy metabolism. In its search for insects and spiders, its diminutive size enables it to creep with jerky mouse-like movements through the undergrowth and other hidden places. This proclivity may be celebrated in the "cave-dweller" scientific name, which also refers to their enclosed nests.

This is one of the most widespread of all European birds, occurring in almost every habitat except the most barren. It has also colonized various islands, where it has evolved distinctive races, such as those particular to small islands of the North Atlantic. There are four such in the British Isles: *hirtensis*, endemic to St Kilda way out in the Atlantic, *hebridensis* (the Outer Hebrides), *fridarensis* (Fair Isle) and *zetlandicus* (Shetland).

ALPINE ACCENTOR

Prunella collaris

The most widespread of the accentors, found from Spain (and N.W. Africa) through southern, central and eastern Europe, and right across Asia. Occurs at altitudes of up to 3,000 m in the Caucasus, higher outside Europe. Most descend to lower altitudes in winter, including ski stations.

The small accentor family is exclusively Palearctic, with most of the 13 species restricted to Asia. Although the two species whose breeding ranges include Europe share many family features, they are utterly different in distribution and abundance. The Dunnock (or Hedge Accentor) is unusual in that it is most common in the lowlands, where it has adapted to life in farmland, woods and urban gardens. The Alpine Accentor, like most other accentors, breeds solely in wild, high-mountain country, on rocky alpine slopes between the tree-line and the snow-line.

It is a more striking bird than the little, shuffling Dunnock, with a more robust build and upright posture – like a cross between a large, dark pipit or lark and a small thrush. It resembles these birds, too, in its strong, undulating flight. Also, its song is more musical than the Dunnock's cheerful scratchy warble. And females as well as males sing to attract mates.

Like the Dunnock, the Alpine Accentor has a complex and hectic sex-life. It breeds in "polygynandrous" groups, a racy sort of sexual society in which two to four females share a large territory with a similar number of males, one of which is dominant. This alpha male tries to monopolize copulation with fertile females, but at the same time the females compete to mate with every male. These conflicts result in the highest copulation rate of any bird, and a relatively gigantic pair of testes, accounting for up to 8 percent of the male's body weight. The human equivalent for a 70 kg man would weigh 5.6 kg!

NIGHTINGALE

Luscinia megarhynchos

A summer visitor to much of Europe but not in the north or north-east. Favours light broadleaved woodland with coppiced shrubs such as hazel, as well as tangles of bramble, blackthorn or wild roses; also occurs among young conifers, on shrubby heaths and in overgrown gardens.

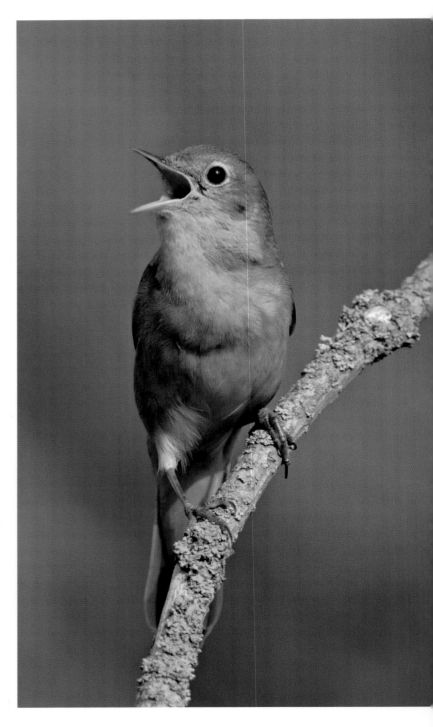

No other European bird is so renowned for its song. Although other species arguably make sweeter, prettier and more melodious sounds, none (save its very similar-looking, more north-easterly relative the Thrush-Nightingale) can rival this plain brown Robin relative for impact. With its melodramatic phrasing and impressive volume, a virtuoso performance from a male can carry up to a mile or more on a still, quiet night. Its fame is, of course, partly due to the habit of singing at night, celebrated by its common name. Nightingales sing by day as well, especially when they are newly arrived back from their African winter quarters, and need to establish a territory and attract a mate.

The uninitiated frequently mistake the nocturnal song of other species, including Sedge Warblers and especially Robins, for that of the Nightingale. But once they have been enthralled by a concert from the master there should be no doubt as to the identity of the real thing. Its unique blend of phrases – slow, melancholy piping or fluting notes on a rising scale, sweet warbling and bursts of deep, rich throbbing or bubbling sounds – are separated by long pauses, heightening the drama.

The bird is self-effacing, usually delivering his torrent of sound from deep within dense cover. Where its range overlaps that of the Thrush-Nightingale, it can hard to distinguish their songs. When both occur, this less dominant bird is far more likely to imitate other species. A German study found that 67 out of 239 of Thrush-Nightingales had mixed songs. Though even louder, the latter's song is slower, more repetitive and staccato and lacks the crescendos of its more famous relative.

BLUETHROAT

Luscinia svecica

Breeds widely in northern Europe, largest numbers by far in Russia; major populations in Norway, Sweden, Finland, Ukraine. Patchily distributed farther south (mostly northern and central Spain, France, the Netherlands). They winter mainly around the Mediterranean and south of the Sahara.

Although the male of this smaller relative of the Nightingale has a coloured throat, he can be surprisingly inconspicuous, skulking deep within thickets or low shrubs, especially during stops to rest or refuel on the long migration to and from Africa. Patience is usually necessary to get a good view, but the wait is amply rewarded when this little bird hops into the light on his long, thin black legs, cocks his red-sided tail and reveals the complex plumage pattern of his front end. From the big dark eyes surmounted by a brilliant white supercilium, the watcher's gaze is quickly led down to the chief glory, the broad cornflower-blue gorget, which has a lustrous richness – blue of such intensity is rare in European species. In its centre, set like a jewel in a choker, is a spot of red or white – red in birds of the northern race *svecica*, white in the central European race *cyanecula*. Below the blue are narrower black and red chest bands. Four other European races have different details, such as no central spot or black band. These decorative patterns are shown to maximum effect as the male puffs out his throat and breast feathers when he sings.

The song is loud, sweet, complex and varied – in some ways like that of a Nightingale but not so wistful, with less rich, full notes, and including bell-like notes. It also recalls the song of the Marsh Warbler. Like the latter, it often incorporates mimicry of other birds the male hears around him (Redwings, Crested Tits, Dunlin, Greenshanks), frogs and insects and even other sounds such as locomotive whistles.

REDSTART

Phoenicurus phoenicurus

Breeds from Britain and Iberia across Europe and beyond to central Siberia, with over half the world population in this continent. Large breeding populations in Russia, Finland, France, Germany. Still very numerous and widespread, but with recent declines. European breeders winter mainly in Africa.

While other redstarts that turn up as vagrants in parts of Europe may be larger or more dramatically patterned, none is more beautiful than the male of this, the commonest and most wide-spread European *Phoenicurus* species. Among the loveliest of all summer migrants to Europe – indeed of all the world's woodland birds – it is one of those species that a novice birdwatcher longs to encounter and which never fails to disappoint.

Often shy and elusive, it spends much of its time in the sun-dappled canopy. It breeds in open woodland, preferring broad-leaved woods in most of Europe, but also pine forests farther north and birch forests in the extreme north. In Wales and south-west England it is one of a triad of songbirds linked with ancient sessile oakwoods (the other two are Pied Flycatcher and Wood Warbler).

Both the common and scientific names refer to one of the most noticeable features of the bird, the bright orange-red rump and tail sides. The "start" suffix derives from the Old English word *steort*, meaning "tail", while *Phoenicurus* is Latinized Greek for "red tail". This feature is shared with other redstarts, and is subtly echoed in the duller russet tails of less closely related members of the chat subfamily, such as the Nightingale. Often, our first view of a Redstart is as it flies off, when it draws attention to its tail by a curious loose flirting action. Its habit of obsessively quivering this terminal ensign when perched seems to invest it with even greater vibrancy and warmth of hue.

ISABELLINE WHEATEAR
Oenanthe isabellina

Breeds from Turkey through the Caspian region and Kazakhstan to W. China and N. Mongolia. European pop. has expanded west since 1960. From S. Russia and Ukraine it has spread into N. Greece, Bulgaria, Romania. Western breeders migrate to Africa. Vagrants have reached as far as Britain and Norway.

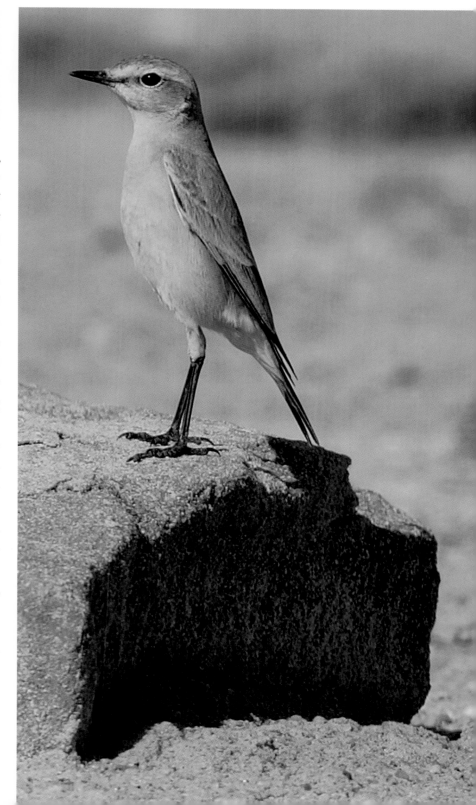

The largest of the eight wheatear species breeding in Europe, this one is like a pale ghost of the others, with a strong similarity to a rather bleached female Wheatear. The unusual adjective of the common name is a modern Latin construction, meaning "of an Isabella colour, greyish-yellow". The story deriving the word from the hue of the Archduchess Isabella's dirty undergarments during the siege of Ostend (1601–4) is unlikely, as "Isabella-colour" was in use at least a year before that date. Related names in German, French, Spanish and Italian refer to a much earlier Isabella, the Queen who with King Ferdinand V of Castile survived the siege of Grenada in 1492, so there may after all be some connection with aristocratic underwear. Another suggestion is that it comes from the Arabic word *izah*, meaning "lion", which has a similarly-coloured pelt.

The plumage makes the bird hard to see against the sandy ground it generally frequents – until it moves, when flashes of white on rump and tail base give the game away. Isabelline Wheatears generally have an upright, almost vertical attitude on the ground, a posture made possible by the relatively short tail. Useful field-marks are the short supercilium, reduced white on the rump compared to Wheatear and silver and white underwing.

The song is far richer than other wheatears' – loud, melodious, varied. Indeed, the bird has been dubbed, with hyperbole, "the nightingale of the desert". It incorporates much mimicry, including barking foxes, bleating goats and bellowing camels, and even – according to some Russian sources – the sound of an entire caravan of travellers passing by!

BLACK WHEATEAR
Oenanthe leucura

Over 95 percent of a declining European population breeds in Spain; most of the rest in Portugal, just across the border. Very local. Apart from birds breeding at high altitudes moving downslope in winter, generally very sedentary. Outside Europe, occurs only in North Africa.

This striking wheatear has the great merit for birders of being confusable in all plumages with only one other species. That is another wheatear, the White-crowned Wheatear, and it occurs in Europe solely as a rare vagrant from Africa. Immatures of that species lack the distinctive white head of the adults, but the Black Wheatear is still easily identified by the complete T-shape of its black tail markings.

As well as their black-and-white tail pattern, all wheatears have a bold white rump, hence their common name. This has nothing to do with ears of wheat, but is a Victorian euphemism for "white-arse". The generic name, *Oenanthe*, Greek for "wine flower", is derived from the fact that Wheatears and Black-eared Wheatears arrive in Greece when the grapes are beginning to blossom. This is one species that doesn't grace the spring of that country, however, being almost entirely confined as a breeding bird in Europe to the Iberian Peninsula, apart from a handful of pairs breeding in southern France. And even in its Spanish stronghold it is sparsely distributed and declining.

This bird suits its sombre plumage by choosing a sunless site for its nest, within a cleft in a cliff or among rocks, in a cave or in a stone wall. This is one of a number of species of songbird worldwide in which the male carries small stones to the nest site and deposits them in piles around the entrance. These may accumulate over several years to form a miniature parapet around the bulky nest. Apart from the possible function of protection, research suggests that this may also attract a mate and provide her with a gauge for assessing his fitness.

BLUE ROCK THRUSH
Monticola solitarius

The male of this striking thrush lives up to its name in being intensely blue – indeed, it is the only such extensively blue bird in Europe. There are various mythical Blue Birds credited with magical powers in fairy stories. This real blue bird may not have magical properties, but it conjures a powerful reaction from those who seek it out in warm rocky country in southern Europe.

Although thrush-like in appearance as well as in name, the 14 species of rock-thrushes, mostly restricted to Africa or Asia, are now classified together with the chats rather than in the main lineage of the thrush family. One of a pair in Europe, the Blue Rock Thrush is less restricted to higher altitudes compared to the blue, orange and white Rock Thrush, ranging from sea level up to about 2,000 m in Spain and Greece. Ironically, it is the national bird of Malta, a country where hordes of heavily bando-liered hunters continue to flout European law and shoot or trap protected birds of all sorts, including Blue Rock Thrushes.

A widespread resident breeder in Iberia and Mediterranean regions, from S. France to Italy and the Balkans, including the Balearic Islands, Corsica, Sardinia, Sicily, Malta and many Greek islands. Found in a variety of rocky habitats. Outside Europe, occurs from Turkey as far east as China and Japan.

Like many mountain birds, it is often shy and elusive, with a tendency to fly with powerful wingbeats over a ridge, behind rocks, even through mine-shafts and tunnels. Fortunately, it is more approachable where it is used to people at ancient ruins and in towns and cities, as in Rome. Here, in the ruined Forum, you can enjoy the sight of a deep blue male, his plumage the colour of sloe berries, as he delivers his far-carrying, simple song, like a cross between a Blackbird's and a Mistle Thrush's, from a prominent perch or in a long, slow, gliding song flight.

RING OUZEL

Turdus torquatus

Breeds in Britain, Brittany, Norway, N.W. Sweden, N. Finland, the Kola Peninsula, and as a separate race in the south from the Pyrenees to the Balkans. A third race breeds in the Caucasus and Asia Minor. Most European breeders winter in S. Spain, N.W. Africa, Greece and W. Turkey. Declining.

This generally scarce, specialized thrush is mostly confined to Europe as a breeder. It is also the only European member of the thrush genus *Turdus* that is almost entirely a summer visitor, and the only one that is mainly an upland and alpine bird. A plethora of old British local names such as Mountain Ouzel, Rock Ouzel, Crag Ouzel and Mountain Colley indicate this habitat preference. Best known is Mountain Blackbird, which celebrates the species' close relationship with the almost ubiquitous Blackbird, as does "ouzel", an old name for Blackbird. Other old names, such as Ring Thrush, as well as most names in European languages and its scientific name ("Collared Thrush"), refer to the crescent-shaped chest band, white and unsullied in the breeding male, duller with dark scaling in the female.

Although it is easy to mistake a Blackbird in brief view or at long range for a Ring Ouzel, and an aberrantly coloured Blackbird with white on the upper breast can cause the heart to beat faster, a good view should clinch identification. With a more rakish, streamlined body, the Ring Ouzel also has longer wings and a longer, sharp-cornered tail. Along with the white chest crescent and pale scaling on the underparts, the most distinctive feature is the pale patch on the closed wing, formed by the silvery-grey edges of the flight feathers. The male's simple, skirling song, with dramatic silences between the remote-sounding, disjointed pipings, epitomizes wild mountain country.

The Ring Ouzel is usually wild and wary, often flying fast and far to hide from view. Near the nest, though, many pairs are aggressive, swooping at predators with loud rattling alarm calls.

ZITTING CISTICOLA
Cisticola juncidis

This tiny songbird, fractionally bigger than a Goldcrest, is the sole representative of the largely African warbler genus *Cisticola* to breed in Europe; the other species include Rattling, Bubbling, Wailing, Whistling, Croaking, Chirping, Churring and Trilling. Zitting Cisticolas are often infuriatingly difficult to see as they are prone to skulking in tall or dense vegetation. A glimpse of one in flight may reveal the short rounded wings, orange-buff rump and rounded tail, and the head and upperparts boldly patterned with dark brown and pale buff stripes like a Sedge Warbler.

In contrast to this general elusiveness, the male forsakes cover in the breeding season to deliver his territorial song, a tuneless series of scratchy *zit* notes at 0.6–1 second intervals, in a strongly undulating flight that covers wide circles. Climbing steeply with a brief flurry of rapid beats of its tiny wings, he sings each penetrating note, then closes his wings and dives a short distance before ascending again, in a repeated pattern. With each

One of the most widespread of all songbirds. In Europe, breeds across most of the south; in France, as far as the north coast; a few in Belgium, none yet in Britain. Badly affected by severe winters. Outside Europe, has a vast range across three more continents, in Africa, Asia and northern Australia.

ascent, he fans his tail to display the black and white edge pattern that gave the bird its old name of Fan-tailed Warbler. Highlighted by the sun, this produces a distinctive twinkling appearance as the diminutive singer, looking as much like an overgrown bee as a bird, bounces around in the blue.

Since the early 1970s the species has spread at an impressive rate northwards. A major factor has been its versatility in colonizing cornfields and other agricultural land once its preferred tall grassland and marshland habitats are filled.

GRASSHOPPER WARBLER
Locustella naevia

Breeds patchily in a range of habitats with dense cover across western, central and northern Europe. Prone to wide fluctuations; but many populations, especially in the west, have declined. Largest populations in Russia, Poland, Baltic states and Germany. European breeders winter in Africa. Breeds across Asia.

The standard common name is a slight misnomer, in that the insects producing the high-pitched reeling song which the song of this small, elusive brown warbler resembles are crickets or bush-crickets, not grasshoppers. The warbler's song is most often heard around dusk and dawn, and may continue all night, with only the briefest of pauses. At a uniform high frequency of about 6 kilohertz, it is at the upper end of the range of sensitivity of the human ear and is one of the first sounds that becomes hard to hear with age-related deafness.

Often this strange sound, also likened to an angler's reel, is the only evidence a bird is present. Pinpointing the singer can be frustrating, for the sound is ventriloquial, and the volume changes as the bird moves its head. Most easily confusable with it are wood cricket and Heyden's cricket, but it is also similar to Roesel's bush-cricket, vineyard mole-cricket and common mole-cricket. An intriguing question is whether this warbler and its close relatives have acquired their strange songs by mimicry of the insects or through convergent evolution.

Although males newly arrived from Africa may emerge periodically to reel out their song from an exposed perch near the top of a bush, later on they sing mainly from dense cover. Here, with their mates and later their young, they live out most of their lives in private. Reluctant to fly, they usually afford no better view than that of a dark-streaked undertail disappearing into the foliage as they slip away with mouselike movements.

AQUATIC WARBLER

Acrocephalus paludicola

This is a fast declining and globally threatened warbler, almost its entire population breeding in vulnerable habitats in central and eastern Europe. It is the most beautiful of all the European *Acrocephalus* reed-warblers, with striking "tiger-stripe" upperparts. In a brief view or in poor light it can be confused with a Sedge Warbler, but its plumage is far brighter, with much greater contrast between the blackish stripes on head and back and the yellowish buff ground colour. The latter forms a pair of prominent pale "braces" extending diagonally down the mantle. and there is a bright yellow-buff central crown stripe as well as the similar broad supercilium. Another distinctive feature is that the strongly graduated tail feathers are often separated at the tips into spiky points, making it look as if the tail had been caught in a paper shredding machine.

Extensive areas of wetlands are needed for breeding. The males require large territories in wet sedge beds, fen mires and hay meadows in river valleys and to a lesser degree among

The entire world population breeds in just 7 European countries. Most are in Belarus, Poland and Ukraine, with some in Hungary, Lithuania, Russia and Germany. Migration is initially west via Belgium or S. England to France for a stopover, then to Iberia before continuing to winter quarters in W. Africa.

coastal marshes. These habitats have been greatly diminished and destroyed or degraded. Loss of insects from pesticides has also been damaging. An international rescue effort is underway, but the bird faces continuing threats from development, including the projected building in Poland (in contravention of EU law) of a major road through the Biebrza marshes.

On a more positive note, the mystery of its precise winter quarters within Africa has been partially solved recently, making it possible now to focus attention on reducing threats at the major site in Senegal and to locate other sites in the region.

MARSH WARBLER
Acrocephalus palustris

As a breeding bird, restricted to Europe, from Britain (very rare) and N. France east to S. Russia. Largest populations in Romania, Germany, E. Europe and the Low Countries. Has expanded into S. Scandinavia, Finland and N.W. Russia. Arrives late from its southern and eastern African winter quarters.

This little dull brown bird produces one of the most amazing of all bird songs. It incorporates astonishingly accurate mimicry of a remarkable number of other bird's sounds – not just those heard in its European breeding grounds, but also many picked up in its autumn stopover areas and winter quarters in north-east and sub-Saharan Africa. The Belgian ornithologist Françoise Dowsett-Lemaire discovered that the species can imitate 212 species – 99 from Europe, 113 from Africa. An individual male can reproduce the sounds of over 76 species. The imitations include many songbirds, but also non-passerines, from Oyster-catchers and Greenshanks to bee-eaters and hornbills. The young warblers acquire the whole of their European repertoire during the first summer after hatching, before they migrate to Africa; there they pick up the entire "alien" part of their repertoire.

Sometimes a male delivers his song from deep within a bush or tall, rank vegetation. Often, though, he emerges to proclaim his presence more dramatically from the top of a bush or a prominent perch in a tree, puffing out his creamy white throat feathers and opening his bill wide to reveal his yellow or orange gape. Males sing at night as well as by day, especially when newly arrived from Africa and eager for a mate.

This is one of a group of extremely similar-looking un-streaked *Acrocephalus* warblers whose visual identification hangs on minutiae. Where two or more species breed together, the Marsh Warbler is usually distinguishable by its song. However, to the frustration of those trying to identify a hidden bird, its reper-toire occasionally includes perfect imitations of Reed Warbler!

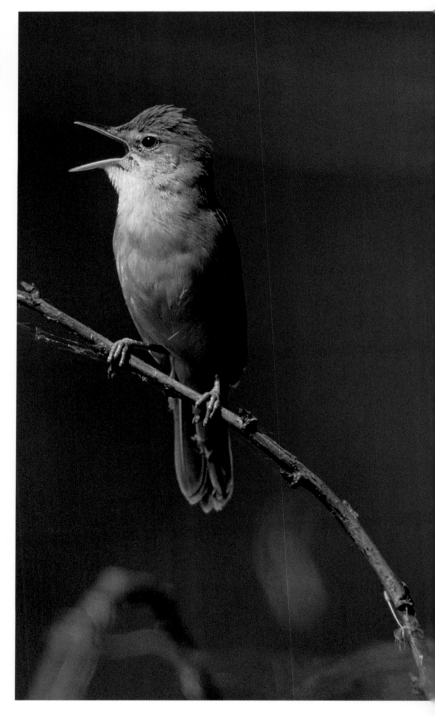

FROM LARKS TO CRESTS **201**

GREAT REED WARBLER

Acrocephalus arundinaceus

The "Great" is well deserved, since this is truly a giant among warblers, bigger than a Skylark and the size of a small thrush. It is the largest of the European *Acrocephalus* warblers, over one and a half times the length of a Reed Warbler and more than twice as heavy, with a longer and far more powerful bill. The nests can break under the weight of a brooding female and her young. Its song is very large, too, of the same general repetitive chattering pattern as a Reed Warbler's but deeper and far louder, carrying up to about half a mile. As well as hoarse churrs and trills, it includes froglike croaks suddenly interspersed with high creaky notes. It also has a froglike or insectlike hard, churring alarm call. On arrival at a breeding site in spring, unmated males often sing for up to 20 hours a day from exposed perches high in the reeds or a shrub, especially on fine mornings, but once mated the performance is usually from deep within cover.

Great Reed Warblers crash about in the reeds if alarmed

Breeds widely across Europe; absent from Britain and most of Scandinavia, Finland and Russia. Major declines in west, central and S. Europe, but has expanded into S. Scandinavia, Finland and Russia (due to climate change). Its range extends across central Asia east as far as N.W. China. All birds winter in Africa.

or when pursuing prey. They tackle large insects, including hawker dragonflies, which they bash to death on a stem, as well as reed beetle larvae, freshwater shrimps and small fish. Many pairs are parasitized by the Cuckoo in parts of its range, as in Russia and in Hungary, where one study found that almost half the nests already containing a Cuckoo's egg later succumbed to a second Cuckoo. The Great Reed Warbler is, along with the Red-backed Shrike, the largest species to regularly receive the attentions of the continent's commonest nest parasite.

BARRED WARBLER

Sylvia nisoria

A widespread but local summer visitor to much of E. Europe. The main populations occur from eastern Germany to Russia, Ukraine and Caucasus, with very small outliers in W. Germany, N. Italy, S. Finland and Scandinavia; beyond Europe it ranges as far as S.W. Siberia and Mongolia.

Few small songbirds have such an angry, even malevolent, look about them as an adult Barred Warbler. With its glaring, bright yellow eyes, grey upperparts and barred underparts, it resembles a miniature male Sparrowhawk minus the hooked bill and long legs with taloned toes – or, less fancifully, a Cuckoo. The only European member of its family with extensively barred underparts, this striking, large and heavily built warbler is the largest of all the 25 species of *Sylvia* "scrub-warblers". Uniquely, the female is larger and heavier than the male. Also, in a genus in which the female is usually duller than the male, the Barred Warbler is not so strongly sexually dichromatic.

Compared with the smallest, most agile Old World warblers, such as Pallas's and Yellow-browed, this species is a sluggish giant. It is often very elusive, and the skulking behaviour of both breeding and passage birds that remain hidden within dense cover and are reluctant to budge is often remarked on.

In late spring and early summer, though, a male may be intermittently more obvious as he pours out his lively song from near the top of a tree, or in a short song flight in which he flies up steeply, singing, then glides down, rocking from side to side and fanning his tail – and often audibly clapping his wings. The song can closely resemble a Garden Warbler's, but as with Common Whitethoat the sweeter warblings are mixed with more rasping and scratchy notes. The song suggests a Skylark's in its rising and falling volume, though it is much briefer.

RÜPPELL'S WARBLER

Sylvia rueppelli

The male of this very local species in breeding plumage is one of the most handsome of all European warblers, like a larger, *de luxe* version of a Sardinian Warbler. As with the latter, his head has a black top, but in this species it is restricted to the forehead, forecrown, lores and an area around the eye; below this is a broad and vivid white moustachial stripe. And instead of the white throat of a male Sardinian, there is a large, neat black bib underneath that forms an instantly diagnostic pattern, isolating the white slash against the black. This striking front end is enhanced further by the reddish eye surrounded by a similarly-coloured orbital ring, like that of a Sardinian Warbler. Some females show a far less solid but clear version of the male's head pattern, with a dark grey face and dark-blotched throat, as if a freshly inked drawing had been hastily blotted. Other females, like immature birds, are trickier to identify, but they share the male's distinctively paler edges to the wing feathers, especially the tertials.

This is one of the least studied of all European songbirds, although within its restricted eastern Mediterranean range it is relatively easy to find, especially compared to many other, far shyer, warblers. Like most members of the family, it is skulking; but it is less nervous and more sluggish, so that once spotted within a bush, it does not necessarily move deeper into cover or fly off to another patch. The males are conspicuous when singing from a prominent perch in a bush or atop a rock, or in a brief song flight. The sound can closely resemble the harsh rattling chatter of a Sardinian Warbler but is deeper and may be interspersed with high, clear whistling notes, especially in the louder version delivered from the air.

Rüppell's forms a species-pair with that even more restricted island endemic, the Cyprus Warbler, *Sylvia melanothorax*. Along with eight other *Sylvia* species, both form a suite of warblers largely restricted to the *matorral*: a zone of evergreen scrub with tough, often thorny, drought-resistant leaves.

Breeds in Europe only in southernmost Greece (including the Peleponnese), the Aegean, Crete and the European coast and islands of Turkey; outside Europe only in southern Turkey, N.W. Syria and N. Israel. Passage migrants occur on Greek islands and Cyprus en route to winter in Africa.

DARTFORD WARBLER

Sylvia undata

With a body almost as tiny as a Wren's, the Dartford Warbler's total length of 12.5 cm is half tail. And it is the long tail, often cocked or in constant motion, that is prominent when this skulking warbler is glimpsed out of dense cover. The best time to gain a good view of this sprightly, dark-plumaged midget with the glowing ruby eyes is when a male is establishing his territorial rights in spring. On warm sunny days, he often declaims his spirited song, a medley of sweet piping notes and hard rattling ones, from the top of a gorse bush or other prominent perch, or sometimes in a brief song-flight. As he turns his head from side to side, raising its feathers into a bushy peak and ruffling his spotted throat, his tail pumps up and down or is suddenly cocked up high. And when he flies off low on short whirring wings, almost touching the ground, with a weak-looking, undulating action, the long tail flicks up and down or wags from side to side as if it were only loosely attached to the body.

The common name was given to the bird in 1773 by the English ornithologist John Latham (1740–1837). He first recognized it as a British bird from a pair shot on Bexley Heath, near Dartford, Kent. At this time, the species was quite widespread on heathland in southern England, but by the early 20th century it was rare. One reason for this was loss of heathland; another, that this bird is vulnerable to the vagaries of the British climate, and went through a series of population crashes in severe winters, which by 1962 had reduced it to 10 pairs. Over the last 30 years numbers and range have increased again, including a few pairs breeding again in Kent – though not on Bexley Heath.

ARCTIC WARBLER

Phylloscopus borealis

This member of the leaf-warbler genus is restricted in Europe to the northernmost forests. However, "Arctic" is a misnomer, as its entire range lies within the subarctic region.

The Arctic Warbler is a little larger than a Willow Warbler but smaller than a Wood Warbler. It has a striking head pattern, with a very prominent creamy supercilium, made even more conspicuous by being sandwiched between a bold dark eye-stripe and a neat dark crown. In these respects, it bears closest resemblance to the slightly smaller Greenish Warbler, whose range lies farther south.

Although there is a clear-cut latitudinal and ecological distinction between the two birds' breeding ranges, both species may turn up together as off-course vagrants along the coasts of western Europe.

The longer wings of the Arctic Warbler are a manifestation of the most remarkable feature of its biology. It makes one of the most astonishing migrations of any small bird.

A rare, local, irregular breeder in Norway and Sweden. Finnish population numbers thousands of pairs; 4–8 million pairs may breed in European Russia. An annual autumn vagrant to W. Europe, esp. Britain (Shetland). Outside Europe, has a huge range, across Russia and into Alaska. Winters in S.E. Asia.

For our westerly breeders this involves a round-trip of at least 16,000 miles each year. Instead of migrating to Africa like the Willow Warblers that may breed alongside them, they fly to southern South-east Asia – right across Russia and then south through eastern China, to avoid crossing the central Asian deserts and the Himalayas. This accounts for its late return to the breeding grounds – not until late June in Lapland, returning in August. This unusual migration is a relic of the Arctic Warbler's distant past, when it bred solely in Asia before extending its range westwards after the end of the last Ice Age.

FIRECREST
Regulus ignicapillus

A widespread, locally common breeder in
west-central and S. Europe, by far the most
in Spain. Since 1900 has expanded its range
to Britain, Low Countries and Denmark, but
remains a rare breeder there. Prefers conifers, but quite common in mixed forest, even
broadleaved woodland, unlike Goldcrest.

This slightly bulkier, bigger-headed and generally scarcer close
relative of the Goldcrest is almost endemic to Europe, apart
from scattered populations in North Africa and Turkey. Along
with its tiny size, its most noticable feature is the brightness
of its plumage. The whiter underparts contrast far more
strongly with the darker, intense greenish-yellow of the
upperparts, there is a dab of bronzy yellow colour on the sides
of the neck, and, most distinctive of all, a dazzling pattern of
black and white stripes on the head. This gives the Firecrest
a more intense, almost fierce expression compared with the
"surprised" appearance of the Goldcrest.

Like the Goldcrest, the Firecrest uses its tiny needle of
a bill to pluck insects and spiders from the foliage, but tends to
dine in the lower storeys of the trees or in the undergrowth
beneath, or in more open areas with bushes, especially on
migration. Both species have the same hyperactive lifestyle,
slipping through the foliage with ease and frequently hovering
in front of a leaf to search out or snap up prey.

This is one of a very small group of birds known
colloquially as "crests" from the vividly coloured, erectile patch
of feathers on the crown, and more formally by their American
name of kinglets. Like the generic name *Regulus*, and the French
and Spanish names *Roitelet* and *Reyezuelo*, this means "little king",
in reference to the brilliant crowns. Formerly subsumed within
the warblers, kinglets are now given a family of their own; they
may be more closely related to tits. As well as Firecrest and
Goldcrest, they include the recently split Madeira Firecrest.

FROM FLYCATCHERS TO BUNTINGS

RED-BREASTED FLYCATCHER

Ficedula parva

To those encountering one for the first time, an adult male of this engaging little songbird may have a very superficial resemblance to the European Robin, owing to the pattern of its plumage. However, the orange-red is less extensive, the legs shorter, and the posture dfferent. The species also has a rather Robin-like alarm call and the spotty juveniles of both species are similar. Any confusion, however, is soon dispelled as the flycatcher frequently flicks its Wheatear-like tail upwards, drawing attention to the large white patches on either side of the basal half, or cocks it over its back like a Wren.

The dwarf among European flycatchers, this is no larger than a Willow Warbler. Indeed, it has some of the character of a leaf warbler, remaining within the cover for much of the time, where it is restless and can be hard to see well. And like a leaf warbler, it hovers in front of a leaf to pick off a caterpillar and also flits out quickly to take insects such as flies and butterflies. It rarely spends more time on the ground than it takes to dash

Within its European range, a bird of the east and centre, breeding regularly no farther west than eastern Germany and S. Sweden. Unlike most summer visitors, which winter in Africa, all populations migrate to S. Asia, but a few head westwards and are found as scarce migrants in W. Europe.

down and snap up a small beetle, although migrants may stay longer to take advantage of food, including earthworms. On the other hand, it is generally tame and unconcerned by a close approach, so patience is often rewarded by close if brief views.

Its song is a good deal more musical than that of other European flycatchers. It is rather warbler-like, often sounding like a mixture of the silvery *stip* notes that begin a Wood Warbler's song and a simpler, more hesitant and inferior version of the Willow Warbler's delicate cascade of sweet sad notes on a descending scale.

BEARDED REEDLING

Panurus biarmicus

Breeds widely, but very local: needs large reedbeds. Range is expanding in much of Europe. Most European populations rather sedentary, but they tend to make eruptive movements after breeding and in winter. Largest populations in Russia, Romania, Ukraine. Outside Europe, breeds across Asia.

This engaging little bird was until recently called Bearded Tit. The resurrection of the old name of reedling avoids this erroneous connection with the tit family – it is the only representative of the small Asian family of parrotbills. "Bearded", though, remains inaccurate: the black markings adorning the male's face are not on the chin but are large stripes that droop on either side like a Chinese mandarin's moustaches. They add a rakish touch to his lavender-grey head and rich ginger upperparts.

These beautiful birds spend so much time deep within the reedbed that a good view is a treat to savour. During the breeding season, they feed on insects at or just above the waterline, or linger at the deep cup-shaped nest, usually woven among reed stems just off the ground. In winter they can sometimes be seen perched near the top of the reeds, passing portions of feathery seedheads through their sharp little bills and nibbling out the seeds. Agile feeders, they may hang upside-down or draw a seedhead nearer with the bill or a foot. They can hold their legs at anatomically improbable angles, and often straddle two reeds with a foot grasping each stem. To help digest the winter diet of hard seeds, the gizzard doubles in weight as its walls thicken, and the birds eat prodigious amounts of grit.

Bursts of loud, metallic, ringing *ping* notes are usually the main sign of their presence. Now and then, small groups take wing low over the reeds before dropping again. The flight is whirring and weak-looking, the long, graduated tail twisting and fanning as it trails behind, so that they resemble tiny Pheasants: another old fensman's name for this bird was Reed Pheasant.

SIBERIAN TIT
Poecile cincta

Breeds sparsely in N. Norway, in an isolated population in the mountains of southern-central Norway, and across N. Sweden, Finland and Russia. Farther east, breeds across Siberia, south into the montane forests of Siberia and N. Mongolia, and into Kamchatka. Also found in the New World.

Along with the Willow Tit, this is the most northerly-breeding member of the titmouse family. But unlike its hugely more numerous and very widespread relative (which outnumbers it here by a ratio of about 25:1), it is restricted in Europe to the north. It dwells in the cold forests of the boreal zone of Scandinavia, Finland and Russia, living almost entirely within the Arctic Circle. It is mainly a denizen of the great dark northernmost coniferous forest belt but also occurs on mountainsides in birch forest. This is the only member of the tit family to occur in both the Old and New Worlds.

This hardy little bird is remarkable for remaining on its breeding grounds all year round, enduring the severest winter weather, when the temperature may plunge to -45°C (-49°F) or below during the long nights, using a variety of adaptations and strategies. These include roosting in mouseholes beneath the insulating blanket of snow, and fluffing out its plumage, which is especially thick and downy; in addition, it is able to reduce energy expenditure to a minimum by allowing itself to become slightly torpid, when its body temperature falls by 5–10°C (9–18°F).

Although Siberian Tits do not depend on humans for food, however severe the weather, they do visit refuse tips around northern towns in winter, as well as feeders. Living in regions with sparse human populations, they are often very tame, even to the extent of perching on your hat. Close to, you can appreciate the difference from their more common European relatives: a mousy grey-brown colour above, with a darker grey-brown cap rather than the black one of Willow and Marsh Tits, most like that of the closely related Boreal Chickadee in North America, whose range it just overlaps. Among Eurasian tits, only the southern Sombre Tit has a brownish cap. Also distinctive is the brownish-black bib: much larger than the neater black bib of a Willow Tit or the even smaller one of a Marsh Tit, and frayed at the edges rather like a male House Sparrow's.

CRESTED TIT

Lophophanes cristatus

This is the only really small European bird that sports such a prominent crest. While a few lark species, especially Crested and Thekla Larks, can erect their crown feathers to form a smallish crest, these well-named tits have a permanent pointed crest that is always visible – though it may be raised or lowered. Its owner can vary the precise angle, perhaps to indicate various degrees of excitement, aggression or other states: it is erected, for example, when driving off rivals of its own or other species, when singing, and by a male ready to mate. When fully erect, it has a conical shape, so that it appears triangular when viewed from the side, from the front or from behind. At other times, it has more of the shape of one of those futuristic-looking streamlined helmets worn by racing cyclists. The black flecks on the white ground make it especially decorative.

Although, like most members of its family, the Crested Tit is not a shy bird, it is not generally as bold or inquisitive as Blue or Great Tits. Often the best clue to its presence is the distinctive call, a purring trill.

Whether in the great sombre pine and spruce forests of Scotland or Scandinavia, the mixed forests in much of its central and southern range, or the cork-oak woodland of southern Iberia, this little bird, like the Coal Tit with which it often shares its habitat, obtains much of its food by assiduous investigation of the fissures in the bark of mature trees. It seems to be especially fond of those with abundant lichens, probably because these support insects such as springtails and bark lice that are in turn eaten by spiders, an important food. Like other tits, it is an inveterate hoarder of food (both seeds and insects, especially moth larvae), which is often secreted among tufts of lichen on trunks or branches. Like lodgers sharing a house and using different shelves of a refrigerator, Crested Tits usually store their food lower down the tree than Coal Tits. The Crested Tit's requirements include mature, decaying trees or stumps, since each year it excavates its own nest hole, unlike most tits.

Almost entirely European in distribution, apart from an area east of the Urals. Absent from Italy and the islands of the Mediterranean, much of S.E. Europe and the far north, as well as Britain (apart from the ancient Caledonian forest of Scotland). Seldom encountered outside extensive forests.

AZURE TIT

Cyanistes cyanus

Main breeding area in Europe extends from central Russia to the Urals, plus a very small area of N.W. Kazakhstan and S. Belarus. Has also bred in Ukraine and (at least as hybrids with Blue Tits) in Finland. It has been recorded as extremely rare vagrant to many European countries, mainly in Scandinavia.

Like a ghostly Blue Tit, the Azure Tit is its eastern counterpart. Together with the Yellow-breasted Tit (*Cyanistes flavipectus*), which overlaps with it a little in the centre of its range, it forms a trio of very closely related species – a "superspecies". This little bird is every bit as enchanting as the Blue Tit but with the cachet of unfamiliarity to excite western European birders, to whom it may be a hoped-for treat on a long trip eastwards.

Slightly larger than the Blue Tit, and with a longer tail, it has far more white in the wings and tail, distinguishing it from an aberrant pale individual of its common sister species. The Azure Tit's plumage is usually fluffier than the Blue Tit's, though not so much so as the superficially similar though much longer-tailed, and unrelated, Long-tailed Tit.

Another difference is that the Azure Tit is generally far more secretive and hard to see than the Blue Tit. Unlike that species, it does not live alongside humans and become tame, but generally keeps well hidden among dense bushes or, in winter, reedbeds. It is ecologically distinct from the Blue Tit, preferring to breed in thickets of birches, willows or poplars mixed with shrubs, especially along the banks of rivers, streams and lakes.

Periodically, Azure Tits embark on waves of westward expansion, especially in winter. The greatest of these was during the 1870s and 1880s, when they reached the Baltic, and some stayed to breed. These advances are always followed by retreats back to their usual range.

CORSICAN NUTHATCH
Sitta whiteheadi

Unlike most of the birds in this book, this is one about which there is no problem in deciding where to go to look for it. The Mediterranean island of Corsica, to which it is endemic, is a place of rugged, dramatic landscapes, and much of the interior is mountainous, with snow-capped peaks towering up to 2,710 m above sea level in the north-west. It is on the Corsican pine forests clothing the mountain ridges running down the centre of the island that this distinctive little Blue Tit-sized bird lives.

Unlike the abundant, widespread Nuthatch, it usually excavates its own nest hole, although it sometimes takes over a disused home of one of the smaller woodpeckers. It does not need to resort to the habit of plastering larger holes with mud to deter predators that is a trait of the common species. Also, in contrast to the latter, there is a noticeable difference between the sexes, although this is by no means dramatic, being restricted to the male's more vivid head pattern, sharply demarcated black and white rather than blue-grey and pale grey.

Found only on Corsica, where it is largely confined to 15 or so high-altitude forests of mature Corsican Pine growing on mountain ridges. Smaller numbers breed in other woodland habitats. Like other nuthatches, highly sedentary, except for local downslope movements in winter, to 600 m or below.

The specific name (and original common name) of the bird honours the English collector John Whitehead. He shot and skinned the nuthatch on his second trip abroad at the age of 23, and thought no more about it until told by the British Museum (Natural History) that the bird was new to science. When he first set eyes on the nuthatch, it was considerably more numerous than it is today. Lightning-caused wildfires are a regular event in Corsica, burning several thousand hectares of forest and maquis every year, and the damage is aggravated locally by logging, so that the birds lose valuable prime habitat.

ROCK NUTHATCH

Sitta neumayer

Breeds along E. Adriatic, in western parts of Slovenia, Croatia, Bosnia and Albania, also Greece (incl. Corfu, Zakynthos, Lesvos), Macedonia, Serbia-Montenegro, Bulgaria, parts of Georgia. Found mostly at 1,000–1,500 m. Outside Europe, breeds in Turkey, Middle East, Armenia, Azerbaijan and Iran.

A cascade of long, clear whistles varying in tempo and dropping in pitch, like a harder, much louder version of a snatch of Woodlark song, may puzzle the birder not familiar with this distinctive, lively bird, as the sound echoes on a mountainside or down a gorge in the Balkans. When the singer is tracked down, it turns out, surprisingly in such a treeless habitat, to be a nuthatch – a rangier, longer-billed, bleached version of the far more familiar Nuthatch. Like its close relative the Eastern Rock Nuthatch, which is bigger and equipped with an even longer and heftier spike of a bill, this south-eastern European speciality is

a resident of rocky country, climbing cliffs and boulders instead of trunks and branches. It prefers areas dotted with trees or bushes in arid limestone country where there are rock crevices for nesting. It often frequents stone walls and old stone buildings such as shepherd's huts or ancient ruins.

Often heard long before they are seen, Rock Nuthatches are very noisy birds, with both sexes giving the far-carrying whistling song; pairs frequently perform duets. Perched erect in a very un-nuthatch-like posture, each singer proclaims territorial rights at full volume. A pair will fly around together, calling to maintain contact; when they stop to feed, one bird will usually perform sentry duty from a lookout point.

The male does most of the work of building the nest. Usually sited on a hollow in a rock face or under an overhang, it is an impressive flask-shaped construction of sun-baked mud strengthened with animal dung, hair, beetle wings, crushed bodies of insects, berries, feathers, raptor pellets and other debris.

WALLCREEPER

Tichodroma muraria

Breeds very sparsely in the high mountains of the Cantabrians, Pyrenees, Jura Alps, Apennines, Corsica, Tatras, Carpathians, S. Balkans, Caucasus. In winter, most descend to lower altitudes: sometimes seen in quarries or on walls. Elsewhere in Europe, an extremely rare vagrant. Also breeds across Asia.

Mere mention of this bird provokes a frisson of excitement among many birders, for it is not only scarce and largely confined to the highest, most precipitous mountain ranges, but also exquisitely beautiful. Although most pairs breed between 1,000 m and 2,000 m, some may nest as high as 2,700 m. They prefer softer limestone to tough granite, since it provides more crevices in which to find food and raise a family. In sheer towering rock faces inaccessible to mammal predators, they find deep clefts at the end of which they build their moss and lichen nests. Often, the site is just above a waterfall or tumbling stream, with the entrance clouded by spray.

Skilled rock climbers, the birds proceed across and up the sheer rock face at dizzying heights with jerky hops and leaps. They are equally agile in their erratic, flitting flight, diving, spinning and sometimes spiralling in updraughts, and resemble giant butterflies as they flash the carmine patches and white spots at the tips that adorn their broad, rounded black wings.

On the rock face they probe into fissures for insects with the long, decurved bill, flicking their wings to reveal the red and white patterns. This often substitutes for vocal communication, since their calls are easily drowned by rushing wind or tumbling water. Uttered by both sexes, the song is a short sequence of whistles of flute-like purity in a pentatonic scale. In winter, they are usually solitary. In exceptionally harsh weather they may seek shelter, warmth or sustenance in a group.

PENDULINE TIT

Remiz pendulinus

Occurs patchily across Europe, from France east as far as the Urals. Although suffering from drainage of wetlands, and declining in some southern countries, it is also expanding its range northwards, as far as Scandinavia and Finland, and westwards, with increasing numbers of vagrants in Britain.

The Penduline Tit is one of very few birds named for its nest. Slung from a tree or a bush, this is a deep pouch averaging about 25 cm from top to bottom, with the top end tapering upward to form the noose by which it hangs and the bottom end broadly rounded. It also sprouts from near the apex a spout-like entrance tube, slanting downwards. To further discourage predators, the nest is suspended from a fork in an outermost twig, often over water. Made of what appears at first glance whitish and buff felt, it looks as though it might have been fashioned by some eccentric craftsman. In reality, it is the work of two birds that are smaller than Blue Tits. The male selects the site and starts weaving together plant fibres, reedmace down, poplar and willow catkins, animal hair and grass. When he has reached the basket stage with the interior still unfilled, he advertises his nest and hotly defended territory to any interested female. If she accepts, she will help complete the shelter by lining it with plant down.

Penduline Tits have a complex mating system that includes serial polygamy by both sexes, and although many females may be monogamous, pair bonds are loose. Like a human single mother rearing a family while making DIY improvements, a female may continue to work on the nest until the young fledge.

Penduline Tits have a striking plumage with a pattern somewhat like that of a washed-out miniature male Red-backed Shrike. The odd generic name *Remiz* is from the Polish name for the birds. Along with relatives in Africa, Asia and North America, they are sometimes regarded as a subfamily of the tits, but often now given a family of their own. Like true tits, they have relatively strong legs and feet, and they are even more agile, climbing along the undersides of branches as well as hanging upside down.

In parts of central Europe, the nests of these unusual birds were traditionally used as slippers for small children, a touching indication of the strength and warmth that ensure the snugness of their own tiny offspring.

GOLDEN ORIOLE
Oriolus oriolus

Greatest numbers are in countries that have a continental climate with hot, dry summers, especially Russia, Bulgaria, Romania, Belarus, Ukraine and Spain. A summer visitor, wintering in central and southern Africa. Outside Europe, breeds in Asia from Turkey to the Altai Mountains and India.

This stunning-looking, slim, thrush-sized bird combines flamboyance with elusiveness. The male is among the most vividly plumaged of all European birds, the intense buttercup yellow head and body rendered even more brilliant by contrast with jet black wings and tail. The scientific name is a double reference to this glorious colour, from the Latin *aureolus* ("golden"). The female is as green above as the male is yellow, sometimes the almost acid green of new leaves, and can be confused with a Green or Grey-headed Woodpecker in the usual brief view.

Almost entirely arboreal, Golden Orioles spend most of their time high in the canopy, hidden by the leaves. They are usually glimpsed only momentarily as they swoop between treetops, with a characteristic upward sweep into the crown.

Like the Jay, this is a bird whose calls are mostly as unlovely to human ears as its plumage is pleasing, being mainly harsh cat-like squalls or screeches. The song could not be more different, with mellow, lazily fluting syllables, often transposed as *weela-wee-weeoo*. An aural equivalent of the sunny plumage, it sounds like the voice of a rainforest bird.

The nest, slung between a horizontal fork in a branch, is a shallow cup of vegetation, often incorporating fragments of cloth, paper, wool or string. Here, the solicitous parents repeatedly swallow and regurgitate brittle-bodied beetles until they are soft enough to feed to their offspring, or squeeze cherry juice into the tiny upturned bills.

RED-BACKED SHRIKE

Lanius collurio

Breeds widely across Europe; not in Iceland, Britain or much of Scandinavia, Finland and N. Russia, also absent from Iberia except extreme north. Declining in the west, mainly owing to agriculture and drought in its winter quarters in southern Africa. Outside Europe, range extends into western Siberia.

In contrast to the four other species of shrike that breed in Europe, this summer visitor exhibits a striking difference in plumage between the brighter male and the far drabber female. With his smart pale blue-grey and chestnut upperparts, black "bandit's mask" and pinkish buff underparts, the male cuts a handsome figure as he perches at the top of a favourite hawthorn, sloe or rose bush on the lookout for prey. Females are usually warm brown above, with dusky-brown scalloping and barring on the cream underparts, though a few have a good approximation of the male's head pattern, while some are even duller than usual.

Like other shrikes, these birds when excited or alarmed tend to swing the tail in a curve from side to side, or flick it up and down, at the same time partly fanning it, an action that in the male flashes the striking white patches at its base.

A Red-backed Shrike can spot a beetle or other prey from a range of up to 30 m. It then launches itself on a long, shallow glide to seize it and carry it back to a perch to eat or take to its nestlings – or it may impale it on a thorn, sharp broken twig or barbed wire, especially when feeding young or to see it through periods of cool or wet weather when insect prey is scarce. Although a great percentage of the diet consists of insects, the Red-backed Shrike also take voles, mice and other small mammals, small or young birds, reptiles and frogs.

Although by far the most abundant and widespread shrike in Europe, it has suffered major declines in recent times, especially in the north and west. In Britain, it is now virtually extinct as a breeding bird: a few pairs nest sporadically in Scotland.

SOUTHERN GREY SHRIKE
Lanius meridionalis

Widespread in Spain, most of Portugal and southernmost France. Mainly resident, although a few birds winter in N. Africa. A rare vagrant outside its breeding range, including a few to Britain. Outside Europe, has a wide range: Canary Islands, Africa, Middle East, central Asia east to Mongolia.

Along with the more northerly Great Grey Shrike, from which it was recently split as a separate species, this is among the biggest of the world's shrikes. Even so, it is only about the same length as a Blackbird. It is a powerful predator for its size, capable on occasion of tackling creatures larger than itself, such as stoats, rats and young rabbits. However, it concentrates mainly on big insects as well as voles, mice, small lizards and snakes, generally eating few birds. Vertebrate prey is usually killed by a bite or bites to the back of the neck, severing the spinal cord. The toothlike projection in the upper mandible, similar to the arrangement in falcons, facilitates this *coup de grâce*. Sometimes the victim manages to put up a spirited defence, and to avoid injury its attacker must hover above it, darting down for repeated onslaughts.

Both these grey shrike species live in open country with elevated perches from which they scan for prey; where their ranges overlap, they do not interbreed. Slightly smaller than a Great Grey, the Southern Grey is darker above and often deep pink below, so that it can resemble the Lesser Grey Shrike, though the two species hardly coincide. Unlike tree-nesting Great Greys, Southern Grey Shrikes nest lower down in bushes in scrubby, rocky country with orchards, olive groves and plenty of thorny bushes. Like other shrikes, they skewer their prey on long, sharp thorns, a habit that earned the family its old name of "butcher birds". As well as serving as a larder, this makes it easier for the shrikes to dismember their victims with their bills.

MASKED SHRIKE

Lanius nubicus

Breeds in very small numbers in parts of S. Bulgaria and S. Macedonia, as well as N. Greece and European Turkey, also on Lesvos, Chios, Samos and Kos, and in larger numbers in Cyprus. Outside Europe, S.E. Turkey has most of the world population. All migrate to winter in subtropical Africa and Arabia.

Smallest of the shrikes breeding in Europe, this species is a south-eastern speciality that is a summer visitor to hot dry country. It prefers habitats with more tree cover than other European shrikes, occurring mainly in open woodland, light forest with thorny undergrowth, scrub and cultivated areas such as olive groves and orchards. It tends to keep low down or perch well inside a bush or other cover, and can often be hard to see well. Sometimes, though, one will take up position on an overhead wire to watch for prey, such as crickets, dragonflies, moths and beetles, as well as lizards and small birds. It can be unafraid of humans when in pursuit of a meal. Also, it is frequently far bolder for a short while in April after returning to its breeding site. At this time the birds utter harsh, rather Snipe-like alarm calls as they cock their tails nervously, and males broadcast a rather monotonous, scratchy song from exposed perches.

Although sharing bold white shoulder patches – and most of its range – with the far more widespread Woodchat Shrike, its head pattern is very different, with a white forehead unique among European shrikes. The fresh spring plumage is attractive, with the delicate apricot tint of the breast and flanks especially extensive in males, but this wears to whitish by autumn.

Its reputation in rural Greece as a bird of ill-omen has contributed to its persecution, which also includes the hunting of migrants in Turkey, the Middle East and Africa. Pesticide use has resulted in declines in parts of this insectivore's range.

SIBERIAN JAY
Perisoreus infaustus

Resident in E. and N. Norway, central and N. Sweden, much of Finland (not south) and Russia, within taiga belt. Prefers stands of Norway spruce and Scots pine; sometimes lives among larch and birches in far north. Its range has contracted over the past century. Extends across Russia to Pacific coast.

This is the smallest and most delicate of all European members of the crow family, little bigger than a Blackbird. It is less flamboyantly handsome than its common relative the Jay, but nonetheless has a subtler beauty of its own. To enjoy this, one must travel up into the far northern coniferous forests of Europe, north of about 60°N. With the softness and thickness common to birds living in the far north, its fluffy insulating plumage is mainly grey-brown, with a darker cap and glowing reddish orange patches adorning wings and tail that are much more obvious when the bird flies. The bill is much shorter than

a Jay's; as with many northern birds, this is doubtless an adaptation to reduce heat loss in the cold climate.

The Siberian Jay is often patchily distributed, and tracking it down can prove tricky. The task is made more difficult in summer by wariness during the breeding season, except at some picnic places and other sites where it has become used to humans and attracted by easy pickings from discarded food. This is in striking contrast to its general tameness in winter.

Siberian Jays are, like most crows, omnivorous. Although feeding largely on insects, berries and seeds, they relish carrion and are more predatory than Jays, eating many rodents and small birds, and especially songbird eggs and nestlings. They carry food in the typical corvid throat pouch, which here shows up as a pinkish bulge when distended with food. They produce extra-sticky saliva which they use to stick berries, seeds and insects together into balls that they glue to the undersides of branches. These food caches help them survive the lean northern winter.

AZURE-WINGED MAGPIE
Cyanopica cyanus

Found in S. and central Spain, with non-breeders extending sporadically to the N.E.; in Portugal, mainly in the S. and along Spanish border. Most abundant Extremadura and W. Andalucia and parts of S. Portugal. Favours cork oak and holm oak woods; also found among stone pines and mixed woodland.

This unique, exotic-looking member of the crow family has an odd world distribution, occuring not only in the Iberian peninsula, but also some 6,000 miles away in eastern Asia. "Disjunct distributions" of this kind may result from continental drift, from competition with other species or from climatic change. The latter cause is most likely here, with the loss of the major central part of the population during the last ice ages. Marked genetic differences between the Iberian race and the various Asian sub-species suggest that the rift happened a long time ago.

The recent discovery of 44,000-year-old fossil Azure-winged Magpie bones in cave deposits in Gibraltar has put paid to the alternative theory that the European population might have originated from birds brought back from China to Portugal in the 16th century by traders and seafarers.

Distinctly smaller and more slender-bodied than the familiar Magpie, this lovely bird is a fine sight as extended families of co-operative breeders or larger autumn and winter flocks roam restlessly in the open woodlands of Spain and Portugal. They spend much time deep inside the cover of the canopy, hopping about with almost parrot-like agility to work the foliage, branches and trunks for insects, seeds and fruit, and uttering curious dry, trilling calls. In shade, they can look quite plain, but when they emerge into bright sunlight they are transformed, as the soft pastel greyish and pinkish buff body contrasts with the glowing, pale powder blue wings and long graduated tail.

NUTCRACKER
Nucifraga caryocatactes

Probably the only bird with the same common name as a kitchen utensil, this unusual white-spotted, mainly chocolate-brown crow is restricted to the boreal forests of the north, and scattered mountain forests far to the south. Its diet in winter consists almost exclusively of high-energy hazel nuts and seeds of Arolla pine, and in the Balkans, Macedonian pine. Along with its sole relative, Clark's Nutcracker of North America, this is the champion avian food hoarder. Every autumn, each adult buries about 100,000 seeds and many nuts in soil and under moss, dead leaves and so on. Remarkably, the birds can relocate the exact position of their hidden stores and find up to 90 percent of the food, even under snow well over a metre deep.

The birds' relationship with the trees that provide their food is deeply mutualistic, particularly with the pines, whose heavy, unwinged seeds are broadcast mainly by Nutcrackers.

Sometimes this relationship breaks down, when populations of the distinct, longer-billed race living far to the

Breeds sparsely in the lowlands of southernmost Norway, S. Sweden, extreme S. of Finland and from N. Poland, Baltic states and Belarus into Russia; also in mountains of central and S.E. Europe. Most in Romania, Russia, Austria, Switzerland, Bulgaria, Italy. Beyond Europe, breeds across Russia to Japan.

east in Siberia experience the failure of the crop of Siberian stone pine seeds on which they depend, and the birds are forced to move west in search of food. Normally rare vagrants to Europe, they turn up in unprecedented numbers, often in places far removed from their normal habitat, especially gardens and parks. In 1968, thousands invaded Europe. As well as feasting on bird-feeder scraps, the starving immigrants resorted to hacking down rodents and House Sparrows or eating dung, the contents of compost heaps and farm crops, while some took food from people's hands or even entered houses.

CHOUGH

Pyrrhocorax pyrrhocorax

With N.W. outposts in Ireland, Wales, Scotland and (recent colonization by a few pairs) Cornwall, breeds across much of S. Europe, where it is found chiefly in mountains; in Britain it is mainly coastal. Has declined, though conservation efforts are in hand. Largest populations are in Spain and Russia.

If Superman were a bird, the Chough would be the species. No creature epitomizes exuberance in the air more than this dapper red-billed, red-legged crow. An appreciation of its prowess involves lots of exercise for your neck muscles. First, you're squinting up to see a pair or small flock wheeling high above a sea cliff or mountain gorge, like scraps of charred paper in the updraught from a bonfire, and the next minute you're craning down to follow one as it plummets in free fall, only spreading out its broad fingered wings at the last moment before striking rock or waves. Their apparent exultation in

defying gravity is echoed in the birds' loud, ringing *cheeow* calls, bouncing off the walls of rock. It is this call from which the name comes, originally pronounced "chow".

The Chough's black cloak of feathers is glossier than that of other European black crows, shot with deep blue and purple iridescence that glints in the sun as it hurtles past. Even more distinctive is its bill, a bright vermilion downcurved spike, while its typically strong corvine legs and feet match it in colour. The beak's shape indicates a specialized diet, unlike all other European crows – including even its less impressive-looking close relative, the Alpine Chough. It is this specialization that has proved its downfall in many parts of its range, notably in the British Isles. For agriculture has "improved" much of the short rabbit-cropped and sheep-grazed turf above sea-cliffs and on mountainsides – and in the process removed the ants, beetles and other insects, many living among animal droppings, that these handsome birds probe and fossick for.

ROOK

Corvus frugilegus

Being privileged to share the land with this intensely gregarious and characterful member of the crow family depends on where in Europe you live. In countries such as Spain, Portugal, Norway and Sweden, Rooks are virtually absent or at best breed in only a few areas. But where they are really numerous, as in the open lowlands of Britain, Ireland, north-west France, Russia, Ukraine and Belarus, it is difficult not to see Rooks. They do almost everything in concert, whether feeding in a field, where they stride about with their rather comical, waddling gait on legs that look like they are clothed in baggy black shorts; stealing one another's twigs and branches high up in the rookery as they repair their nests at winter's end; or flying in long wavering ribbons of black between food and home, with a regularity you can set your watch by. As the writer and Rook devotee Mark Cocker puts it: "Farm workers used rook flights as a means of knowing when to down tools."

It is not just the sight of Rooks that helps define the fabric of the countryside where they are most abundant: their calls too are an integral part of the landscape. The collective conversational sound that emanates from a big rookery is utterly distinctive yet infinitely variable. When the birds are gathered together in noisy assembly high in the topmost branches of their swaying treetop communes, the more familiar hoarse "cawing" notes are interspersed with softer crooning sounds, high-pitched creakings, gurglings, rattlings, raspings, almost human mutterings and other noises, in seemingly endless variety.

The roosts and rookeries are among the most obvious and impressive gatherings of any European landbird. Although most rookeries contain fewer than a hundred nests, the biggest comprise more than 2,000 pairs or even twice that number, while there may be over 60,000 birds at some roosts. The function of these great assemblages, drawing birds from distances of up to 30 miles, may be to serve as information centres where knowledge of good feeding sites is shared.

During the breeding season at least, associated in Europe with lowland farmland (with grassland for worms and clumps of tall trees for colonial nesting). Birds from northern, central and eastern Europe migrate in winter westwards and southwards. Beyond Europe, breeds across Asia to as far east as China.

RAVEN
Corvus corax

Breeds all over Europe, large populations in Russia, Spain, Ukarine, Belarus, Norway and Sweden. Big increases over past 40 years but in western Europe is numerous and widespread only in western and northern British Isles, Brittany, mountain ranges of central and southern Europe and across much of Iberia.

Bigger than a Buzzard, this imposing black bird is the largest of all the 5,800 or so species in the great order of passerines, or perching birds. Its power and typically corvine adaptability make it a versatile predator, capable of killing a wide range of smaller mammals and birds, and bigger ones too that are sick or injured; but it relies far more on carrion for much of the year. Its great meat cleaver of a bill is equally suited to killing a rabbit or slicing into a dead sheep. The extraordinarily wide diet ranges from beetles, slugs and spiders through hares and pigeons to the carcasses of dead whales.

No bird in Europe is more steeped in myth, legend and history, from serving as corpse-cleaners at prehistoric burial mounds to being mentioned in half of Shakespeare's plays. Ravens were endowed with supernatural powers, as omen-bearing messengers of the gods. Most of the associations were with death or disaster – in part because they attended the aftermath of battles to feed on slain warriors. Much of the folklore has portrayed them as cruel, treacherous or downright evil: two old nouns for a flock are an "unkindness" or "conspiracy" of Ravens.

After centuries of persecution, more enlightened attitudes today mean that Ravens have made a comeback. Where persecution has ceased, they have the potential to increase their numbers dramatically. They rival the Wren, at the opposite end of the size spectrum, in adapting to different landscapes. Their supremely aerobatic flight and sonorous croaking calls can be admired in habitats as diverse as the high Arctic, the wave-lashed sea-cliffs, the rolling steppes and the highest mountains.

ROSE-COLOURED STARLING
Sturnus roseus

A bird of the steppes. In Europe most breed in Russia, Ukraine, Romania. Has declined, perhaps partly owing to use of pesticides in controlling locusts. Outside Europe, breeds across central Asia to as far east as Mongolia. Wintering range large, throughout the Indian subcontinent and also in Sri Lanka.

Like its relative the Starling (*Sturnus vulgaris*), this is an intensely sociable bird, but it is a far more localized and sporadic breeder in Europe, almost entirely in southern Russia, the Ukraine and the Balkans, which lie on the fringes of the species' mainly central Asian range. At roughly eight to ten year intervals, but often more irregularly, large numbers travel up to 750 miles beyond their normal range into south-eastern and central Europe. These irruptions probably follow rapid population growth after a run of years with exceptionally successful breeding, and may also coincide with shortages of insect food. Although they may anger orchard and vineyard owners with their depredations on fruit in summer and autumn, the birds more than make up for this by their fondness for locusts. In the past, the major incursions took the flocks much farther west.

Vagrants to western Europe are usually singletons, and are seen as far west as Britain and Ireland. There are particular concentrations in the Isles of Scilly in autumn, mostly of juveniles, migrating in the wrong direction. Adults and first-year birds occur in spring and summer, especially in Shetland.

A brief view of an abnormally coloured Starling can set the pulse racing, but with its pale rose pink and glossy bluish, purplish and greenish black plumage, and its long drooping crest, an adult Rose-coloured Starling is a far more exotic-looking bird than its commoner relative. The pink to yellowish bill is shorter and blunter, and together with the rounder outline of the head, this gives the bird a gentler demeanour compared to the spiky-billed, angular-headed Starling.

SNOWFINCH
Montifringilla nivalis

Breeds locally at high altitudes in Alps and mountains of S. Europe, including the Cantabrians, Pyrenees, N. Apennines, Balkans and Caucasus. May roam from breeding ranges in winter but rarely descends below 1,500m. Outside Europe, breeds in Turkey and central Asia east to Tibet and Mongolia.

Despite its common and scientific names – *montifringilla* means "mountain finch" – this subtly attractive little bird is actually a member of the sparrow family. A clue to this relationship is its rather hesitant, jerky song of varied chirrups, though these are mixed with dry trills to produce a rather superior sound. And compared with a House Sparrow, this is a distinctly bigger, less dumpy bird, its elongated appearance emphasized by long wings and a long tail. The "mountain" part of the name is, by contrast, accurate. Indeed, the Snowfinch is one of the greatest alpinists of all passerines. It lives on bare mountainsides at 1,900 to 3,600 m in Europe – even higher in central Asia, where it breeds up to 5,300 m in Tibet. It inhabits the zone above the tree line up to the permanent snowline.

Spending most of its time on the ground, it can be quite hard to find, its complex pattern of ash grey, earth brown, black and white rendering it almost invisible. When it takes flight, though, it becomes a much more conspicuous bird, as it reveals the almost entirely snow-white inner wings and tail. Fortunately for birdwatchers keen to make a positive identification, its range does not overlap with the similarly patterned Snow Bunting.

Snow Finches thrive alongside humankind: sometimes they build their bulky nest cups of dry materials in niches on mountain huts, ski stations, or ski lift pylons. In most places, they nest in small, loose colonies of up to half a dozen or so pairs. In winter, they are more gregarious, joining up to form flocks of about 20 to two or three hundred birds. These often forage for human food scraps, becoming as tame as town sparrows.

BRAMBLING

Fringilla montifringilla

Widespread and common from Norway across northern Europe to Russia. Most abundant in Russia (10–15 million pairs) and Finland (1–2.5 million); 1–2 million in Sweden and more in Norway. A few breed in Iceland and Scotland. European breeders winter widely south and west of breeding range.

This northern relative of the ubiquitous Chaffinch is distinguished by a bolder, tortoiseshell, pattern. This is particularly striking in the male's breeding plumage, with the black head and mantle contrasting with the sunset-orange breast and shoulders and the white belly and rump. In contrast to the Chaffinch, in which the female is much drabber than the male, the sexes look far more alike in the Brambling, especially in winter. At this time, the male is duller, owing to the pale fringes of the feathers on head, nape and upperparts. These wear away, and by early spring the black areas of the mantle are still flecked with paler edges to give it a scalloped pattern until it, too, becomes solid jet black.

Bramblings are very common in the northern forests, and during spring their simple, rather mournful wheezing song is as monotonous as the Chaffinch's is merry. Their nests are as beautiful as the neatly woven cups of their close relative, but bigger, more free-form and with a warmer feather lining. Up to 40 per cent or more of nests are destroyed by predators such as Hooded Crows, Ravens, stoats and weasels plundering them for eggs or young. They are also parasitized by the Cuckoo: the Brambling is one of its major hosts in Finnish forests.

In irruption years, immense flocks roam over wide areas in search of their favourite winter food, beechmast (beech nuts). Their roosts in central Europe at these times can contain up to 20 million birds, and may comprise much of the European population in just one small valley.

CITRIL FINCH
Serinus citrinella

At first glance, the plumage of these characterful little birds can recall that of the much larger Greenfinch – but Citril Finches are clothed in cooler hues. Their upperparts are dark-streaked greyish green; males are bluish grey on the rear crown, nape, ear coverts and neck sides, while the females have an even more extensive, duller grey wash, like the rocks or scree among which they sometimes feed. Similarly, the cold, broken-glass tinkling and twittering of the little mountain-dweller's voice contrasts with the Greenfinch's rich, drowsy wheeze. Taxonomically, the Citril Finch is most closely related to the tiny Serin, and is only a fraction bigger.

This is one of a very few mountain birds endemic to Europe. In mountain ranges over parts of southern and central Europe, these little sprites delight the birder who takes the trouble to search them out along the edges of conifer forests and adjacent alpine meadows. Their presence is often betrayed

Breeds mainly in conifer forests (especially pine, larch, spruce) at 700–1,500 m in Spain (Cantabrians, Pyrenees etc), France (Vosges, Massif Central), the Jura, much of the Alps and mountains of northern Italy and Slovenia. Favourite feeding sites include forest clearings, ski-runs, roofs of alpine huts, scree.

by the distinctive calls. They feed mainly on the ground but also in trees and shrubs, on the seeds of grasses, wildflowers and conifers. Like most alpine birds, Citril Finches escape the harsh winter by moving downslope, where they can then be seen in large flocks, often with other finches.

In Corsica, Sardinia and the tiny islands of Capraia and Elba is a race of Citril Finch now given full species status with the name Corsican Finch, *Serinus corsicanus*. It enjoys a wider range of habitats, at lower altitudes as well as in the mountains.

TWITE

Carduelis flavirostris

Scarce in Europe, breeding only in W. coastal and N. Norway, Lapland, with a declining population in Ireland, N. Scotland, a small part of N. England, and in the Caucasus. Easier to see in winter, when flocks of migrants from the far north join birds making local migrations to coasts on both sides of the North Sea.

Apart from major populations in Asia, this unassuming finch breeds nowhere but in Norway and its fringes, far across the North Sea in northern Scotland, the Pennines of northern England and coastal western Ireland, and much farther away in the Caucasus. During the last Ice Age, birds from the ancestral stock centred on Tibet are thought to have expanded across the tundra of central Asia into central Europe. Then, as the climate warmed, some colonizers followed the retreating ice into north-west Europe while most fell back to their original home in Asia. This adds to the species' uniqueness, as the only European bird derived from the Tibetan avifauna. It is also one of the few European birds that feeds almost entirely on seeds.

Twite are easily missed by walkers out on the hills: they are a real "birder's bird". Their similarity to females and especially juveniles of their close relative the Linnet combines with their very restricted range and general scarcity to give them status as a challenging species to find and identify. Twite are often very hard to see well as flocks tend to hunker down among autumn heather or saltmarsh vegetation on a winter estuary. Also, they are restless, suddenly erupting with a chorus of hard twittering calls into a dancing flight that takes them high and far.

The name is onomatopoeic: once pronounced "tweet", it approximates to the hoarse nasal call. An old English name was Mountain Linnet, and various dialect names, as well as the Welsh *Llinos y Mynydd*, provide variations on the same theme.

ARCTIC REDPOLL

Carduelis hornemanni

This is one of those bird species around which a blizzard of disagreement has swirled as to its taxonomic boundaries, owing partly to considerable variation between individuals as well as between species and subspecies. Interpretations have ranged from recognition of no fewer than seven species by the American Elliott Coues in 1862 to the Dane Finn Salomonsen's 1951 approval of just a single species. The most recent research suggests that a more sensible figure might be three. In addition to the Arctic Redpoll, this scheme also recognizes the Lesser Redpoll and Common Redpoll.

Such uncertainty has caused headaches for birdwatchers as well as taxonomists – especially on a freezing, windy winter's morning. To start with what the birds have in common: they are all small, plump-bodied finches, dark-streaked brown or greyish above, paler beneath with a white belly and streaked flanks, and sporting a black chin and a red patch on the forehead; the males have a pinkish-red wash to the breast in breeding plumage.

Those breeding in Europe belong to the race *exilipes*, which lives in the far north of Scandinavia, Finland, Russia and N. America. The other subspecies, *hornemanni*, breeds in N. Canada and Greenland. Lesser Redpolls live in Britain and N. and central Europe; Common Redpolls in N. Eurasia and N. America.

The main feature of Arctic Redpolls is their extreme paleness. Birds of the European race *exilipes* are whitest of all, with a long, very white rump that looks as if it is covered in frost – hence the name Hoary Redpoll. Other distinguishing features include the virtually unstreaked flanks, the very small stub of a bill, and the white feathering extending down onto the legs, like tiny white shorts. These ghostly white and grey birds look like little balls of snow when they fluff out their dense plumage to keep warm. Most birders will see them as winter visitors in variable numbers, often in mixed flocks with other redpolls.

SCOTTISH CROSSBILL

Loxia scotica

Restricted to Highlands of Scotland: lives year-round in remnants of the ancient Caledonian pine forest, and in old conifer plantations. There may be as few as 1,500 adults. Analysis of sonograms of calls should soon provide a more accurate estimate. Currently seen as threatened.

As well as being one of very few birds whose range lies entirely within Europe, this is the only bird species endemic to the British Isles. That simple statement omits a long and tangled history that revolves around the niceties of taxonomic adjudication.

Like all the species in the genus *Loxia*, this plump little sparrow-sized bird has the unique characteristic of a bill whose mandibles cross over one another at the tip – a highly evolved precision tool for prising apart the tough protective scales of conifer cones to extract the nutritious seeds hidden within.

The exact blueprint varies slightly from species to species, to suit the extraction of different tree seeds, so that the birds have been able to avoid competition even where their ranges overlap. The deeper, wider beak of the Scottish crossbill is adapted for feeding on the seeds of Scots pine. It is intermediate in size between the usually smaller bills of Common Crossbills, with a diet based on spruce seeds, and the massive bills of Parrot Crossbills, which eat mainly Scots pine seeds. Both the latter breed within the range of the Scottish bird, especially after irruptions following the failure of their seed crops in northern Europe.

The differences between the three birds are very subtle, and often impossible to discern in the field. Recent studies have shown that their calls can be distinguished by examining their sonograms, that the birds choose mates with a similar call and bill size, and that bill size is inherited. This led to the decision to promote the Scottish Crossbill to full species status.

TRUMPETER FINCH
Bucanetes githagineus

In Europe truly wild birds live only in extreme S.E. Spain; those in Portugal's Algarve are thought to be feral. From the original colonization in the 1960s from N. Africa, has increased in numbers and range since the 70s, moving east into Murcia. Outside Spain, occurs in the Middle East and across Asia.

This is an unusual North African and western Asiatic species that colonized the Canary Islands some 7,000 years ago and which has expanded its range far more recently to gain a toehold on a third continent. Here, in the south-eastern corner of Spain, it finds the extreme habitat to which it is adapted.

This is a little bird, only fractionally larger than a Serin, and with that species' portly shape. At a distance, the male's breeding plumage looks drab pinkish-grey and featureless, with the greyer head and pinker breast and rump visible only at close range. More noticeable is his bulbous, gaudy sealing-wax-red bill. Both plumage and bill are duller in winter, and females and immature birds are duller still.

Trumpeter Finches can survive in the most inhospitable desert, with the shadows cast by the baking rocks providing the only respite from the intense sun. They spend much of the day resting in the shade, feeding in the couple of hours before sunrise, when their big eyes help them find food. They can tolerate such temperatures only if they have daily access to water, for the seeds they eat contain virtually none. To ensure this, they are prepared to fly considerable distances, often at sunset, when it is cooler. At night, they may need to huddle together for warmth.

Trumpeter Finches can easily be missed, but males draw attention to themselves with their remarkable song, with nasal notes like a child's toy trumpet, often interspersed with equally strange buzzing, as well as clicks, whistles and wheezes.

GREAT ROSEFINCH

Carpodacus rubicilla

Breeds in Europe only in the N. Caucasus (N. Georgia, S.E. Russia). Often found near glaciers in upper reaches of deep river valleys. Has declined in last 30 years, possibly to fewer than 5,000 pairs, due partly to nest predation by Alpine Choughs and destruction of habitat. Main range is in central Asia.

This is the biggest of all finches to breed in Europe, averaging a little longer (though not bulkier) than the Pine Grosbeak. It is far bigger than the continent's only other member of the mainly Asian rosefinch genus, the Common Rosefinch. Whereas the latter is widespread across much of northern and eastern Europe, and is still in the process of a remarkable westward expansion from its original range in Asia, this far more spectacular finch is a very restricted range species in Europe, as one of the most exciting specialities of the Caucasus region.

In summer this bird dwells above the rhododendron zone in alpine meadows and on scree-slopes and boulder-strewn mountainsides, mainly at altitudes of 2,500–3,500 m, nesting in rock crevices. Here pairs or small flocks spend much of the day feeding. They may fly downslope in winter, but usually no lower than 2,000 m. It is only after very heavy snowfalls that groups of mainly young birds descend lower to more sheltered valleys.

The size of a Starling, the plump-bodied Great Rosefinch has a stout, seed-cracking bill and strong legs for a life spent mainly on the ground or rocks. Difficult to approach, it will usually fly off when still about 30–40 m away. Its size and undulating flight and dark brownish upperparts can make it look like a small thrush or a large lark. The male is one of the most impressive of all finches, peppered with a constellation of silvery white spots on his head and underparts. This gives him a lovely frosted appearance, as if tiny snowflakes had fallen on his soft, ruby-red plumage. He serenades his dowdy mate with a loud whistling song, bobbing about on a boulder, head pointing skywards.

PINE GROSBEAK
Pinicola enucleator

A scarce breeder in far north, in pine and birch woods. Most in Russia; also Sweden and Finland, and a few in Norway. In most winters, make local movements, to central Scandinavia and Finland. In an irruption year, may reach central Europe. Outside Europe, breeds in Siberia and northern N. America.

This far northern forest speciality is the bulkiest of all the finches in Europe, the size of a small thrush. This is especially true in winter, when it fluffs out its soft, dense plumage to trap heat. The rather small, neckless head and stout but stubby bill look out of proportion to the bulky body and long tail. Pine Grosbeaks often remain in one place, moving slowly or not at all for long periods, giving rise to the Canadian nickname of "Mope". But they are also acrobatic birds for their size, hanging upside-down from slender twigs when feeding, and using their slightly hooked bills as third limbs to help them clamber around, like crossbills – and parrots (an old Swedish name for the species was *Svenske Papegoja*, or Swedish Parrot). But unlike the highly specialized conifer seed extractor that is the crossbills' trademark, the Pine Grosbeak's uncrossed bill has evolved to deal with a diet similar to that of its close relative the Bullfinch: for much of the year these birds feed mainly on buds, shoots and fruits of shrubs and trees and soft seeds of wildflowers.

Although often elusive, living in more remote areas except in winter, they are not at all shy. Indeed, some of the local names for this species in Scandinavian languages such as *Dumskalle* and *Dumsnut* refer to their tame behaviour. This proved their undoing in the past when they were caught for the cagebird trade. They are particularly fearless in winter when many move south and west in search of good crops of red rowan berries, including those on trees lining the streets of towns. They almost allow themselves to be touched. At such times, these unusual finches brighten up the trees like Christmas decorations.

The striking difference in colour between the sexes again recalls the crossbills. Males are especially bright, the blue-grey ground colour of much of their plumage suffused with raspberry red on the head, back, rump and breast; while the colour that mottles the females is very variable, ranging from a subtler greenish-yellow to a lovely bronzy-gold with much more of the grey showing through on the flanks, rump and back.

HAWFINCH

Coccothraustes coccothraustes

Widespread but patchily distributed across Europe (not far north). Breeds in broadleaved woodland, at highest density in oak and hornbeam; also found in orchards (esp. with cherries), olive groves, parks. Large populations in Germany, Poland, Czech Republic, Slovakia, Hungary, Romania, Croatia, Ukraine.

The legendary shyness of this extraordinary finch is only too well known to most birders. Often, even those who study the species must be content with a flash of white on wings and tail as a small flock flies heavily but fast from one tree canopy to another. To add to the difficulty, Hawfinches can be relatively silent for much of the year. The best hope of good views is during winter when they take fallen seeds from the ground. Although all of this is very much true of the bird in most of its European range, in the south it can be surprisingly confiding.

So much about this big finch is special: its size (at 18 cm long it is the third biggest European finch); its subtly beautiful colour scheme of tawny orange, ash-grey and wine-brown set off by a small black eye patch and bib; its very short tail; the strangely notched sixth to tenth primary feathers and handsome green and purple gloss to their jet black hue – and, of course, that colossal bill. Blue-grey in the breeding season and yellowish ivory for the rest of the year, its pale colour and neat black lining of feathers at the base make it look even more conspicuous. Capable of cracking cherry and olive stones, it has a pair of horny pads on the palate and two nubs opposing them on the lower jaw to hold the stone firmly while the bird deals with it. The pressure exerted via the massive jaw muscles is equivalent to a human jaw delivering over 60 tonnes. Further evidence of power comes in the bloodied fingers and injured knuckles of ringers handling these birds.

BULLFINCH

Pyrrhula pyrrhula

Widespread: often in broadleaved woodland in west of range, conifers in north and east. Has expanded in north and west, but with huge declines in some parts, especially Britain. Larger, brighter race *pyrrhula* from the north and east is a partial migrant, moving south and west. Also breeds across Asia to Japan.

With his glowing pinkish-red, blue-grey, black and white plumage, the male Bullfinch is one of the finest of all European songbirds. The more soberly adorned female has her own subtle appeal. This is one of the more monogamous songbirds, and pairs spend much of their time together. Generally rather secretive, their presence is betrayed mainly by their melancholy piping contact calls. Although soft, with a hesitant, absent-minded quality, these can carry far. Every now and then, the plump, bull-necked birds will emerge from a thicket or overgrown hedge to delight the eye before flying off again with a flash of the white rump. The escape flight usually takes them back into cover, in contrast to many finches, which fly up and away or into the top of a tree.

The unusually intimate pair bonds are maintained by a metaphorically – and literally – touching display in which the birds swivel their tails towards one another and momentarily touch bills, nibbling in silence. They then turn away to one side before "kissing" again, often repeating the performance over and over. Although the female tends to be more dominant, performing a ritual attack on her partner when they first meet, there is a remarkable lack of aggression between the two thereafter.

By plundering seeds from different food plants as they come into season, they can extend the breeding period, and raise two or even three broods. When the seed crop is poor, Bullfinches may visit orchards, where they can eat fruit buds at the rate of 30 or more per minute. Huge numbers of offenders used to be trapped and killed to prevent this, although with only a temporary effect on the local population.

SNOW BUNTING
Plectrophenax nivalis

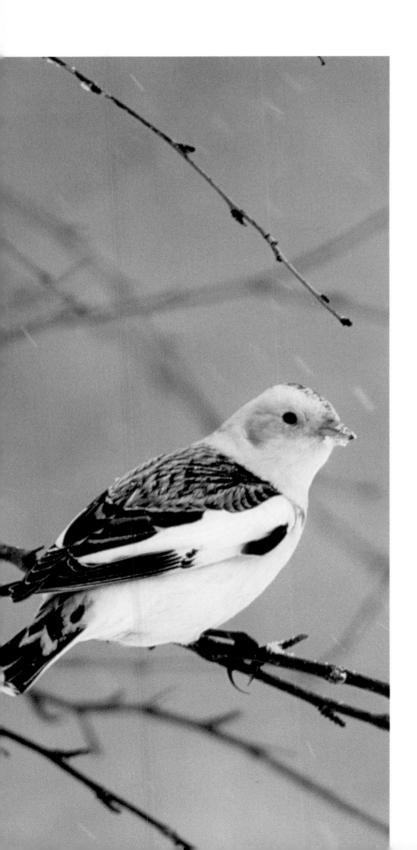

In north of range breeds on rocky tundra and coasts; good sites in Iceland, including Lake Myvatn; also Norway (eg Dovrefjell), Sweden (eg Abisko NP), Finland (eg Kevo NP). Winter visitors appear along coasts, including eastern Britain; especially shingle and sandy beaches and on saltmarshes.

An old name for this striking member of a large, mainly New World family is Snowflake. Indeed, in winter, birders in Europe can encounter flocks drifting low over shingle beaches or saltmarshes like a living snow shower of feathers, to the accompaniment of soft, rippling contact calls. When they land, the birds appear long, low-slung and almost legless, as they shuffle along, with their plump snow-white bellies almost touching the ground. Constantly on the move, they search for seeds or sandhoppers, with a distinctive habit of playing leapfrog, the birds at the back of the flock making short flights over the backs of those in front. They are generally very tame and approachable in winter, rarely moving far away even when disturbed.

Snow Buntings are at their most striking in breeding plumage, the males in gleaming white with contrasting coal-black back, wingtips and central tail feathers. To see large numbers in spring and summer, you have to go to the far north, to Iceland, Norway or northern Sweden and Finland. The tiny breeding population in the Scottish Highlands – the great majority in the bleak, high-mountain tops of the Cairngorm massif – is a southern outlier of the main Arctic population. They are most easily seen foraging for scraps in car parks or by ski-lift stations. It appears that these belong not only to the Icelandic race *insulae* but also to the race *nivalis* from Fenno-Scandinavia. Another recent, and welcome, revelation has been that there are far more of these buntings in the breeding season in Highland Scotland than was hitherto thought – maybe as many as 100 pairs. On the other hand, global warming is likely to reverse this trend.

CINEREOUS BUNTING

Emberiza cineracea

Breeds in Europe on a few Greek islands, mainly Lesvos (with 100–250 pairs); fewer on Chios and Skyros. Probably winters mainly along the Red Sea. There, and at migration stopovers (eg Cyprus, Syria, Jordan, Israel), where they are very scarce, they are often among other buntings, and easily overlooked.

This is one of Europe's rarest and least known songbirds, with a total of only 110 to 300 or so pairs on several of the Greek Aegean islands. The European population is nonetheless important as the species breeds elsewhere discontinuously in a few parts of Turkey, a very small area of adjacent Syria and Iran and possibly of Iraq – and nowhere else in the world.

As well as being rare and sparsely distributed in its limited range, this enigmatic bird is generally shy and hard to see. In contrast to the distinct sexual dimorphism of most other buntings, there is not such a great difference in appearance between the sexes. "Cinereous" means "ash-grey", a good description of much of the adult plumage. This is virtually unstreaked and rather sombre and washed-out, although brightened somewhat in the male by an olive-yellow head and neck and a brighter yellow eye-ring and throat.

On the Greek islands, it favours dry, rocky slopes or plateaux, such as those in the species' European stronghold, in the wild, rugged country of western Lesvos. Numbers here appear to be stable. Potential threats include changes in grazing pressure by sheep and goats (too little deprives them of open feeding sites, too much and their ground nests are are risk from trampling) and disturbance from increased tourism.

The song matches the plumage in being a plain, simple affair, with four to six rapidly delivered, rather hard, hoarse notes that usually rise in pitch and then end with a couplet.

CRETZSCHMAR'S BUNTING
Emberiza caesia

Generally patchily distributed. Scarce in S. Albania and N. Greece, abundant in some places, such as Chios. Breeds in greater numbers in W. and S. Turkey. Also breeds on Cyprus, and in parts of Middle East bordering the Mediterranean. Winters in N.E. Africa and perhaps also in the Arabian peninsula.

The 19th-century German physician and anatomy lecturer who gave his name to this pretty little bird unwittingly provided many birders with a spelling challenge. This is one of those species with a very restricted global range, being endemic to the Western Palearctic and breeding in a small part of the east Mediterranean. In Europe it occurs mainly in Greece, on the mainland and many islands, with small populations in southern Albania.

It is closely related to the better-known Ortolan Bunting (greatly prized as a delicacy by rich gourmands) and to the non-European Grey-necked Bunting of south-east Turkey to Iran and central Asia. This trio are all birds of dry, open habitats. The plumage pattern of all three is similar, but most alike in Cretzschmar's and Ortolan, both with contrasting markings on the head and throat, especially pronounced in males. The male Cretzschmar's has a blue-grey head and chest band (rather than the greenish-grey ones of Ortolan), while his moustachial stripe and bib are orange rather than grey. The rest of the plumage in both is an attractive rufous colour, darker and richer reddish orange in Cretzschmar's. The latter's simpler song is a quite spirited but brief, monotonous sequence of three to four rather mournful notes at the same pitch, the last one longer. At most the singer alternates between a phrase of thinner, scratchier notes and one in which they are rather sweeter and more fluty.

Where Cretzschmar's and Ortolan occur together, they compete for similar resources. One or the other species takes to the higher ground. Usually, Cretzschmar's occupies more barren habitats, mainly at higher altitudes, up to 1,300 m.

RUSTIC BUNTING
Emberiza rustica

Widespead and numerous in N. Sweden, N. Finland and N. Russia, having spread westward and southward over the past 100 years. A few breed in Norway and Latvia. Outside Europe, has a huge breeding range across N. Eurasia. Almost all winter in China or Japan; a few vagrants reach W. Europe in autumn.

This smallish bunting has a habitat preference not found in any other European (or indeed Western Palearctic) bird, for marshy ground dominated by spruce but also with birch and an undergrowth of grasses and low, dwarf shrubs. But it will also colonize sphagnum bogs dotted with cloudberry shrubs or willow scrub edging fens or river banks. In places, it breeds in damp conifer forest, especially in central parts of its European range, in Russia; while in the west, in Lapland, some nest in drier heathland, with birches and scattered juniper bushes.

The male's brief but delightful song is far superior to the simpler utterances of most buntings. In their neat, well-concealed nests the greenish eggs, intriguingly, lack the scribble-like markings of most other buntings' eggs: instead, they are heavily spotted and blotched, like those of many other ground-nesting birds, in this case with brownish or olive grey.

Males in breeding plumage look like no other bunting, the head featuring a pattern formed by a broad black crown stripe and a very broad black one below, standing out against white; the silky white underparts are smudged with big rufous streaks. But winter males and females and the immature birds that may turn up as vagrants are confusable with Reed and Little Buntings or even Asiatic species that very rarely turn up in Europe, such as Yellow-browed, Pine and Meadow Buntings. Often they show a slightly peaked crown. Unlike most other buntings they often elevate their tails as they hop about on the ground.

BLACK-HEADED BUNTING

Emberiza melanocephala

Largest European populations are in Russia, Greece (including many Aegean islands), Cyprus (but not Crete), Macedonia, Albania, Bulgaria; also breeds in parts of S. Italy, Slovenia, Croatia, Bosnia-Herzegovina, Serbia-Montenegro, Georgia, Ukraine. Winters in India, where it often forms huge flocks.

The boldly plumaged male of this south-eastern speciality is hard to ignore as he proclaims ownership of his territory from an overhead wire with the endlessly repeated, simple two-part song. This is an often faltering, widely spaced series of sharp, dry *zit* notes followed by a brisk cheerful warbling. With his combination of soot-black hood, sunflower-yellow breast and rich chestnut back, reminiscent of a tropical African weaverbird, he is one of the brightest and most easily recognized of all buntings. Even after his partial post-breeding moult in summer, when the black and brightly coloured areas of plumage are rendered much paler and duller by pale fringes to the feathers, the basic pattern remains and identification is straightforward, aided by the species' general tameness. As usual with buntings, females and non-breeding males are rather trickier: in very worn plumage, females can look like even more washed-out and more colourless versions of worn males, but otherwise they have the typical streaky brown female bunting plumage. The key features here are lack of any white in the tail and the yellow undertail coverts.

These big, sturdy, long-tailed buntings favour open country that provides them with their three basic needs: feeding places on or above the ground, where they can find seeds and grains as well as insects; nest sites low in cover; and song posts for the males, in trees, shrubs or roadside wires. Sometimes, though, a male may instead launch himself on a song-flight, with shallow, flickering wingbeats and dangling legs like a Corn Bunting, or more rarely involving a parachuting performance like a pipit's.

BIBLIOGRAPHY

The following list includes major references used during the writing of this book. However, there were many additional sources consulted occasionally, which cannot be listed owing to lack of space. Among these are many site guides to different European countries and regions. Similarly, I drew on the knowledge contained in a very large number of journal and magazine articles and online sources. The following were especially useful: the journals *British Birds*, *Birding World*, *Dutch Birding*, *Alula* (Finland) and *Nos Oiseaux* (Switzerland) and the magazines *Bird Watching*, *Birds Illustrated* and *Birdwatch*.

Bannerman, D., *The Birds of the British Isles*, Vols. 1–12, Oliver & Boyd, Edinburgh and London, 1953–1963

Blomdahl, A., Breife, B. & Homlström, N., *Flight Identification of European Seabirds*, Christopher Helm, London, 2003

Cocker, M., *Crow Country*, Jonathan Cape, London, 2007

Cocker, M. & Mabey, R., *Birds Britannica*, Chatto & Windus, London, 2005

Cramp, S., Perrins, C. et al (eds.), *Handbook of the Birds of Europe, the Middle East and North Africa (Birds of the Western Palearctic)*, Vols. 1–9 OUP, Oxford, 1977–1994. Also, with updates, on interactive DVD-ROM as *BWPi*, BirdGuides, Sheffield and OUP, Oxford, 2004

Davies, N., *Cuckoos, Cowbirds and Other Cheats*, T. & A.D. Poyser, London, 2000

Delin, H. & Svensson, L., *Philip's Guide to Birds of Britain and Europe*, Philip's, London, 2007

Elphick, J., *Birds: The Art of Ornithology*, Scriptum Editions, in association with the Natural History Museum, London, 2004

Elphick, J., *The Birdwatcher's Handbook*, BBC Books, London, 2001

Ferguson-Lees, J. & Christie, D., *Raptors of the World*, Christopher Helm, London, 2001

Forsman, D., *The Raptors of Europe and The Middle East*, T. & A.D. Poyser, London, 1999

Gaston, A., *Seabirds: A Natural History*, T. & A.D. Poyser, London, 2004

Gorman, G., *Birding in Eastern Europe*, Wildsounds, Salthouse, 2006

Gorman, G., *Woodpeckers of Europe*, Bruce Coleman, Chalfont St. Peter, 2004

Hagemeijer, W. & Blair, M. (eds.), *The EBCC Atlas of European Breeding Birds*, T. & A.D. Poyser, London, 1997

Heath, M. & Evans, M. (eds.) *Important Bird Areas in Europe*, Vols. 1 & 2, BirdLife International, Cambridge, 2000

del Hoyo, J. et al (eds.), *Handbook of Birds of the World*, Vols. 1–11, Lynx Edicions, Barcelona, 1992–2007

Hume, R. & Pearson, B., *Seabirds Behaviour Guide*, Hamlyn, London, 1993

Huntley, B., et al, *A Climatic Atlas of European Breeding Birds*, Lynx Edicions, Barcelona, 2007

Jobling, J., *A Dictionary of Scientific Bird Names*, OUP, Oxford, 1991

Kear, J., *Ducks, Geese and Swans* Vols. 1 and 2, OUP, Oxford 2005

Kear, J., *Man and Wildfowl*, T. & A.D. Poyser, London, 1990

Knystautas, A., *Birds of Russia*, HarperCollins, London, 1993

Marsh, K., *The Good Bird Guide*, Christopher Helm, London, 2005

Mearns, B. & Mearns, R., *Biographies for Birdwatchers*, Academic Press, London, 1998

Mikkola, H., *Owls of Europe*, T. & A.D. Poyser, Calton, 1983

Mitchell, P. I., Newton, S., Ratcliffe, N. & Dunn, T., *Seabird Populations of Britain and Ireland*, T. & A.D. Poyser, London, 2004

Mullarney, K., Svensson, L., Zetterström, D. & Grant, P., *Collins Bird Guide*, HarperCollins, London, 1999

Ogilvie, M. & Pearson, B., *Wildfowl Behaviour Guide*, Hamlyn, 1994

Olsen, K. M., & Larsson, H., *Gulls of Europe, Asia and North America*, Christopher Helm, London, 2003

Tucker, G, & Evans, M., *Habitats for Birds in Europe*, BirdLife International, Cambridge, 1997

Tucker, G. & Heath, M., *Birds in Europe: their conservation status*, BirdLife International, Cambridge, 1994, with online updates

Voous, K., *Owls of the Northern Hemisphere*, William Collins, London, 1988

Wernham, C., et al (eds.), *The Migration Atlas*, T. & A.D. Poyser, London, 2002

Wheatley, N., *Where to Watch Birds in Europe and Russia*, Christopher Helm, London, 2000

Witherby, H., Jourdain, F., Ticehurst, N. & Tucker, B., *The Handbook of British Birds*, Vols. 1–5, Witherby, London, 1938–1941

INDEX

Common Names

The common names used in this book are the "user-friendly" ones favoured for everyday use by many birders. Also given below where applicable – in parentheses – are the more "official" names that are useful in an international context. An index of scientific (Latinized) names is given on page 254.

INDEX

Scientific Names

PHOTO CREDITS

INTRODUCTION
2–3 Golden Plover/David Tipling; 4–5 Black Grouse/David Tipling

FROM WILDFOWL TO GAMEBIRDS
12–13 Steller's Eider/David Tipling; 14 Bewick's Swan/David Tipling; 15 Bean Goose/Jari Peltomäki; 16 Lesser White-fronted Goose/Jari Peltomäki; 17 Barnacle Goose/David Tipling; 18–19 Red-breasted Goose/David Tipling; 20 Ruddy Shelduck/Mike Lane; 21 Pintail/David Tipling; 22 Garganey/Roger Tidman; 23 Marbled Duck/David Tipling; 24 Ferruginous Duck/David Tipling; 25 Steller's Eider/David Tipling; 26 King Eider/David Tipling; 27 King Eider/Jari Peltomäki; 28 Harlequin Duck/David Tipling; 29 Velvet Scoter/Markus Varesvuo; 30 Long-tailed Duck/David Tipling; 31 Barrow's Goldeneye/Markus Varesvuo; 32 Smew/David Tipling; 33 White-headed Duck/David Tipling; 34 Ptarmigan/David Tipling; 35 Black Grouse/David Tipling; 36 Capercaillie/David Tipling; 37 Caucasian Snowcock/Giorgi Darchiashvili; 38 Grey Partridge/Markus Varesvuo; 39 Quail/David Cottridge

FROM DIVERS TO FLAMINGOS
40–41 Dalmatian Pelican/David Tipling; 42 Black-throated Diver/Arto Juvonen; 43 Black-necked Grebe/David Tipling; 44 Fulmar/David Tipling; 45 Cory's Shearwater/Roger Tidman; 46 Manx Shearwater/Chris Gomersall; 47 Leach's Storm-petrel/Steve Young; 48 Dalmatian Pelican/David Tipling; 49–51 Gannet/David Tipling; 52 Pygmy Cormorant/David Tipling; 53 Bittern/David Tipling; 54 Squacco Heron/Richard Brooks; 55 Cattle Egret/Jari Peltomäki; 56 Great Egret/David Tipling; 57 Purple Heron/David Tipling; 58 Black Stork/Richard Brooks; 59 White Stork/Igor Shpilenok (Naturepl); 60 Bald Ibis/Mike Lane; 61 Glossy Ibis/Roger Tidman; 62 Spoonbill/Bence Máté; 63 Greater Flamingo/David Tipling

FROM RAPTORS TO BUSTARDS
64–65 Osprey/David Tipling; 66 Honey-Buzzard/Dave Watts; 67 Black-winged Kite/David Tipling; 68–69 Red Kite/David Tipling; 70–71 White-tailed Eagle/David Tipling; 72 Lammergeier/Philip Mugridge; 73 Griffon Vulture/David Tipling; 74 Black Vulture/Roger Tidman; 75 Short-toed Eagle/Jordi Bas Casas (NHPA); 76 Montagu's Harrier/David Tipling; 77 Goshawk/David Tipling; 78 Spanish Imperial Eagle/Jürgen & Christine Sohns (FLPA); 79 Golden Eagle/David Tipling; 80–81 Golden Eagle/Markus Varesvuo; 82 Bonelli's Eagle/Roger Tidman; 83 Osprey/David Tipling; 84 Lesser Kestrel/Chris Gomersall; 85 Lesser Kestrel/David Tipling; 86 Red-footed Falcon/Richard Brooks; 87 Eleonora's Falcon/Richard Brooks; 88 Gyr Falcon/Markus Varesvuo; 89 Peregrine Falcon/David Tipling; 90 Baillon's Crake/David Tipling; 91 Corncrake/David Tipling; 92 Purple Swamphen/Steve Fletcher; 93 Demoiselle Crane/David Tipling; 94–95 Common Crane/David Tipling; 96 Great Bustard/David Tipling; 97 Little Bustard/Bill Coster

FROM WADERS TO SANDGROUSE
98–99 Knot/David Tipling; 100 Black-winged Stilt/Richard Brooks; 101 Avocet/David Tipling; 102 Stone-Curlew/David Tipling; 103 Collared Pratincole/Jari Peltomäki; 104 Kentish Plover/Dave Kjaer; 105 Dotterel/David Tipling; 106 Golden Plover/David Tipling; 107 Sociable Lapwing/Hanne & Jens Eriksen; 108 Lapwing/David Tipling; 109 Knot/David Tipling; 110 Sanderling/David Tipling; 111 Temminck's Stint/Markus Varesvuo; 112 Curlew Sandpiper/David Tipling; 113 Ruff/David Tipling; 114–115 Ruff/Chris Knights; 116 Great Snipe/Terry Andrewartha (FLPA); 117 Woodcock/Chris Knights; 118 Black-tailed Godwit/David Tipling; 119 Curlew/David Tipling; 120 Spotted Redshank/Markus Varesvuo; 121 Greenshank/Markus Varesvuo; 122 Terek Sandpiper/Jari Peltomäki; 123 Red-necked Phalarope/David Tipling; 124 Long-tailed Skua/Jari Peltomäki; 125 Great Black-headed Gull/Jari Peltomäki; 126 Slender-billed Gull/Hugh Harrop; 127 Audouin's Gull/Arto Juvonen; 128 Glaucous Gull/Jari Peltomäki; 129 Ross's Gull/Chris Schenk (FLPA); 130 Ivory Gull/Nigel McCall; 131–133 Kittiwake/David Tipling; 134 Caspian Tern/Bill Coster; 135 White-winged Black Tern/Jari Peltomäki; 136 Roseate Tern/Chris Gomersall; 137 Arctic Tern/David Tipling; 138 Brünnich's Guillemot/David Tipling; 139 Little Auk/Nigel McCall; 140 Puffin/David Tipling; 141 Pin-tailed Sandgrouse/Yoram Shpirer

FROM PIGEONS TO WOODPECKERS
142–143 Eagle Owl/Markus Varesvuo; 144 Turtle Dove/David Tipling; 145 Great Spotted Cuckoo/John Hawkins (FLPA); 146 Cuckoo/Chris Gomersall; 147–149 Barn Owl/David Tipling; 150 Scops Owl/Richard Brooks (FLPA); 151 Eagle Owl/Arto Juvonen; 152 Snowy Owl/David Tipling; 153 Snowy Owl/Markus Varesvuo; 154 Great Grey Owl/David Tipling; 155 Hawk Owl/David Tipling; 156 Pygmy Owl/Markus Varesvuo; 157 Tengmalm's Owl/David Tipling; 158 Long-eared Owl/David Tipling; 159 Nightjar/David Tipling; 160 Swift/David Tipling; 161 Alpine Swift/Bill Coster; 162 Kingfisher/Bence Máté; 163 Bee-eater/David Kjaer; 164 Hoopoe/Jari Peltomäki; 165 Roller/Bence Máté 166 Wryneck/David Tipling; 167 Grey-headed Woodpecker/David Tipling; 168 Black Woodpecker/Hannu Hautala (FLPA); 169 White-backed Woodpecker/Markus Varesvuo; 170 Lesser Spotted Woodpecker/David Tipling; 171 Three-toed Woodpecker/David Tipling

FROM LARKS TO CRESTS
172–173 Waxwing/David Tipling; 174 Dupont's Lark/Roger Tidman (FLPA); 175 Thekla Lark/John Hawkins (FLPA); 176 Woodlark/David Tipling; 177 Skylark/David Tipling; 178–179 Horned Lark/David Tipling; 180 Crag Martin/Phil Mugridge; 181 Red-rumped Swallow/Harri Taavetti; 182 Red-throated Pipit/David Tipling; 183 Water Pipit/David Tipling; 184 Citrine Wagtail/David Tipling; 185 Waxwing/David Tipling; 186–187 Dipper/David Tipling; 188 Wren/David Tipling; 189 Alpine Accentor/David Tipling; 190 Nightingale/David Tipling; 191 Bluethroat/Markus Varesvuo; 192 Redstart/Markus Varesvuo; 193 Isabelline Wheatear/Neil Bowman (FLPA); 194 Black Wheatear/David Kjaer; 195 Blue Rock Thrush/Bill Baston (FLPA); 196 Ring Ouzel/David Tipling; 197 Zitting Cisticola/David Tipling; 198 Grasshopper Warbler/David Tipling; 199 Aquatic Warbler/Martin Woike (FLPA); 200 Marsh Warbler/Terry Andrewartha (FLPA); 201 Great Reed Warbler/Markus Varesvuo; 202 Barred Warbler/Markus Varesvuo; 203 Rüppell's Warbler/Richard Brooks; 204 Dartford Warbler/David Tipling; 205 Arctic Warbler/Markus Varesvuo; 206–207 Firecrest/Hugh Harrop

FROM FLYCATCHERS TO BUNTINGS
208–209 Bearded Reedling/David Tipling; 210 Red-breasted Flycatcher/Markus Varesvuo; 211 Bearded Reedling/David Tipling; 212 Siberian Tit/David Tipling; 213 Crested Tit/David Tipling; 214 Azure Tit/Jari Peltomäki; 215 Corsican Nuthatch/Mike Read; 216 Rock Nuthatch/Frederic Desmette; 217–219 Wallcreeper/David Tipling; 220 Penduline Tit/John Hawkins (FLPA); 221 Golden Oriole/Weiss (FLPA); 222 Red-backed Shrike/David Tipling; 223 Southern Grey Shrike/Bill Baston; 224 Masked Shrike/Richard Brooks; 225 Siberian Jay/Haari Tavetti; 226 Azure-winged Magpie/John Hawkins (FLPA); 227 Nutcracker/Markus Varesvuo; 228 Chough/David Tipling; 229 Rook/David Tipling; 230–231 Raven/David Tipling; 232 Rose-coloured Starling/John Holmes (FLPA); 233 Snowfinch/David Tipling; 234 Brambling/David Tipling; 235 Citril Finch/Hugh Harrop; 236 Twite/Jari Peltomäki; 237 Arctic Redpoll/David Tipling; 238 Scottish Crossbill/David Whitaker; 239 Trumpeter Finch/Richard Brooks; 240–241 Great Rosefinch/David Tipling; 242 Pine Grosbeak/David Tipling; 243 Hawfinch/David Tipling; 244–245 Hawfinch/David Kjaer; 246 Bullfinch/David Tipling; 247 Snow Bunting/David Tipling; 248 Cinereous Bunting/Richard Brooks (FLPA); 249 Cretzschmar's Bunting/David Kjaer; 250 Rustic Bunting/Haari Tavetti; 251 Black-headed Bunting/David Kjaer

ACKNOWLEDGMENTS

It is customary in a book to mention one's closest and dearest allies last, but here I am overturning convention to indicate the overwhelming importance of the contribution made by my wife Melanie. Quite apart from reading my words and suggesting many improvements, the blessing of her wise advice, good humour and support in countless other ways is incalculable. I also thank my children, Tom, Alys and Becky, and grandchildren Jacob and Callum, for tolerating my long absences, both in the field and at the desk.

I owe a great debt to my parents Walter and Mimi, and my brothers Michael and Richard, for encouraging my early enthusiasm for birds and for natural history generally. Others who supported me early on include my inspirational biology teacher Tony Angell, the ornithologist and ecologist Peter Hope-Jones, and an entire family of remarkable birdwatchers, Peggy, Fred, Peter, John and Frances Walton.

Among many people who made valuable comments on my manuscript were Hans Fried, one of my oldest and truest friends. Angie Brewer not only read some of the text with a writer's eye but also, with her husband Mike, extended hospitality on visits to their beautiful old house and land in central France, where a wealth of birds such as Golden Orioles and Melodious Warblers gave much pleasure. Others, from Simon Smith and Sian Stickings in Moscow to Encarna Guillen in Spain, ensured that visits to various parts of Europe were especially enjoyable and productive.

Of all my fellow hewers at the book face, I respect none more than my dear friend Mark Cocker. A true corvophile, it was he who noticed the initial omission of one special bird, the Rook. During many talks and walks he has given me the benefit of his deep knowledge of birds and his huge talent as a writer.

Detailed critical reading was undertaken by Katrina Cook, whose knowledge of so many aspects of ornithology still astonishes me. Her many marginal comments, reflecting great erudition and experience, were often couched with such wit that even when critical they were easy to swallow.

Having collaborated and travelled with David Tipling before, I knew that working with him once more would be a delight, and so it proved. I hope that I have done justice in my writing to his fine collection of images.

Finally, I have to thank, as always, my agent Pat White, for her professionalism, support and advice, and those at DBP who have worked with David and me all through the publishing process. Bob Saxton, the Editorial Director, has combined his customary sensitivity to words and pictures with a real passion for the subject. His keenness to see birds brought a bonus in that some of the discussions about the book were conducted while enjoying its subjects in such delightful surroundings as the North Norfolk coast. In Manisha Patel we could not have had a more sympathetic and accomplished designer, always prepared to go the extra mile to get things just right; while Sailesh Patel spent much time and effort on preparing the maps.

A Note on Taxonomy

Bird taxonomy varies from one authority to another, and it is in a state of constant change as new research, including the study of their DNA, reveals more about the relationships between birds. No one list can claim to be *the* list. The main sources on which I have drawn for the sequence of birds in this book and for their scientific names are: The British Ornithologists' Union's list of British birds, *The British List*, 7th edition, July 2006, updated 28 March 2008, and available online from the BOU website; the online list associated with *Handbook of the Birds of the World*, created by Lynx Edicions, Barcelona, the publishers of this monumental multi-volume work; The Howard and Moore *Complete Checklist of the Birds of the World*, 3rd edition 2003, edited by E. C. Dickinson and published by Christopher Helm, London.

The arrangement of the families and species in the book reflects the birds' evolutionary history, beginning with the most ancient and ending with the most recently evolved. In a very few places, a bird has been placed slightly out of sequence, for design reasons.

A Note on Map Sources

The information from which these maps were prepared was based upon numerous sources, including various published Europe-wide maps in field guides and other books, as well as ornithological atlases of particular countries and regions, maps and surveys in journals, and unpublished records of mine and others. Particularly useful for checking and updating in the preparation of this synthesis were the maps in Philip's *Guide to Birds of Britain and Europe* (Håkan Delin and Lars Svensson, Philip's, London, 2007) and *BWPi 2.0: Birds of the Western Palearctic Interactive DVD-ROM* (OUP/BirdGuides Ltd, Edition 2, 2006). It should be borne in mind that at the scale used in this book the maps cannot convey fine details of distribution.